King of the Middle Class
by
Tim Larkin

Dear Virginia,

Trust us for all your financial needs.

Timothy D. John 12/07

King of the Middle Class, Inc.

West Sayville, New York

King of the Middle Class
© 2006 by Tim Larkin

ISBN: 0-9785586-0-X

Printed in America

10 9 8 7 6 5 4 3 2 1

Editor: Bob Spear
Interior Design: Bob Spear
Cover Design: Angela Farley

Disclaimer

Published by:
King of the Middle Class, Inc.
69 Main Street
West Sayville, NY 11796
631-589-8898
info@kingofthemiddleclass.com
www.kingofthemiddleclass.com

Acknowledgement

This book is dedicated to my old man, Henry G. Larkin. If it were not for his money and wisdom coupled with his untimely death, this book would not have been possible.

A special tribute goes to my mother, Patricia A Larkin, an angel, who earned her wings on September 10, 2005, when she mysteriously died.

I would also like to acknowledge my loving wife Jacqueline, and our four beautiful daughters, Amanda, Lexi, Alyssa and Samantha. Their special powers helped me overcome the greatest obstacle in my life: myself.

A special thanks goes to my foster brother Abe Delgado, who was rich enough in thought to drop everything and join me on this mission. Abe was "Too Stupid To Quit," and one day he will be richly rewarded for that virtue.

I would like to salute my editor, Bob Spear of Sharpspear Enterprises for putting up with my cacography long enough to finish the edit. A special shout out goes to Angela Farley, the award winning illustrator and creative genius behind our custom designed book cover and logo.

Special thanks to Dan Poynter (the Godfather of self-publishing), John Kremer (the book marketing Wizard) and WBJB internet radio (the Voice of self-publishers).

And most importantly I would like to thank the college students of America in advance for giving me the opportunity to share my father's rich wisdom.

Table of Contents

About The Author

Timothy Larkin, born March 9th 1965. Devoted Son of Henry G. and Patricia A. He was one of two naturally born children of Henry and Patricia. His parents also raised many foster children, some of whom they adopted. Tim grew up in Long Island New York. Graduated from East Islip High School in 1983. From there he attended SUNY Stony Brook College in fall of 1983.

His first year in college he made the dean's list by earning a 3.96 cumulative grade point average. His second year in college he attained a 3.780 cumulative grade point average, earning him membership into the prestigious Sigma Beta Honor Society. He was well on his way to becoming what he thought he wanted to be; a highly compensated, well respected attorney at law.

But while attending college he started learning about how his father made his wealth, and remembering what his Old Man always told him, "Follow your dreams whatever they may be," Tim decided his dream wasn't to be a lawyer anymore. It was to follow in his father's footsteps and become *A King Of The Middle Class*.

Tim has always been a dreamer and now he has a new dream, to teach college students how to follow *their* dreams. He will teach you what his father taught him; how to take a dream and make it a reality.

Roll out the Red Carpet...A King of the Middle Class is coming...

As his mortal body lay dying, his perpetual soul came to life. The old man wanted to talk some more. He said, **"Son, I don't know what crime in life I committed to deserve such a harsh penalty as a death sentence."** I am not prepared for the journey, I am about to take. I don't know what to pack for the afterlife trip that I am about to embark on. I am afraid no training in the universe can prepare a man for such an odyssey. I will soon, rather reluctantly, have the opportunity to experience one of life's most horrifying events; physical death of the host body that houses my perpetual soul. I will soon be able to answer the age-old question of what happens when you die. I will cease to exist in your world. I will be a non-event, like I never happened. In time, no one alive will ever even know I was here. My jokes will be forgotten; my life stories lost, and I will fade away from anybody's memories. The wonderful experiment called life will be over for me. One hundred years from now, when no relatives, friends, or family members are left that knew me, I won't even be talked about. I will be a forgotten name on an unvisited tombstone, silenced by death. My pass in life will be expired. Eventually everyone I touched in life will no longer be around to keep the memory of my life alive.

"I implore you, as my son, to make a promise to me. Promise to keep the memory of my life alive so that the time I spent in this wonderful world wasn't a worthless, trivial, forgotten event. I won't be able to carry out this mission where I am going; I pass the torch to you on this one. I hope you love me enough to carry out this mission. I just want to be remembered by your children to be and possibly, dare I dream, their children-to-be. I will donate whatever time is left in me to help you do this; it's not like I have somewhere important to go. My only dream for what is left of my life is to be fondly remembered.

"The illusion of my monetary dreams has been evaporated; money is just meaningless, worthless, valueless paper to me now. I won't be needing it where I am going. I just don't want my life and the rich things I did in life to become as devalued as the money I leave behind for you after I check out. You are my greatest treasure. I know now, from this vantage point, that the greatest assets in life one can accumulate, are people not money. I now know the only reason, I amassed a fortune in monetary gains is because I placed a higher value on the truly valued assets in life—the people that helped me along the way. My last dream before I leave this planet is for you to promise me that you will do everything in your power to keep the memory of my life alive in the hearts and souls of your children to be. It is your job to pass on this family tradition. I will leave you all the money possible to carry out this endeavor, but ultimately only your love and respect for me will make this dying man's dream realized. Son, don't let me die in vain." He nodded off.

The old man awoke from his dream and proclaimed, "Son do you know what happens to your dreams when you die?"

I said, "**Real** dreams never die, Dad; they are immortal. They are impervious to time. There is no limit or boundary line for a **real** dream because there is no limit to the imagination that creates the dream. Your imagination is infinite. Nothing can stop a **real** dream from happening, not even physical death. **Real** dreams survive many deaths. You can ask Martin Luther King Jr., when you meet him, he'll tell you. Why do you think OJ Simpson was exonerated? Because he didn't care how much money it cost to realize his dream of freedom. He spent his entire fortune and then some on a Dream Team that helped him realize his dream. He is living proof that dreams do come true. Dad, I am your dream team.

"Dad, I will make your last dream come true. I will prove to the world that dreams **really** do come true. My dream in life will be making sure your last dream in life becomes everyone else's reality. I won't do it for me, Dad. I'll do it for you. I figure I owe you that respect. I will spread your word, like a loyal servant. I will not fail in my mission. I will feed the starving young minds of America, and they will feed the rest of the world. I will rescue them from their poor thoughts and feed them with your rich wisdom. Most people have a Plan B, a back-up plan, just in case the real plan doesn't work out. They have something to fall back on, like an aspiring actress has a waitress job, I too have a Plan B. My Plan B is not to screw up Plan A, because my plan B is my Plan A. The best way to protect your future is to create your future with the endless power of your dreams. My Plan B is to properly carry out Plan A, because my Plan B is my Plan A. All or none, the man on a mission only knows one speed, **forward**, no matter what adversity or doubts or setbacks, nothing compromises the integrity of the mission. The mission will be accomplished no matter what the odds or personal sacrifices."

Translation: There is no plan B on this one, Dad. My plan B is not to mess up Plan A. Plan A is Plan B. Plan A is the only plan. I am only focused on accomplishing one thing in life, and one thing only: properly executing Plan A. I am a marksman with only one bullet in the chamber; this is my one shot, and I am taking it for you, Dad. I am stepping up to the proverbial "plate" and swinging my idea at America. I am not going to borrow your dream and pretend it is mine. NO!! I am going to take your dream and make it my **real** dream. I will inherit your dream along with your money and use it to make my dream of you being fondly remembered, a **reality**.

"It is my dream; no one can steal it from me. It is not for sale. Dreams are earned, not bought. No amount of money in the entire universe could stop me from accomplishing my dream. The message will be delivered. I am as unstoppable as a fully packed eighteen-wheeler barreling down a slick hill with no brakes. My whole life was preparation for this journey. I will prove, 'If you can dream it, it can be done.' In my mind, my dream is already accomplished; I am just looking back from my future and marveling at how I wrote a book and accomplished my dream. That's how sure I am that this dream will come true. It is a foregone conclusion. It is a done deal. It's history already. I am just a time traveler who wanted to go back in time and relive it again. My wild dream will become everyone else's calm reality. You should get accustomed to the fact, that it is already done, Dad, because I am not going away until I live to see my dream successfully fulfilled."

My old man thanked me in advance for conquering my errand—our dream—and reminded me of one very important thing: real dreams are only accomplished when you discard your old notion that "Seeing is believing" and replace it with the correct notion that "Believing is Seeing."

I replied, "Yes, I know, and that is why I will do one thing for you in the future, Dad." I will gather all your grandchildren, the ones who knew you and the ones who knew of you, and we will ceremoniously correct the epitaph on your tombstone in Laurel Cemetery to properly reflect my conviction to grant you your last **Dream.**

Your Epitaph, for all the world to see, will read:
Henry G Larkin
Still Living
His Dreams

The old man mused, "So you are going to write a book about me, huh?"

I said, "Absolutely, it's the only way I could realistically think of to make my dream truly come true."

What have I done in life that warrants such kudos?" the old man asked.

I said, "Number one, you performed a miracle; you created me, and number two, you accomplished a dream that eludes many struggling Americans—the dream of financial freedom. I will share your accomplished dream with the world and accomplish my own dream at the same time, because, Dad, dreams do come true. I will prove it. I will show the youth of America, in your memory, what this country was really built on; the backs of tireless dreamers like you. Dad, I will earn your place in history by showing the world that dreams do come true. Once people understand that dreams **really** do come true, maybe a new revolution of thinking can sweep this great country and immobilize our youth to aspire as far as their dreams conjured in their vivid imaginations will take them. All society will benefit from our example."

My old man had the desire and tenacity to accomplish the dream of being truly rich, rich in thought and rich in monetary gain. And I am here to show you how to do it as well. All I ask is for you to fondly remember my old man after this book helps you conquer your dream of being truly rich.

The old man said, "Remember, Tim, always be a friend; never talk above, below, or at people. Enrich your life experience and **talk with** people because:

'The true mark of a friend is to be genius enough to have the ability to take large chunks of complicated subject matter and translate the meaning into small pieces of understandable thoughts that can be easily digested by all,' or as Albert Einstein used to say, 'Everything should be made as simple as possible, but not simpler.'"

* * *

As Chairman of the Board of Sonline Realty Corp. and Sonline Funding Corp. based in Sayville, New York, "America's Friendliest Town," it is incumbent upon me to pay respectful homage to my mentor and fulfill an obligation I made to him on his deathbed. I told my old man that I wouldn't let his ideas die with him. I promised that I would preserve his legacy by sharing his teachings with the world. In essence, I am here to immortalize my mentor and his ideology by recruiting you as my protégé to spread his message and profit from his beliefs. I am your guide to his kingdom of knowledge. I am the son, in-line to the throne, and I am here to assume my position as your mentor, and to teach you how my old man conquered his **dream** of retiring early by properly investing in real estate, and became a "King of the Middle Class."

I am here so that my mentor's voice will not be silenced by his death. I am here to pass his wisdom posthumously on to you. I am here as your tutor, to take you under my wing and gently guide you step-by-step through the metamorphosis of thinking required to become like my mentor, a "King of The Middle Class." I am here to earn your friendship and respect by showing you how my old man made his **dream** of being rich in real estate a **reality;** a system of real estate investing that was passed down to me by my dearly departed mentor and father, my old man, Henry G. Larkin, a professional real estate investor for over twenty-five years.

My old man was a smoker—a heavy smoker. A smoker looks at things differently than a non-smoker, a lot differently. The non-smoker pays taxes and works hard for years and eventually, upon retirement, say sixty-five years old, looks forward to getting social security money from the government. The smoker doesn't think that far ahead. My old man knew the perils of smoking; it actually changed the way he invested his money and how he lived his life. A smoker's timetable is much shorter; the prospect of an early death looms large in the smoker's world and results from activities, like investing have to come sooner rather than later. The smoker can't sit around waiting for investments to pan out. Smokers demand instant gratification from their investments; they never know when the addiction will prevent them from enjoying the benefits of their invested dollars.

My father was a gambler, and he knew the odds of him and any other heavy smoker living long enough to collect any social security payments were against them. He would always tell me that the reason the government allows tobacco companies to exist is so smokers could subsidize the retirement income of non-smokers. He would always say if it weren't for smokers dying every year, social security would have gone bankrupt years ago. Barring any unforeseen events, social security is a great retirement plan for the non-smoker, but what do you do if you are a smoker? You either learn how to quit smoking or get a new retirement plan.

My father was too hooked on cigarettes to quit, so he got a new retirement plan. He had to figure out how to get paid today because tomorrow might not be coming to him. He wanted his fair share of social security while he was alive and able to enjoy it. He wanted to collect his pension at forty instead of sixty-five or seventy years old. My old man got his wish, and I am here to show you how he did it. But before you can use his system, you have to know a thing or two about the man behind the plan. My old man had a unique way of looking at life and it definitely affected how he invested his dollars. As Abraham Lincoln once said, **"It has been my experience that folks who have no vices have very few virtues."** The old man had many virtues, and I am here to share them with you.

In late February, 1997, at the ripe old age of fifty-four, my father's smoking finally caught up with him and he was diagnosed with an inoperable cancer called Oat Cell. I was devastated. My best friend and mentor was checking out of the game of life. Before he moved on, I vowed to spend as much time with him as possible. When he got admitted into Southside Hospital, I dropped everything and spent two weeks camped at his bedside, I don't know if it was the morphine talking or that my old man just had a lot to say before he passed on, but the pearls of wisdom were flowing out like a river of knowledge. I couldn't shut him the hell up. After the first day, I wised up and got a notepad and starting writing it all down. My father was adamant. He wanted to teach me how to live life and how to invest my money before he faded into oblivion. He was dying, and he had a lot of things he wanted to get off his chest. He flapped at a fever pitch; he told me he didn't have much time and had a lot to cover. The old man wanted to give me my inheritance, and I was eager to collect it.

He started out by telling me, "Never be afraid of dying; be afraid of not living." Dying is a natural event; not living is something you control. Do not deny yourself the simple pleasures of life—that is not living.

As he lay in the hospital bed, half the man I remember him to be, he declared, "Don't pity me. I am more alive then some of the people walking around in life. Some people who walk around don't even realize that they are alive."

My father called people who didn't enjoy life and experience all that life has to offer, "the Walking Dead." The walking dead's primary function in life is to live as long as possible by avoiding any activity that will prevent them from living as long as possible.

My old man quipped, "The walking dead think they can cheat death and live forever, not your father, the King; the king lives for today because he doesn't know how many more todays he has. The only thing the walking dead accomplish is to cheat themselves out of the joys of life. The walking dead aren't fully alive—they are half alive—the hesitation to fully commit to life's experience stops them from getting the full effect of life. They ride the speedboat of life at half throttle, never experiencing the thrill and exhilaration of full speed."

The old man said you should live your life at warp speed, as if you instinctively knew you would die early, at say thirty-seven; you would have no hesitation or guilt or regrets; you would go for it; you would throw all caution to the wind and seize the opportunity to experience any and all of life's wonders; you would be "running" at a hectic, frantic, whirlwind pace trying to squeeze eighty years of life experience into a thirty-seven-year span. You would be totally alive. You would not be "walking around half dead." The old man said, if you made it past thirty-seven years, you would consider yourself lucky, a man living on borrowed time, and you would be even more alive, and more willing to experience life's thrills, because you know it's only a matter of time before your bonus time runs out. He said, "You never know when the lease on your time is up."

Some walking dead won't even take vacations for fear of crashing and dying in a plane accident. They would rather avoid the excitement of a fun in the sun vacation, just so they wouldn't have to face the risky possibility, albeit small, that the unlikely event of a crash could occur. My old man would say it's not how many years you live; it's how good you live those years that matters. "There are no do-overs in life. You get one shot at a great life; make it count."

Once you are gone, you never come back. At least not in the same exact form. Don't get me wrong; the old man believed in the afterlife experience, you know, reincarnation. My father believed the body was borrowed; just a host for the soul. You could use and abuse the body—it didn't matter. Every lifetime you got a spanking brand new one. The old man believed the soul is immortal, only the body dies. The old man said if the government had proof that the afterlife existed, it couldn't alert the general population. There would be mass suicides of horny, ugly people, you know the genetically screwed who want to get laid so desperately they would kill themselves hoping to score by being reincarnated into pretty people. The old man felt the only reason divorce rates were so high in our country was because the institution of marriage was a fallacy; it only existed so horny, ugly people could be guaranteed sex. The rest of the population needlessly suffered under this restrictively archaic system of servitude. My father said the trick to this life is to forget you have an afterlife; live this life like it is your only life, because if you are wrong and this is the one and only show that you are given, you should hedge your bet and live this life to the fullest. That way you win the game of life no matter what the deal is.

The walking dead are people who deny themselves all the sinister pleasures of life like tobacco, sugar, mayonnaise, chocolate, a fatty steak, alcohol, butter, marijuana, etc, just so they can live longer. The walking dead allow their doctors to decide what their taste buds experience. If a great tasting food is deemed unhealthy, the walking dead avoid it like the plague. Not my old man. My old man couldn't live without flavor. First, he sniffed the food to excite the taste buds, and then he tasted the food in all its glory, judging the food by its taste, *not* its nutritional value. The old man told me, "Certain tastes are universal." Rich or poor, they are the ultimate choice for the maximum experience i.e., Hellmann's™ mayo on a cold cut sandwich, Heinz™ ketchup on fries or the after dinner cigarette with your coffee.

The old man started rattling on about the merits of coffee and cigarettes. "You know, Son, if it weren't for coffee and stooges, I wouldn't be rich."

Coffee drinking and cigarette smoking are the best networking vehicles in business, believe you me, better then golf. Maybe not as healthy, but a lot more profitable. Almost all of my customers and clients either drank coffee or smoked; that common thread is how we met."

He went on to tell me that, "I can't tell you how many deals I got just by having a cup of Joe or hanging out in the smoking section or going outside and having a puff and casually meeting and greeting fellow smokers and giving them my business card. Smokers love to do business with other smokers, there is a certain bond, a kindred spirit if you will. It's the desperation and exhilaration of the addiction that binds smokers to each other," the old man retorted.

Smoking a cigarette together is a great way to break the ice. People tend to put their guard down and open up and are more willing to become your friend. Once you become their friend, they are more willing to trust you with their business. The old man said the best way to make friends with a fellow smoker is to buy him a cup of coffee and share a smoke. The coffee was like go-go juice to my old man; it fueled his ambition and gave him the energy he needed to conquer his goals and successfully run his business. If the coffee was real good, you know—top shelf, he would walk around proclaiming *San-Dan-Das-e-us, San-dan-das-e-us*—(gesturing to the sky with the mug in his hand)—"The nectar of the gods—Columbia's finest—coffee fit for a king."

My old man was on a 24-hour non-stop coffee frenzy; at home he would brew a full pot and pick at it all day, and if the well ran dry or guests popped over, he would brew a fresh pot. On the road he was a regular fixture at several 7-11's; all the clerks knew his name, brand of smokes, and what he did for a living. He was Mr. Real Estate. He got so much business networking with fellow coffee drinkers and smokers at the 7-11, that he actually called Southland Corporation looking to expand his networking circle by opening his own store.

My old man used to say, you can tell how healthy a food is by how terrible it tastes—the worse the taste of the food, the better it is for you. He believed in quality of life not quantity of life. He told me it is better to celebrate life for 50-60 years like a decadent pig rather then live in fear of death for 80-90 years like the saintly walking dead. He would say the walking dead eat all the right bland foods, get yearly physicals, and do all the right exercises like jogging and working out, yet they fail to realize that in the end we all wind up in the same place—DEAD! In the end, good or bad habits, we all wind up dead. Dead is dead; it doesn't matter how long it takes to get there. The final result of physical life is the same—non physical life. You could do all the right things—eat the right foods; take the right pills; avoid dangerous activities; watch your cholesterol and blood pressure; and basically live the life of a saint; and your end result, your reward for abstaining from the forbidden pleasures of the carefree pigs is your body is dead in say 84 years, instead of 60. My old man used to say, 50-60 exciting years of experiencing the pleasures of life or 80—90 boring years of sacrificing taste and pleasure for longevity. It's your choice, Son. Door A or Door B, you both end up at the same place upon your demise, DEAD, so you might as well enjoy the ride."

Obviously, my old man chose Door A. He chose the greasy, fatty exciting and succulent bacon double cheeseburger over the boring healthy lean veggie burgers. My old man used to say, **"Life**

is not a contest to see who lives longer; no one can control that. Good strong genes and no freak accidents control that."

He knew tomorrow was guaranteed to no one. He would say no matter how healthy a life you lead, if you're crossing the street and the Mack truck is gonna get ya, it's gonna get ya. It won't matter how healthy your lungs are or what your cholesterol count is when the truck hits you, so enjoy the ride. We never know when the ride of life will end. My old man didn't jog or workout—the only exercise he got was sex—a pleasure he rarely denied himself. While all the health freaks were out conditioning their bodies and trying to live forever, my old man was vigorously exercising his most important muscle with their wives or girlfriends inside the house. My old man got around like a coke dealer at a narcotics anonymous meeting. He was always welcome, and he was always everybody's friend. He was Mr. meet and greet. His wit made him the life of the party. If you were a female, he wanted to know you, really—really get to know you, and believe you me, most of the female talent wanted to get to know him too. He had a hypnotic personality; once you were under his spell, it was hard to resist him. My father was like eye candy for the ladies. They all wanted a taste, and he was always eager to share. The shop was always open 24/7 like a reliable 7-11. The private liaisons, the sneaking around invigorated him. He got off on it. The old man would say, "You never know when the party's over, so you might as well get as much as you can for as long as you can."

When I probed him further for more details, he shouted, "Hey, the King never kisses and tells," it cheapens the thrill and lowers the odds of scoring again. Son, if you keep your mouth shut, you might get seconds and thirds. The king always eats well. What you do behind closed doors stays behind closed doors."

I tried to pry those details out of him, but even on drugs, his lips were tight, or as he would say, his lips were as tight as a crabs ass, and that's water tight.

My old man tasted more life in 54 years then most 80-90 year olds. My old man never held back. He knew the truth of life. Every day above ground was a great day. He used to tell me, "Taste all that life has to offer."

My old man didn't worry about the consequences of what he ate or what he did. His sole mission in life was to experience all he could in this lifetime. The old man lived a life of impunity. He used to say the odds of you being you are like 20 million to one—20 million sperms fought for the right to fertilize that egg—you were the winning combination—you beat out over 19,999,999 different versions of you—that makes you special. Just being here means you won the game of life. You won the race to the egg—the prize is your life. How valuable is that life? It is an irreplaceable, unique, priceless gem. It is the single most expensive commodity in the entire universe. As Albert Einstein used to say, **"There are two ways to live your life. One is as though nothing is a miracle. The other is as though everything is a miracle."**

A single life has an expiration date; it's called your lifetime. The only thing you can control in your lifetime is how you decide to live your life, not how much time you have to live it. No one ever knows beforehand what the expiration date is. You could expire in 37 years, like my best friend Jerry, or you could live into your 90's; you know, long enough to experience the thrill of shitting yourself in your grown up diapers.

Translation: You never know for sure how much time you have to enjoy this miracle called life, so before you throw away those pleasurable cancer causing cigars or tasty high-cholesterol shrimps, you should ask yourself, do I see myself hanging around life long enough for these devilish treats to kill me?

It would be such a shame to refrain from enjoying these nasty delights unless we knew proof positive that it would prolong our life experience. The trick is, we don't. You are born with an internal clock. You just do not know what the dial is set to.

My old man used to say from the moment you are born, you are dying, "The timer starts ticking the moment you pop out the womb." You never know how many ticks of the clock you have. You don't know if you are going to live a short or long life; it's a cosmic crapshoot, the old man said. If we knew our time span, we could regulate our lives. My old man believed his lifetime was a preordained event. The exact number of ticks was decided long before he popped out the womb. He believed no matter what you did or how you did it, the exact number of ticks never changed. When it was your time to check out, it was your time to check out, no stragglers. If it was decided before you were born that you would live to 100 years old, then that is what would happen no matter what you did or didn't do in this world. You could smoke like a chimney, drink like a fish, eat like a pig, and screw anything and everything in your path like a wild alley cat; it didn't matter. If it was your destiny to live to 100, then that is what happened. He believed in free will, but his free will had a time limit. That time limit was agreed upon before he entered the forum of life. My old man knew that he could do anything he wanted to do in his lifetime, but he only had a certain amount of preordained time to work with. My old man didn't know how much that time was, so he figured he didn't want to miss out on anything. He basically tried everything that made him happy—Screw the consequences. My old man would say, **"The worst consequence in life is living life so safe and secure that you never experience the thrills of a naughty consequence."** If he saw a beautiful woman, he didn't worry about infidelity. He stepped up to the plate and went for it. He would say, "Why would they make women so beautiful and alluring if they weren't meant to seduce weak men like me." You almost have to go against your nature to resist this one, Son. It is unnatural to not want to experience her.

The old man never believed in going against his own nature. He always blamed his nature for his actions. He was attracted to other women like an uncontrollable twitch. He couldn't help himself. He would always say, " Don't be a slave to your conscience." When you leave this planet, you don't want to leave any regrets laying around. You want to suck the marrow out of the life experience.

The old man was faithful to himself; he would never rob or cheat himself out of the exhilaration of experiencing another woman. No wedding ring or vows ever got in his way.The old man said, **"A cheater may lie to his wife, to spare her feelings, but he would be cheating his own feelings if he didn't act on his desires."** The old man said, "Unlike other men who fantasize away their wanton desires by masturbating, I have the strength to be true and honest to myself by not denying my carnal appetite, and actually eating the forbidden fruit." Shame on those that fight their own nature and deny themselves the experience of enjoying such exotic pleasures.

The next morning I was abruptly awoken by the playful voice of a burly nurse: "Oooohhuuuuuu!!, someone is up early," she shrieked.

The old man adjusted his morning wood and announced the king is happy, very happy. He turned to the nurse with a sly grin and proclaimed, gesturing towards his manhood, "You can make a dying king ecstatic with a Major Release."

The nurse shot back, "I wouldn't want to deprive your hands of the only meritorious exercise available in a hospital bed, Self Love."

The old man took his cue and turned to me and said, "When it comes to love, Son, LOVE YOURSELF FIRST. Love who you are as a person; always be true to yourself. You are the only you that is You. Love who you are as a person. If you're fat, stupid, tall, skinny, ugly, deformed, short, gay, geeky, it doesn't matter; love yourself. Only when you truly accept who you are as a person and love yourself can you give love out to someone else. How can you give love to someone else, if you have no love inside you to give? Love yourself so you can truly experience the full effects of giving this magnificent gift to some other deserving soul."

The old man said the most powerful force in the universe is LOVE. Love is so great it can cross barriers; it can transcend time. If your love is strong enough, it can be felt immediately in any dimension; it can stretch across other galaxies faster than any speed known to mortal man. Love is the fastest known speed in the universe, much faster than the speed of sound and much faster than the speed of light used by angels. Love is Godspeed— instantaneous motion—before the thoughts of where you want to be are formulated, you are already there. As you send it, they feel it immediately no matter where they are in the universe—the physical realm or the metaphysical realm. Love is the invisible bridge, connecting the physical real world with the metaphysical spiritual, dream world we simultaneously live in. The old man said, love is how you take your dream from the metaphysical reality of the dream world into the physical reality of the real world. Your love to make your dream come true eventually makes it a reality. Love is the intangible force at the core of your soul that can instantly drive your spirit anywhere it desires. Anything is possible with love, even impossible dreams. The morphine kicked in as he drifted into REM sleep.

When he awoke in the wee hours of the morning, the old man couldn't contain himself. "WAKE UP, SON!!! WAKE UP!!!!"

For a split second I instinctively tensed my body and assumed my defensive posture as the authority in his tone of diction sent me reeling back to my mischievous childhood and the fear of his wrath that accompanied it. It was 3:00 am, and the old man wanted to talk some more. As I cleared my lethargic eyes and realized where I was, I repositioned myself on the cot next to his bed, and I reluctantly obliged the old man. I knew by his firm voice that he was having another moment of clarity, a lucent break from his self-induced morphine stupor. I welcomed the opportunity to talk to my real father again. He was straight, and he wanted to do what he always did when he straightened up—talk incessantly. It was like he was trying to catch up for all the time he lost sleeping his life away, wasted on morphine. He fought the pain and started talking rapidly. He was like a teenager that finally figured out the rubik's cube; he was beaming with enlightenment. "Son, I had a wild dream. I have to tell you about it before I fall back to sleep and forget it.

"In my dream, I was walking down the street, smoking a Lucky, when I struck up a conversation with a destitute bum, who grubbed a stoggie. As he lit it up, he said, 'Thank you, God.'

"And I responded, 'I am not God, you poor fool.'

"He snapped back, 'It is you who is foolish enough in thought to miss that rich truth in life. Not only are you God, so am I. So is everybody and everything.'

"I said, 'That's impossible, you heathen.'

"He said, 'God didn't create us from the physical world of the possible. God created us from the world where the impossible is possible, the metaphysical world. In the beginning, God was a non-physical being only, an omnipotent spirit of pure energy, freely roaming the metaphysical realm, limitlessly creating at will, anything and everything possible. It was in this world of unlimited possibilities that God conjured and then created a comparable physical world. Basically, God used some of its unlimited energy to create a world, our real physical world just so it could fully experience a thrill it had never experienced in the metaphysical realm; the limitations of physical life. God wanted to experience everything and anything physically possible at the same time, all the time, so it created physical objects, hosts if you will, to house its metaphysical existence in, so it could experience on a physical level a world it created in the spiritual metaphysical world. The human being is one of many physical hosts that God uses to experience the sensation of corporeal physical life. The human being is metaphysical God (the creator) expressing itself in a physical form (its creation).'

"The bum said, 'Harry, only the most enlightened few in the mortal world of the physical have enough love in their soul to cross this bridge of thinking. We are all part of one spiritual being experiencing the thrill of physical existence.'

"I finished my smoke, and as I walked away, the bum shouted, 'Harry, have enough love in your soul to realize you are the metaphysical creator enjoying the thrill ride known as the physical human experience.'"

I said, "WOW, Dad, that's a heavy dream, what do you think it meant?"

He yawned a few times, cleared his throat, and said, "I think it means that once you realize you are the creator, only then will you possess the love that allows your metaphysical creations to cross over into our physical world. Your love will make you the creator realize that you control both worlds of the universe, the natural, rational world of the possible—the physical realm—and the supernatural, irrational world of the impossible—the metaphysical realm. Once you know that you control both worlds, you can create anything possible, physical or metaphysical. Love is the cosmic glue that keeps both of these worlds harmoniously attached. A metaphysical dream only comes to life in our physical world by the love of its physical creator." He nodded off.

When he awoke he proclaimed, morality is for people who have no direction in life. Some people are lost without rules to guide them. Society inflicts rules on people to control their actions and maintain order. The religious get their rules from holy books and the agnostics get man-made rules from politicians. The end result is someone else or someone else's rules or laws or regulations are deciding how you experience life and the king, my father, would have nothing to do with anything that restrictive. He would say, Son, "The king's authority will never be usurped by someone else's will. The king's rules are hardwired in from birth; you are born with a morality code instilled inside you. You know the difference between right and wrong from birth; it's your natural instinct; it guides all your decisions in life—basically if it feels right, just do it, and if it feels wrong, don't do it. I don't need a religious book to tell me killing another man is wrong; my inner intuition, the voice inside my head, the genetic code of reasoning I was born with does that."

I wasn't born with the desire to kill; it wasn't programmed into me. But my old man would be quick to tell you, you never know the contents of that morality code until an unsavory experience challenges who you are as a person. My old man would tell you that it doesn't matter who you are in front of the cameras or the spotlight, it's who you are behind closed doors where no one is looking and you can be who you really want to be that matters. A non-killer can be a killer in an instant. My old man said if the right circumstances existed, even a staunch pacifist could be convinced to take a life. If a piece of vermin entered your domicile, and proceeded to rape your woman, all the morality you thought you had from the good book or the laws of the land is out the window. The morality code inside you will instruct you to kill or be killed. You will either become animalistic aggressive and fight, or you will become docilely stunned and take flight. Some people think their nature won't allow them to kill, but until they are thrust into a life or death situation, they will never know.

Translation: The only way you would know how to react to different circumstances and situations and challenges in life is if you knew what the code inside you was beforehand or you already experienced it firsthand. Once we go through a frightening experience the first time, we know what to expect the second time, and how to react. It's not as scary.

The code is not learned. It is built in. If you were illiterate and lived on an isolated island, it wouldn't matter; what you read and where you live doesn't affect your morality code. The morality code inside you that tacitly and robotically guides your decisions in life is already pre-set from birth. The morality code inside you is not spoken or written down somewhere. It is more like a feeling, a gut feeling, a visceral benchmark of your being—it is what makes you—You. The code is universal to you. The code determines how you want to experience this wonderful gift called life. The code inside you will never let you down. It is the invisible force inside you like ambition and desire that guides your life experience. In essence, the code is the core of your human nature. My old man used to say no matter what you say or do, you can never violate or change your nature. You will always revert back to who you really are. The code is who you really are. No one in the entire universe shares the same exact code; it is exclusive only to you.

Basically, the morality code is the rules that were given to each and every one of us to play the game of life. The rules were ingrained into the core of your being, so you can never lose them or forget what they are. There is no strenuous thinking involved with these rules, the rules are understood simultaneously, and they govern your every action. It's an automatic process. It is your personality, and it is unique only to you. My old man would say, "Do you have to think about breathing? No!! It just happens naturally, automatically, like it is supposed to happen.

It's the same way with the rules of your code; they are natural and automatic. You can't control what your nature or temperament really is so don't fight it; go along with it; go with the flow. The code will not allow you to go against who you really are. It kicks in automatically. You don't have to think about being an extrovert or an introvert. You just are. It's your nature. It's your personality. It's the single most unique thing about you. No one is better than you at being you. You are the best you to you.

The old man dozed off. When he awoke, he was in rare form. The old man said, "Son let me give you some great advice before I die: A. Don't be the 'walking dead' and B. Be a 'King of the Middle Class.'"

I asked the old man, "What is a King of the Middle Class ?"
The King, my father, declared, "I am a King of the middle class, and when I am through guiding you, you too will have the distinct honor of being dubbed a King of the Middle Class. My days as a King are numbered, Son. It is now time for me to pass the torch to you while the fire of desire still burns inside me. Son, I am going to give you the best seat in the house, front row dead

center. I want you to concentrate all your energy, like a focused laser beam, on what I am about to unfold to you. It could forever change your life experience. I am giving you the proverbial keys to the city, the blueprint, the personalized guide to your life, the philosophy and ideology of a superior lifestyle that I call 'King of the Middle Class.'"

The old man said everyone thinks that there are only three parties going on in life:

- The Freebie Poor
- The Lonely Rich
- The Struggling Middle Class

1) Poor—"the freebie party" They get everything in life handed to them for FREE; they are spoiled wards of the state; they are used to: free money for not working (collecting welfare or disability or unemployment), free housing (section 8 /social services), free medical coverage (Medicaid) with a free drug card, free food (food stamps/Wic program), free education, free dental, free utilities (Heap), and since they are probably not working, plenty of free time. The only problem with this party is they have all the time in the world but not enough free money to throw a great party. Their party is limited and restricted by a low budget. Don't get me wrong; this is not a stupid party. Some of these party-goers (the rare ambitious ones) know how to get over on the system and increase their budget by abusing the privileges. They collect all the freebies from the government, and then they collect more free money by working off the books, collecting non-reportable, tax-free cash from an employer in the underground economy. These party members enjoy a better quality of life than their poor brethren, but all in all, monetary constraints limit this party. Another problem with this party in life is that eventually the freebies could run out. The government could suspend

or cut the programs, and then where would they be? Imagine the horror on their face, when they realize the party's over and they could be forced to get a j. o. b., a job—short for **J**ust **O**ver **B**roke, not a happy prospect.

Nobody in this party wants to have to work for their money; they have grown accustomed to getting paid for not working. The old man said, "You live like a king when the democrats are in office, but once the republicans take over, you go back to being a peasant." But don't worry, the freebie party takes care of all its brethren, be it democrat or republican. If your benefits get cut, the party has a built in back up plan. It's a barter system, quid pro quo. It's a take off on the oldest profession in the world. It's called a sugar-daddy or sugar-mama. Instead of Big Brother sponsoring all of your freebies, a private individual, aka sugar-daddy or sugar-mama, (usually with deeper pockets than yours), steps in and assumes the responsibility of paying for your free ride by picking up your tab in return for sex. It's the sex for money program. It's privatized "welfare" for good-looking, poor people. It's not prostitution. Prostitution is when you make nickels and dimes by having sex with hundreds or thousands of strangers. The sugar-daddy system is exclusive sex with one person, your sugar-daddy or sugar-mama, in exchange for lots of money and plenty of free gifts and trips. No sharing, your financial sponsor is paying good money for this exclusive privilege. You will not be disrespecting yourself by working the streets trying to score another trick, Hell No! You will be respectfully tucked away in a free rental unit, with plenty of food, beautiful clothing, gorgeous furniture, and if you're really good, a weekly expense allowance. The only people that will know how you make your money in the world and pay your expenses, are you and your sugar-daddy or sugar-mama. And no self respecting sugar-daddy would ever kiss and tell, so it's safe to say that to the rest of the world, you are not perceived as a hooker; just a real horny, available on-command girlfriend, a goomata to the Italians. You are respected as the husband's girlfriend, or a wife's boyfriend, not some cheap tramp. You have sex on a regularly scheduled basis. You are not a one-night stand; you are a daily or weekly event. You are a paid, consistent lover. You are on call 24/7, always on stand-by. You never know when you will be called up for active duty. Your one and only priority in life is pleasing your meal ticket, so a broken wallet doesn't interrupt your free ride in life. Some goomata's are so well schooled in the art of luring men into sugar-daddy servitude, that they make enough money to leapfrog out of poverty and into prosperity.

This party in life has lots of friends, tons of free time (You can get wasted all day.), but not enough guaranteed dough to throw a good party. It's a great party to be in if you don't want to pay any income taxes, or if you have a drug problem that precludes you from getting a real job. This party in life does not discriminate; that would be un-American. It rewards drug addicts with money not to work as well. Drug addicts love free money for drugs. If a drug addict gets busted for drugs, the freebie party takes care of its members. It provides a free attorney via legal aid and if the charges stick, the government will once again pick up your tab and give you, as a privilege of freebie party membership, free room and board, free medical and dental, possible free education, three square meals, free clothing, easy access to liquor, drugs, sex, and weapons—it's called prison; the vacation of choice for the freebie party. It is not uncommon for party members to take five or ten year vacations. All expenses are paid; they have plenty of idle time on their hands; and they don't have a real job that could get in the way. Some really lucky freebie party members get the

LIFE vacation—full time free ride for as long as you live. Permanent Vacation. Poor man's jackpot. Free everything. The service might not be the best, but the price is right. How does the freebie party member earn the right to have such an extensive vacation? Commit a felony or two or three. In NY, Rockefeller created an overcrowding situation at most vacation sites in the state when he: loosened the admission requirements substantially and allowed low level nickel and dime drug dealers, with only three convictions in. Three strikes and you were in; you got the coveted lifetime free ride. The only problem was too many freebie party members wanted to take advantage of this wonderful opportunity, and there were too many reservations and not enough rooms. Not to worry, these vacations are guaranteed. When they run out of room for you, they'll just get the taxpayers to foot the bill and build a more modern facility to accommodate a guest of your stature. Don't worry; they will always make room for you at the inn. You worked hard for your free ride. They won't disappoint you. The best thing is you have the option of working on this vacation, and you won't even have to switch jobs; you can deal just as much, if not more, drugs from your furnished suite...er...cell. My old man said, "The highest paying job in the freebie party is crime, and that's a full-time, round the clock, day and night job." It is the only job that never goes on vacation. The only drawback to the job was if you got caught, they locked you up and gave you lots of free stuff. Not much of a deterrent. Other cultures cut off your hands or publicly hang you for nefarious acts like rape, robbery, and murder. Not us, we reward these hard working felons with a lifetime free ride down easy street. Of course, you could crap out and get the death penalty, and then they really treat you harshly. While you appeal, they give you your own private room on prestigious death row; you actually get to shit without an audience. Hell, you earned the honor, and when your day of reckoning comes, instead of dragging you out like the dirty dog that you are, you get fed like a king, or some star-studded celebrity. You choose the contents of your last meal—sky's the limit. No unreasonable offer will be refused. The wait staff aims to please. You are well-fed for your final journey. Hey, freebie party membership has its perks. Go figure.

2) Rich—"the lonely party"—They have all the money and time in the world, but they lack the single most important element of a good party experience— friends. Real Friends. Rich people do not know if you are their real friend or you are being their friend just to get at their money. This realistic hesitation to fully commit to a real friendship limits the life experience for the rich people. They have the money to throw all the best parties but have few really trustworthy, sincere real friends with which to share the party of life. Rich people can never truly know who their true friends really are because they meet a lot of plastic phonies in life—the "always say yes" people, the paid help, the **professional ass-kissers**; professionally trained people who shower your ego with whatever it takes to remain friends with you—their meal ticket. Everybody wants to be a millionaire's new "best friend," so they can help separate him/her from their money. Most rich people are lonely because their money gets in the way of finding fresh, new real friends. For the right price, your childhood chum could befriend you—you are constantly worried about people wanting to steal your bag of gold—it clouds your judgment and stops you from experiencing a complete friendship. You don't know whom to trust—**"money makes people funny."**

Your own brother/sister/uncle or other relation could void your friendship for the right price. It is a very lonely feeling when you have no way to know who your true friends really are. A rich person can be at a party with a room full of so-called "friends" and still feel very much alone.

3) Middle Class—**"the struggle party"**—The constant struggle to make ends meet and "get ahead" is a crisis in the middle class that unites people and forges real friendships. Surviving this struggle with real friends is how the battle to be rich is eventually won.

The middle class is the infantry of the economy. These loyal workhorses and their tax contributions are the only reason the "freebie party" even exists. They pay the bulk of the taxes that magnanimously subsidizes all social programs. They are the lifeblood of the robust American economy; the **real taxpayers.** The rich use accountants, financial planners, and lawyers to legally hide their taxable income, shielding their money in corporations and off-shore accounts and using loopholes and creative accounting and deductions to legally avoid paying their fair share of taxes. The poor use social workers and legal aid workers to legally collect benefits (free money) that are not taxed. So while the rich are creatively avoiding paying taxes and the poor are draining tax dollars by sucking on the proverbial tit of the government, the end result is the struggling middle class is stuck paying the tab. Their rewards for altruistically subsidizing our country's voluntary tax coffers—lower wages, lost pensions, and unaffordable health insurance premiums. The old man said, the only reason the furious middle class hasn't revolted is because they firmly believe in the system of capitalism and free enterprise that can catapult them out of the middle class into the stratosphere of the rich. They know democracy is a fair system; it allows any American regardless of starting position to be as rich or as poor as they want. The struggle to rise out of the monetary constraints of middle class life is a small price to pay for the opportunity to live "the great American dream" of being rich.

The old man said, the middle class believes this dream because it is a proven truth. Many struggling middle class Americans have successfully conquered the dream and become millionaires. The system really works, and the struggle is definitely worth the cost of admission. The old man said, **"Beating the struggle is how they got rich. Appreciating the quality of the struggle (the ride) is how they became richer."**

The old man said, everyone thinks there are only three parties going on in life:

- Poor—all the time and plenty of friends but not enough money to throw a good party
- Rich—all the money and time, but not enough real friends to throw a great bash.
- Middle class—They struggle, but they always find a way to have enough money, time, and good friends to host a smash party.

But there is another party going on, and it is by invitation only. This book is your invitation to that party. You only gain admittance by knowing someone at the party, and you only find out about the party from another party member. It is not public knowledge; it's a "member's only" party. You have to know a member to gain admittance. Membership grows daily; other members are constantly recruiting other members. The only people who are invited are people who have lots of money and plenty of time and friends to share it with. It's the Mardi Gras of parties, the best party in town, where all the fun people are, the fourth class of people, Kings or Queens of the middleclass. It's like a splinter group of the Masons. These are rich people who know how to be truly rich. They have the knowledge and business acumen to be monetarily rich. Once they reach that apex, they are rich enough in thought to realize that the life journey of the **grand** rich class **is common** and the life journey of the **common** middle class **is grand**.

The old man said, if you have a lot of money, you could live life any way you want to live it. If your wish is to live among the common people, to share the struggles, the pitfalls, the enriching victories in life, you can. Your money gives you the freedom of choice. You can live in an exclusive neighborhood detached from everyday people and their concerns, or you can live like a King inside the middle class attached to the most important assets in life: loving family, friends, and relatives, where the quality of life is more down to earth. A King of the Middle Class is someone who has the money and brains to go to the next level of wealth, but chooses to remain behind to enjoy the middle class ride. To a King, the middle class ride is the most enriching experience in life. A King marinates in the succulent juices of the rich middle class life journey. It's the perceived struggle that adds excitement to life. A King of the Middle Class has the values of the struggling middle class (hard work ethic, family, self-sufficiency, education, discipline, loyalty, respect, honor, integrity) but enriches his/her middle class experience by having the money to eliminate the only drawback to the middle class ride in life, the constant struggle to make ends meet. A King chooses to experience life in the realism created by the common struggle of middle class people, without any money struggles to screw up the ride. Real rich people already conquered the dream of being rich, and now they are looking for something that they can't possibly buy for any amount of money— the rich experience of living the middle class life.

A King hangs out in the shadows of the middle class and has all the time and money in the world to enjoy this exhilarating experience. He/She attends social events, kids events, school events, religious events, birthday parties, graduations, community events, local sporting events, family events etc....Kings don't let money stop them from missing any of life's "once in a lifetime moments." Kings own all those wonderful moments, that's why they became a King or Queen. Their only true work in life is enjoying some of the rich privileges of middle class life, like the camaraderie of good friends, the love of family, and the thrill of raising your own children.

A King of the Middle Class knows the best way to prosper in life:
1. Eliminate all financial pressures in life by making enough money in your investments to casually pay all bills. The stress of bills is almost non-existent.
2. With no money worries in life, your mind is relaxed; a calm rich euphoria sets in.
3. This stress-free environment clears your mind and frees your soul. You now have the time and money to let the ambitious juices flow and freely dream.
4. You can now spend all day with your unclogged rich thoughts, dreaming up new ways to make you richer.

You would never know it if you met a true King of the Middle Class. They don't broadcast their wealth; they hide undetected in the midst of the middle class environment. They blend in like wallpaper. They go un-noticed. Instead of arrogantly displaying their status as rich people, they are rich enough in thought to enjoy the full experience by being private. The reason they are private and hide their wealth is that they do not want to derail their rich middle class experience by subjecting themselves to some of the casualties of being openly rich, like car jackings, extortion attempts, robberies, kidnappings, lawsuits, gold-diggers, scam artists, home invasions, embezzlement from hired help, etc. Being a victim of your own wealth is a sensation in life, a King of the Middle Class tries to avoid by being humble enough in life not to get carried away by his hubris. A king doesn't corrupt his middle class ride by arrogantly thinking he is better than his fellow man because of the wealth in his pockets. A King sheds his ego and maintains a low profile so he can remain on equal footing with his most precious asset in life, his true wealth: people. His real friends know he is monetarily rich and respect his genuine humility and modesty by rewarding him with one of the richest experiences of life: true friendship.

" True Friendship is a plant of slow growth, and must undergo and withstand the shocks of adversity, before it is entitled to the appellation."

George Washington

The old man said you can trace the roots of the King of the Middle Class lifestyle all the way back to one of our founding father's: our first president, George Washington. After the war was over, George was so popular that the gullible colonists didn't even question his $449,261.51 (approximately $4,250,000 in today's dollars) worth of dubious expenses. They loved him so much they were willing to throw democracy away and make him their King. A movement swept the country to elect victorious George Washington as our first King, instead of our first President. Oddly enough, it was George himself who squashed this movement by rallying for the ratification of the Constitution. George gave up a lifetime of unlimited power as a King, to magnanimously protect our democracy. Four point two million dollars was a small price to pay King George for our priceless Freedom.

The old man said, once George became President, he and his Masonic lodge members continued this protection of our democracy by concocting the concept of King of the Common Class. Originally a King of the Common Class was like a rich guardian secretly living among the ranks of common people. Democracy was a relatively new concept and certain rich people felt that common people had to be protected against any one man becoming so popular, so rich and powerful that he could charismatically unite the majority of people and usurp the Constitution and become sole ruler. This is why the Constitution was devised with separation of powers, a system of shared power known as checks and balances. Power was purposely decentralized so no one branch (Executive, Legislative, or Judicial) had all the power. Each branch had certain powers, and each of these powers were limited or checked by another branch. This was the cornerstone of democracy and the Kings were strategically placed among the common masses to ensure that this decentralization of power remained intact. Initially they were protectors of democracy; rich volunteers sprinkled into the common mix, sworn to protecting the integrity of the Constitution. Nowadays, this long tradition still survives. It morphed into a whole new lifestyle of living creating a 4th class of people known as Kings/Queens of the Middle Class.

What is a King of the Middle Class?
- An alternative lifestyle created by: A silently rich person looking to maximize his life experience by concealing his wealth and hiding in the obscurity of the middle class, without enduring the financial hardships or monetary limitations of the struggling middle class.
- A rich person who chooses to live life like a king in the middle class rather than live life like a peasant in the rich class.
- A middle class person that invests his money wisely enough to live like royalty in the throes of the middle class.
- An evolved middle class thinker who has successfully "retrained his brain" and conquered the dream of being rich and purposely decides to secretly remain behind in the anonymity of the struggling middle class to enjoy the spoils of his financial victory.
- A rich person who has the bankroll to live in a Park Ave. penthouse but chooses instead to experience the bucolic life of Main street middle class America.
- A millionaire who enjoys his wealth by living well below his means, by hiding in the shadows of the middle class.
- A rich person who chooses to get lost in the chaotic fun of the middle class rather than graduating to the next level of wealth and joining the rich class.
- A rich person who decides to use his wealth to be the **"poorest rich man"** rather than the **"richest poor man."**

Poorest Rich Man	Richest Poor Man
Lives well below financial means	Lives well above financial means
Manageable debt	Out of control debt
House paid off	Mortgaged to the max
Hidden Ego—wealth hidden in plain sight via investments	Large Ego—ostentatiously displays wealth
Plenty of free time to enjoy wealth	Limited free time to enjoy wealth. Constantly working to support overextended lavish lifestyle
Stress free—No money worries	Stressed out—always worried about making money
Really Rich	Pretend Rich
King of the Middle Class	Peasant of the Rich Class

How do you become a King of the Middle Class?

One King usually learns the ropes from another King, it is like a rite of passage; my old man passed these skills down to me. A King does not become a King by accident. It is all well planned. A king is taught this system of wealth, more like a superior lifestyle to live by. There are rules, a game plan of action, and a mentor— a fellow King to guide you. You only get indoctrinated into the system by someone else who is already enjoying the benefits. Now I am looking to reach out and become your teacher, because Kings are not Kings by mistake. It is a conscious decision. A King doesn't just know how to live. A true King knows how to live well. The old man said, this is how you become a King of the Middle Class: First you **Change the way <u>You</u> think,** so you can **Change the way <u>You</u> invest,** so you can make enough money from your investments to monetarily qualify as a reigning King/Queen.

Part 2—Change the way you think

The old man said, the only way to be a King of the Middle Class is to change the way you think. To be a King, you have to think like a King. A King knows the days of studying hard, landing an entry level job out of college, staying thirty years at the same company, working your way up the corporate ladder and retiring rich aren't guaranteed anymore. Nowadays, <u>you</u> **can't count on your employer to protect your future.** The safety of a secure job; steadily increasing wages, full benefits (Health insurance, life insurance, disability insurance, 401k, tuition reimbursement, dental, vision etc.), and a pension is being eroded by a system of corporate greed known as globalization. Globalization is a euphuism employed by corporations to justify replacing hard working Americans with foreign cheap labor. With globalization, the American employee, even those high up on the food chain, are one corporate decision away from the unemployment line. Nobody's job is safe in America today.

Translation: You better stop falsely thinking that getting a good job is the best way to get rich in America. Those days are long over.

The old man said, "**Times have changed, <u>You</u> can't even count on your own government to protect your future.**" The social security system designed to protect the future of all working Americans could theoretically be wiped out by the time you reach retirement in your "golden years," leaving you old and broke.

Translation: You better stop thinking social security will bail you out in your old age, if your employer "downsizes" you out of your future. The benefits you thought you were entitled to at retirement could be gone by the time you need them.

The old man said, there is only one way to protect your future today; **you have to count on yourself today.** The best way to protect your future is to create your own future. The best way to create that future is to be like a King of the Middle Class—a self-employed owner of a business. The old man said the best way to get rich in America today is not to work for the man, but to *be* the man. In today's economic climate a standard job is riskier than being self-employed. Years ago, being self-employed was an option; now it is almost a financial necessity. Nowadays self-employment is the best way to make the coin needed to monetarily qualify to be a King of the Middle Class. The old man said, self-employment is the best way to be a millionaire in America today. After the old man's death, this fact was well confirmed by a best selling book called *The Millionaire Next Door* by Thomas J. Stanley and William D. Danko. According to the book, self-employed people make up less than twenty percent of all workers in America, but account for nearly two-thirds of all millionaires. This book validated the old man's wisdom by proving that self-employed people are four times more likely to be millionaires than those who work for others.

Further proof of the millionaire making power of self-employment, touted by the old man, comes from *USA Today*. According to an article in USA Today, the worst odds of becoming a millionaire in America are via winning the lottery @ 12 million to 1. The same article says the best odds of becoming a millionaire in America is through the avenue of self-employment. Self-employed business owners have a realistic 1,000 to 1 shot at becoming a full-fledged millionaire in America.

Translation: **The best chance <u>You</u> have to actually live your dream of being a millionaire in America is <u>NOT</u> the lottery at 12,000,000 to 1, it's self-employment at 1,000 to 1.** Self-employed people are four times more likely than lottery players with nine to five jobs of becoming millionaires.

Armed with this knowledge, why aren't more Americans becoming millionaires through self-employment?

1. <u>Paucity of qualified teachers</u>—
Total population USA—approximately 298 million
Source—www.cia.gov

According to CNNMoney.com in an article entitled "Number of Millionaires Hits Record" (May 25, 2005) by Les Christie, CNN/Money Staff Writer and I quote, **"The number of millionaires in America reached record highs in 2004, hitting 7.5 million, acording to a new survey."**

According to this research, less than 3% of the total population are actually millionaires. That means 97% of the general population are not qualified to teach you how to make a million dollars in life, because they haven't even been able to teach themselves how to do it.

Translation: there aren't enough self-employed millionaires willing to stop making money long enough to teach <u>**You**</u> how to do it.

2. <u>Almost 80% of Americans sell their dream of being rich to their employer for the mere cost of a salary and benefits</u>—
The top talent in this country is being paid off with a salary and benefits to bow out of the Get Rich self-employment game. The owner of the business gets to live his/her dream of being rich by paying <u>**You**</u> for not being self-employed and trying to live your dream of being rich. For six figures or less, most educated Americans would foolishly settle for a job in life instead of wisely pursuing the best chance they have in life of becoming a millionaire—self-employment.

Translation: it is almost impossible to dream of being a millionaire when you are spending all your time helping someone else (the self-employed owner of the business) live their dream of being a millionaire instead.

3. Fear of Selling—

The old man said the number one reason most people do not start their own business is not lack of funds or lack of desire or fear of failure, it is fear of selling. No business in the world can exist without sales and most people have misconceptions about their ability to sell. The old man said you have to conquer your fear of selling if you ever want to live your dream of being rich via self-employment.

The old man said, a King of the Middle Class knows how to conquer the fear of selling because he knows the truth about selling—**ANYBODY CAN SELL**

Myth: The ability to sell is an inherited trait. A natural born salesperson is born with the ability to sell—It is genetically encoded into your wiring. You have the gift of gab, a Type A personality, an extrovert, a cunning BS artist, ie., a liar. If you're a convincing liar at a young age, your parents, friends, relatives will usually comment that so and so will make a great salesperson someday. (What a misconception)

Reality: The ability to sell is a learned skill, a trade, and a craft. Selling is an art, not a natural birthright. The great ones didn't become great by accident; they were trained. Anybody can be a salesperson, if they are willing to put in the time and energy required to learn this craft. Great salespeople never lie; they sell through the convictions of the truths inside themselves. They believe in what they are doing. This belief or conviction or attitude or truth inside that salesperson is what makes the sale possible. They acquired this conviction by feeding their mind with books, tapes, and seminars that gave them the education and comfort level to actually believe what they were learning.

Myth: If you have a charismatic personality and a silver tongue and talk a mile a minute at your client, (only taking breathers or shutting up when you ask a closing question), your mouth will land you the sale. So you have to be a smooth talker with elusive answers and quick-witted responses.

Reality: Your mouth is only 7% of the sale. The mouth is only one of the five senses and not a very powerful one; that's why they say a picture is worth a thousand words. People believe what they can see much more than what they can hear. I'll prove the point, three people can tell me with their mouths that someone stole a cookie from my cookie jar, but a 4th person with a digital camera snapped a picture of that someone in the act. Who are you more likely to believe? Obviously, the 4th person, he wouldn't even have to open his mouth to convince you. The power of sight would sell you. The old man said, remember the classic movie *Scarface*? Pacino says, "**The eyes, Chico, the eyes never lie.**" Tony Montana knew the eyes were the doorway to the soul and he would trust people based on how sincere the eyes looked not the words coming out of someone's mouth. Your attitude, convictions, beliefs, your inner core, your moral fabric, your essence, what you are really made of, who you are when no one is looking, that's 93% of the sale. When you sell from your soul, the clients always say, "I don't know why I used him/her. We just clicked; we just connected; it just felt right; he/she touched me in a certain profound way. The good salespeople sell with their mouths only; the great ones sell with their mouth, heart and soul. The great ones want people to experience them through all five senses (sound, sight, smell, touch and taste). The great ones understand that there is a flow of energy between people, and they want to tap into that energy at five levels, not one.

Myth: Great salespeople are born with the ability to instinctively know when to say, what to say, and how to say the magical words that land the sale. It's inborn—They just WING IT—They do not need to practice or study—the gift of gab will carry them (Genetic Luck).

Reality: Great salespeople are not great by accident. They spend years honing their skills. They practice scripts and role-playing. They practice how, when, and what to say to people so many times, it seems natural. Outsiders think the great ones are winging it—insiders know the truth and the power of proper preparation.

The old man said, there is a direct correlation between rejection and landing the sale; a ratio. It's all in the numbers. Your skill level dictates ratio number. A poorly trained salesperson might land one out of ten sales leads; a well-trained salesperson might land three out of ten sales leads; and a greatly trained salesperson might land five out of ten sales leads. Anybody can beat anybody else in sales. It depends on how many prospects you hit. If a poor salesperson goes on 100 sales presentations, he/she might land ten deals (ratio 1 of 10); the great salesperson might go to ten sales presentations and land five deals (ratio 5 of 10). The top salesperson this month would be the poorest trained salesperson because determination beats skill level in the sales game.

The best way to be a King of the Middle Class is to be self-employed

Here's why;

1) **Total control of time**—as your own boss, you are in total charge of the most valuable commodity in life, your time. There are no set hours, you can come and go as you please. A King has all the time in the world to build his financial future.

2) **Unlimited earning potential**—no cap on salary; income is not limited; you can make as much as you want. Self-employment is your ticket to the magic kingdom of unlimited wealth. Unlimited wealth is the best thing that happens to the self-employed business owner. Bankruptcy is the worse thing that happens to the self-employed business owner. The old man said, if you are self-employed, you have to be willing to face the risk of poverty to receive the reward of attaining the great American dream of being truly rich. That's the truth of self-employment. **Only those willing to risk it all get it all; that's the American way.**

3) **Safest job in America**—You run the ship. You chart the course. You control your own fate. You can never get fired from this job.

4) **Unlimited dreams possible**—There is no limit to what future you can create, when you are totally in charge of creating it. Your business is your creation. You brought it to life. You willed it to exist. You created it. As the creator you are in charge of the show. You answer to no one. You call all the shots. You are in total charge of your future. Your future is only limited by the size of your dreams. You can be whatever you dream yourself to be; no one can stop your dreams from happening except you. You decide what dreams in life you want to live. You are the sole custodian of your dreams in life. You have no boss to blame for your unfulfilled dreams in life; you are the boss. As the owner of your own business, you are in total charge of making your dream of being rich actually come true.

The old man said, "Before you can live your dream of being rich, you have to know how to make a dream come true. I have learned from my own experience how to actually make a dream come true."

How the old man made his dream of being rich in real estate come true

1) He Believed—

He had to believe his dream of being rich in real estate before he actually lived his dream of being rich in real estate. This was not some positive thinking mumbo jumbo BS. He spent the time, money, and energy required to realistically believe this dream could be his new reality. He replaced the erroneous notion of, "Seeing is believing," with the correct notion of, "Believing is seeing." He said, real dreams can only be manifested through conviction of belief. He got this conviction of belief through self-education.

2) Self-Education—

He filled his head with real estate knowledge; books, tapes, seminars, conventions, etc...He put a million dollars worth of information in his mind first before he actually believed he could make a million dollars in real estate. Every book he read, every seminar he attended, every tape he digested slowly built up his confidence in the real estate industry until he actually **believed** he had the real estate smarts to **see** himself actually conquer the dream of being rich through real estate.

3) **He followed his own System of investing developed through self-education**—See Part 3: Change the way you invest.

4) **He Took Action**—He put the wheels in motion and used the confidence he obtained from his self-education to realistically GO FOR IT!! The old man said you can spend time and money on seminars, books, and tapes that can teach you how to change your life or make tons of dough, but if you do not act on the information, it is useless to you. The best way to act on this information is with written goals. If you fail to plan, you plan to fail. Written goals direct the action. The old man always put his goals in writing, because if his ambition ever faltered for whatever reason, he had written proof, a constant reminder of the commitment he made to himself. Written goals allowed the old man to **see** the steps necessary to make his dream come true, so he could actually **believe** it could happen (Seeing is believing). The old man said, written goals are your "coming out" party; they announce to yourself your serious intentions of making your dreams come true. Written goals are the directions that allow you to direct your energy and chart the path to accomplishing your dreams. Without written goals, the energy that creates these dreams has an opportunity to dissipate or evaporate; without written confirmation of your plans, you tend to forget or put off activities that could make these dreams a reality. The old man said, when you get lost in life's worries, written goals are like a Hagstrom—a path back to your dreams. That makes it easier to believe these dreams because you can see the steps necessary to make these dreams a reality. Written goals keep you

on track. In case you get derailed from your dreams and aspirations, you have a map that guides you back to that place inside you that conjured up those ambitious thoughts.

The old man said, without written goals it is like being in a speeding car with no clear direction as to where you are going, and eventually you will wind up running out of gas and forgetting the whims of your dreams instead of arriving at your destination and realizing your dreams. The old man said written goals are the compass that allows you to stay focused in one direction. With written goals, you will always know where you are going and how to get there; you are less likely to get lost. Written goals are how the old man "took action" and remained steadfast in his conviction to accomplish his dream of being rich in real estate.

5) He was "Too Stupid to Quit"—
Ten years after the old man entered the real estate industry, he ran into an old classmate, a fellow student from his 45-hour licensed real estate salesperson course at the <u>American School of Real Estate</u>. The fellow classmate asked the old man, "Harry, are you still in real estate?"

The old man responded, "Yes, I am a broker now and own my own company called Guardian Real estate. How about you? Are you still in real estate?"

The fellow classmate said, "I was too smart to stay in that cut throat business; it only took me six months to figure out the real estate business was a dead-end for me. Honestly, Harry, I don't know how you survived all those years in real estate. What's your secret?"

The old man said, "I guess I was just **too stupid to quit.**"
The old man said smart people have too many choices in life. They can try something, fail at it, QUIT, and then try something else. When smart people fail, they use their

expensive educations to rationally switch gears and move on to bigger and better things. Smart people never stick around long enough to make any business work. The old man said, why do you think "A" students eventually wind up working for "C" students in life? It's simple, "A" students are smart people that quit a business before it has time to be a success. "C" students are stupid people that NEVER QUIT. They go through the failures necessary to make a business a success.

The old man said, stupid people don't realize they have other choices in life; they try something, fail at it and keep on trying and trying and trying and trying and trying until they succeed or die trying. Stupid people NEVER QUIT, they don't know any better; they blindly follow their dreams, impervious to the reality of failure. They are too stupid to be smart enough to know that they should realistically quit. The old man said the best way to guarantee success, is to rule out the possibility of failure like stupid people and NEVER QUIT. The old man said it's ironic; most people think I got rich by educating myself and being **smart**, but in actuality, I got rich because I was **stupid** enough to **never quit** trying until my dream of being rich in real estate eventually came true. The old man said, **"being stupid and rich is a lot better than being smart and poor"** because sometimes in life, being stupid is being smarter.

I learned this lesson firsthand as a child growing up in Brentwood, NY. When I was growing up, I knew a foster kid named Mark. Mark loved music. He loved music so much that he would spend countless hours listening to records and mimicking the beats with his mouth. Eventually, he got so talented at this it was hard to tell if you were listening to a real record or Mark's extraordinary mouth. After a while Mark mastered this skill so well, he dreamed of doing it for a living. The only problem was there weren't many job openings in America at the time for a talented **"human boom box."** This stark reality did not stop Mark's passion; he was determined to make music his life, even if he had to help create a whole new genre of music to do it. And that's what he did. Even though the smart kids in school ridiculed him and told him he couldn't sing, Mark was stupid enough not to listen to them and opted to blindly follow his dream instead.

Eventually Mark helped pioneer a whole new style of music that embraced his rare talent: RAP! He started putting words to his beats, and wouldn't you know it; Mark or **"Biz Markie,"** as you probably know him, became a household name. The song *Just a Friend* soared and made him a celebrity. The song is still popular today. Who knows what would have become of Mark had he listened to all those rational "smart" people, who told him he was wasting his time following the foolish, unattainable dream of being a singer. Thank goodness Mark was like my old man—**"Too Stupid to Quit."**

To be a King of the Middle Class, You Have to Avoid Anchors

Anchors—Perpetually pessimistic people who try to unwittingly drag you down into the miserable abyss of their existence. They are a contagious breed of negatively infected people. They are people on a bad trip in life and they want **You** to come along for the ride— Misery always loves lots of company. The trials and tribulations of life have robbed these people of their dreams. They are realists, devoid of any dreamy ambitions. They are broken down, beaten people with a negative attitude that clouds their judgment.

These are people who have tried in vain to get rich for so many years, that now they are preconditioned to think it is a futile endeavor. They instinctively stop trying to get rich because the experience of failing has tricked them into believing it can't be done. They have come to the erroneous conclusion that being rich is an event in life that is not meant to happen to them. They rationally stop wasting any energy or time on the useless, unattainable effort of trying to be rich. Eventually, they accept the fact that being poor is their pre-determined destiny. The old man said, some anchors will actually justify their poverty by migrating to misguided fortune-tellers or psychics that cosmically confirm that being rich is just not in their cards.

The old man said, "Why do you think an elephant trainer only needs a thin rope attached to a stake in the ground to leash a massive four-ton adult elephant? Because adult elephants are so pre-conditioned to failure, they don't believe success (escape) is possible. The trainers use the elephant's greatest asset; its incredible memory to trick it into believing success (escape) is unattainable. As baby elephants, the trainers leash them with thick, heavy steel chains that make it nearly impossible to escape. Each time the baby elephant tries and fails to successfully escape, it remembers this futile act until years later it becomes engrained into the elephant's memory banks as something that cannot be done. Eventually the smart adult elephant, remembering all its past failures as a baby elephant stops trying to succeed (escape) and gives up. Unfortunately, some people in life possess this same "elephant mentality," they have been so educated at being a failure, they QUIT trying to be a success. The old man said, if **You** are hanging out with Anchors that drag you down and demoralize your spirit, LOSE THE EXTRA WEIGHT; it's the only way **You** will rise to the top and conquer your dreams in life.

A whole new standard of excellence has been painstakingly developed and **You** are the harbingers of these fledgling thoughts. Use the power of creation wisely as **You** shape and mold your financial future, in your head first and more importantly in your subsequent actions. Everyone wants to be rich, a select few take the steps necessary to reshape their reality and make that dream come true. I hope **You** are like my old man and me, dreamers that were TOO STUPID TO QUIT.

Unless someone instructed you to this page or you just got lucky randomly scanning this book I will assume that you read all the material up to this point. Either way, I will reward you with information that some naïve few would unwittingly believe appears at the end of a book, the conclusion. I purposely put the conclusion in this spot, and deliberately made no mention of this in the back of the book. This is my test to see if you were seriously reading this book and not just wasting my time by sightseeing. We penalize dilatants, people who give half-effort to something that deserves full effort, with lack of enlightenment. They have no right to this information; they have to earn it the old fashioned way, the way *you* earned it. They have to read the book. You will earn my friendship and respect if you keep this information private and confidential.

The conclusion is exclusively reserved for future millionaires in training, such as yourself. **Wannabes** who can't even read a complete book need not apply. Only *you* deserve the right to become a *self made man* of wealth. You did the work necessary to get to this point; you read the book; you get the prize of the good life. You just proved to yourself that you are better than the people who were too smart to keep reading on. You were intelligent enough to be **too stupid to quit**, a key ingredient needed to be a bona-fide King of the Middle Class. You are well on your way to being what you want to be. You are doing the work required for the position. You are retraining the brain. You are open to allowing this change to really happen. Being rich is not an accident; it is a well-planned event. The preparation for this planned event is reading books that give you the tools and confidence you need to revolutionize your thinking and successfully carry out this mission.

Please earmark this page and return to it when you to successfully complete part three—Change the Way You Invest. No peeking!! Don't take my word for it; instead, take the word of someone you probably already trust and respect; your loving mother. If your mom was here, she would probably tell you, "Good things come to those who wait." Heed her sagacious advice and refrain from being so impetuous that you blow your much deserved finale. Good luck on the rest of your journey and don't worry, **I got your back**, you earned it.

<u>The Real Conclusion</u>—Why did I go so far out of my way to bury the climax of your book? I purposely designed it that way to augment your training. Believe you me there is method to my madness. I wanted to prove a point to <u>**You**</u>. This book is not about me, it's about **You**. I am a total stranger to **You**. **You** don't even know me. **You** don't care about me. **You** care about **you** as well **you** should. **You** didn't buy this book to make me rich. **You** bought this book to make the person you care about *most* rich—**YOU**. **You** needed to prove to **you** that **you** have what it takes to be truly rich. **You** just did it. **You** just learned by your own actions, what the number one quality to be a truly rich person really is.

What it takes to be truly rich:
1) **You** have to be a **self educated** professional dreamer who pays attention to details.

One small mistake (Like not reading the books that give you the knowledge and confidence to believe the imagination that creates **your** dreams) **can be significant enough to change the result of everything** (like living your dream of being rich).

The amateur dreamers with all their education haven't figured this one out yet. They are still dreaming that their expensive college educations alone will guarantee their riches. They didn't get the message from the professional dreamers like Bill Gates, Paul Allen, Steve Jobs, Michael Dell, Andrew Carnegie, Ray Kroc, Henry Ford, John D. Rockefeller Sr., H.L. Hunt, David H. Murdock, Kirk Kerkorin, Richard Branson, Larry Ellison, Dhirubhai Ambani, Edmond Safra, and Subhas Chandra Goel. They were so focused on their dreams or vision, they couldn't afford to lose any valuable time on the distraction of the college education experience. Their passion for learning transcended the structured environment of the classroom. They didn't limit their educational experience to formal schooling only, they had the courage to free their minds from the conventional constraints of structured education and learn from a reservoir of unlimited education; their imagination. They were too busy working on another experience—making their dreams (formed in their imagination) come true. They made all that money because they were smart enough to forget about the money and the traditional path to money (college) and had the vision to follow their own carved path instead—their dreams. Dreams pay big dividends in the hands of the professional dreamer.

Amateur dreamers are so over-educated, they lack the imagination and foresight to realize such colossally high returns. I am here to even the playing field and correct this unfair advantage. I am here to educate the educated. As for you parents, I am here to educate your kids. I do not want you to blindly trust me on this one. I implore you to read my book and prove to yourself that I can really get the job done. If you don't like what I have to say, I respect your opinion. Please extend that same courtesy to me. Your kids will receive this message, the power of my dream, and the large tentacles of the internet; the social mind of the youth will assure that. I am thanking you in advance for the privilege, the honor of allowing me to shape the impressionable young minds of your loved ones. I will not violate that trust.

In time, I hope you see the value of my mission because I know it is "hard to teach old dogs like you new tricks." As for you kids, don't let your loving parents inadvertently kill your youthful **dreams** with their well-intended **realistic** views. If your **dream** is to make the world a better place to live in by pursuing an altruistic career like a volunteer firefighter, ambulance driver, environmentalist, peace activist, social worker, actor, musician, writer, poet, etc... and your doting parents assassinate your character with quips like, "You'll Starve!! Stop **dreaming.** Get a **Real** job," don't despair. Maybe it is time for you to become the teacher of your parents, and your parents to become the students of **You**. Maybe it is time for **You** to be true to yourself and not go against your nature by living a fake life or being a sell out by choosing a career based solely on mommy and daddy's monetary yardstick. Maybe you'll show your parents how much you *truly* love them by following your own heart and conscience and choosing the career of your **dreams.** Maybe you'll show them that "Stop **Dreaming**, Get **Real**," is just the opposite; it's really, **"Start Dreaming to be Real."** As Jim Morrison said, **"The most loving parents and relatives commit murder with smiles on their faces. They force us to destroy the person we really are: a subtle kind of murder."**

Translation: College education **alone** doesn't guarantee you will be a billionaire.

That training is up to **YOU.** There is no course in college that manifests the ambitious thoughts your imagination requires to live out your wildest dream of being rich.

That fire starts in your mind when you start filling it with sparks of new ideas obtained from your life experiences. Those little sparks cluster in the imagination, and like magic, they collide and form a burning desire. That burning desire either dies as a capricious whim or unfulfilled goal or that desired goal swirls deeper into your conscience and morphs into a full-fledged inferno called ambition—an ambitious fire raging inside you, a fire so intense, it explodes your doubts and fears out of your rational mind and forms a powerful laser beam of focused energy that grips the tireless thinker with the energy level required to expand those ambitious thoughts into a full fledged DREAM.

A star is born. The star is **You.** The star is so powerful it can be whatever it **dreams** itself to be. I am here to make you the star of your own life. You are in college because you are trying to figure out who you are and what you want to do in the **real world**. I am a professional dreamer, and I am here from a **real** world, the future world still under construction in your mind, not yet created by your dreams. I am here to enrich your college experience and make your future brighter by making you rich—rich in thought and rich in monetary gain, if that is truly your **dream.** I guess anything is possible once the star of the show in life (you) decides to turn that possibility into a **real** dream. I will help you build the future you haven't dreamt up in your head yet. The answer to what you want to do in life is unwritten in the real world. It resides inside each and every one of **You**, hidden somewhere in your dreams. I am from that dream world of your future, and I am here to show you how to get here. I am your navigator. I am here to show you how to launch the dreams that create your future.

I'm here to give you back that spark, that spark you had as a kid. You had no fear when you were young, you didn't know any better, society's jaded world didn't corrupt your fertile mind yet. I'm here to relight the ambitious fire burning inside each and every one of **You**. I am your servant, I was willed here by your insatiable desire to learn. This is not about me. This is about **You**. You are Your future, and we need to train **You**. You need to know the trick to life.

" **You have to Be who your imagination says you already are**." When you wake up one day, and you decide that you don't want to be anybody, other than the person you envision in your wildest dreams, then, and only then, are you ready to be that real person. You have to BE the person you want to BE, Now!! He/She who hesitates gets lost in the limitations of the real world. Don't fantasize away your dreams; BE your dreams. Consider this book a vacation from yourself and venture into the uncharted confines of your mind that establishes your limitations and stifles your aspirations.

I am here to evolve your thoughts. I am a worthy mechanic and I am here to give you a mental tune-up. I am here to twist your mind, rattle your soul, wake up your five senses, and align them in a new direction. I am here as a catalyst, to jumpstart the new **YOU**. The kids already know this message, but as adults we tend to forget. My daughters always sing to me:

"**You** can be what you want to be, anything you want to be, as long as **You** believe."

I am your guide. I am going to bring you inside a world you might not have explored before, I am going to bring you inside your own mind so we can reprogram the limitations of your imagination and let your dreams flow again. Maybe you forgot when you were little and a dreamer. Your mom and dad would ask you, "What do you want to be when you grow up?"

"Mommy, I want to be a firefighter, police officer, astronaut, millionaire, famous rapper, movie star, teacher…." The list was as endless as your dreamy imagination.

Wise Mom's stock answer, "You can be whatever you dream, son (daughter)."

I know my wise mom was right because I am living that dream right now by honoring my father's memory and teaching you how to **dream** so you can live any possible future you imagine in your **real** world. I am here to clean out your clogged thoughts and give you a new perspective on life. I am here to show you the future you can have, at a critical stage in your thinking—COLLEGE. I will lead you out of the dark labyrinth of confusion created by the real world and into the bright light of untapped potential waiting inside you, in your dream world. This is your life, not a dress rehearsal for some other bigger show. Every nanosecond of every day counts. This is the real deal. The only show in town, your own custom form of existence, your gift, your **LIFE.** This is the play known as your life, and you are the star attraction, so assume your leadership position and take charge of your life. The star always runs the show. Now run the show called your life. Stop letting other people decide how you enjoy the gift of your life. You are the star; now shine. Shine Bright. The star can be whatever it dreams itself to be, you just got to start the sparks flying.

Where do you get those sparks of new ideas that can fuel the dreams of your future? **Education.** The old man used to say every worthwhile idea in a book you read leaves a permanent scar on your soul; sparks always leave their mark. As Walt Disney once said, **"There is more treasure in books than in all the pirate's loot on treasure Island…and best of all, you can enjoy these riches every day of your life."** Don't get me wrong; there are other sources for these sparks such as TV, radio, movies, video games, magazines, seminars, conferences etc…and the most important one of all, life's experiences, the best generator of sparks. But the granddaddy of all sparks, the proverbial incubator is the college experience. College is a breeding ground of innovative, imaginative sparks swirling around in the young minds of the thinkers who go there to find their station or calling in life. College is an environment where dreams are allowed to flow freely. College is a soul-searching mission; it's about finding your **dream**. Some students dream of being doctors or lawyers or accountants or teachers or etc. Then they confirm the conviction of their **dream** and make it **real** by declaring a major. Then they fill their minds with the right knowledge that makes that **dream** a **reality**. Then they leave college and live their **dream** in the **real world**. The graduation is only the beginning of that **dream.** The true scholars will tell you, your self-directed educational journey really begins when you graduate college; it's called a commencement or beginning for that reason. Education never ends. As Albert Einstein used to say, **" Wisdom is not a product of schooling but of the life-long attempt to acquire it."**

The old man used to say, "The only way you will ever live your dreams in the real world is if you enter the reality of the dream world."

I gave him a quizzical look, and told him to stop hitting that morphine button; it was slurring his thinking.

He retorted, "Is it so hard to believe a dream world really exists? You watch TV don't you?"

I said, "Of course, who doesn't?"

The old man said, "Don't you go to another world in your mind for thirty minutes to an hour when you watch your favorite show, especially on the premium channels with no commercial interruptions from your wandering thoughts?"

"Yeah, but I am fully aware of the physical reality around me; I don't leave this physical reality to enter a purported dream world."

The old man said the beauty of the dream world is that it exists simultaneously in the same plane as the reality world. They exist side by side, complementing each other. You don't have to leave the real world to enter the dream world; you exist in both worlds at the same time. The only difference is the mock dream world created by the TV you watch in the real world has maybe

900 channels from which to choose. The real dream world that exists in the universe has unlimited channels, infinity channels; you never run out of material. The programming is as unlimited as the imaginations that create its content.

In nature, everything has an opposite; it's the cosmic symmetry that balances the universe. How would you know what dark is, if you didn't have light? How would you experience wet, if you could never be dry? How could you experience the horror of evil, if the benevolence of good didn't exist? How could you confirm your **real** physical world actually exists, if you didn't have a metaphysical **dream** world to compare it to? The dream world is *yin* to the real world's *yang*. The **dream world** is where the **impossible happens**, and the **real world** is where only the **possible happens**. Together they allow you to be a total free spirit, capable of experiencing the full ride in life without any restrictions.

College doesn't necessarily decide the real winners in life; that is a fantasy, a **dream.** That majestic honor is the privilege of the professional dreamers amongst you, who forgot about the money long enough to follow their **dreams** in the **real** world. Anything is possible in your dreams. Don't take my word for it; prove it to yourself. Let's see what our history shows when you forget the money and go for your dreams. How big do dreams pay off?

Fifty-Six Men who Signed the Declaration of Independence-
They all shared a once in a lifetime **dream**—to liberate themselves from the tyrannical rule of an oppressive, powerful government and build a new nation, their own nation. They were nation builders. A powerful group of professional dreamers that cast aside conventional wisdom and embraced their own radically unique form of self-government.

What caliber of men were they? According to the Connecticut Society of the Sons of the American Revolution (heretofore referred to as the Society) **"...Twenty–four were lawyers and jurists. Eleven were merchants; nine were farmers and large plantation owners, men of means, well educated. But they signed**

the Declaration of Independence knowing full well that the penalty would be death if they were captured."

These were all men of wealth and high social standing. They weren't looking to birth a nation to get rich; they already experienced the thrill of that dream. They were here for a much grander, much nobler dream: to preserve the future of all colonists by establishing a new nation based on the revolutionary concepts of democracy, freedom, and liberty for all. They wanted to experience the thrill of building a nation from scratch. They were so strongly opposed to what the British tyrants were doing; loss of money, social status, and even their own lives didn't matter. The integrity of the quality of life that they were going to leave behind to their heirs, took full precedence. They used their fortunes and business connections they amassed as second class British citizens (referred to as rebel rousing ruffian colonists by first class Brits living in the mother land) to live their dream of making us well respected 1st class free citizens of our own spanking brand new nation. They were so focused on accomplishing their dream of building this new nation for us that they were not concerned about the consequences of their actions. The Dream was going to be accomplished no matter how much money or lives it took; it was more important than any one man's wealth or status. It was a collective effort by a group of men inspired by their rich thoughts instead of blinded by their rich monetary gains.

What happened to some of these wealthy men that signed this nation-building document? According to the Society, **"Five signers were captured by the British as traitors, and tortured …Twelve had their homes ransacked and burned…Two lost their sons in the Revolutionary Army…Another two sons were captured…9 of the 56 who fought died from wounds sustained from the hardships of the Revolutionary War."**

They even named names, according to the Society;

"Carter Braxton of Virginia, a wealthy planter and trader, saw his ships swept from the seas by the British navy. He was forced to sell his home and properties to pay his debts, and died in rags."

"**Thomas McKean** was so hounded by the British that he was forced to move his family constantly. He served in Congress without pay, and his family was kept in hiding. His possessions were taken from him, and poverty was his reward."

"Vandals or soldiers or both, looted the properties of **Ellery, Clymer, Hall, Walton, Gwinnett, Heyward, Ruttledge, and Middleton.**"

Furthermore, according to the Society:

"At the battle of Yorktown, **Thomas Nelson Jr.,** noted that the British General Cornwallis, had taken over the Nelson home for his headquarters. The owner urged George Washington to open fire, which was done. The home was destroyed, and Nelson died bankrupt."

"**John Hart** was driven from his wife's bedside as she was dying. Their 13 children fled for their lives. His fields and his grist-mill were laid to waste. For more than a year he lived in forests and caves, returning home after the war to find his wife dead, his children vanished. A few weeks later he died from exhaustion and a broken heart."

"**Norris and Livingston** suffered similar fates."

Their lives were torn apart and ripped to shreds. Life as they knew it didn't exist anymore. They were wanted men. They just declared war on the single greatest military power of its time—the empire of Great Britain, and now there was a bounty on their heads. They were treasonous infidels. They were instant enemies of the largest war machine around. Their status as loyal, subservient, 2nd class British citizens was unconditionally revoked. There were no laws protecting them now. Those laws only applied to British citizens, not outlaws like them, who were looking to start their own country. It was open season on their heads. They were instantly labeled radicals or militant non-conformists, and Great Britain wanted to expunge them like a malignant growth. The rich lifestyle they had grown accustomed to was officially over. No more social parties or community events or casual fraternization with people. They had to flee the comforts of their loving homes and lose contact with their most precious assets in life, their friends, family and relatives. They were on the lam. They had to live like fugitives in any exile they could find. They couldn't afford to be seen in public, for fear of reprisals from British assassins or overzealous pro-British citizens.

They were viewed as a public relations nightmare, and they had to be silenced before their radical rhetoric spread. They were to be hunted down and eliminated before they infected the rest of the colony. They were marked men; make no mistake about it. They knew that the second they put their signature on that document. There was no rewind button or turning back. It was full speed ahead. They knew failure meant death, and they were all willing to risk that fate to conquer their dream of birthing a new nation. They were on the run for their lives. Their **real** lives depended on conquering their **dream**. They knew their only chance of living through this insurrection was winning the war and subsequently conquering their dream. Amateur dreamers would have tested the waters first, and had a way out, if things didn't pan out, not these fifty-six professional dreamers. They didn't have an escape plan if things didn't work out. There was no back up plan. It was ALL or NOTHING for these fifty-six dreamers. There was no reward for second place in this contest. Second place was death. It was first place or no place. That's the dedication and commitment level these pros possessed on their quest to fulfill their **real dream**.

The Revolutionary War wasn't won on the battle fields alone; it was also won in the minds of men. Battle by battle, the radical concept of democracy was slowly taking root in the consciences of the colonists until it took firm hold and became acceptable mainstream dogma that ignited the revolutionists in their crusade to win the war and live their dream of being a free sovereignty.

If it were not for these professional dreamers, we would not have the greatest environment in the world to live our dreams, the country that was born of a dream: our United States of America. The land of the free. The land of the brave. The land of dreamers.

Why do you think so many foreigners risk their lives just to get in? They want to live the American Dream and they are so determined to make that dream a reality, that they are prepared, like our fifty-six dreamers were prepared, to die for what they believe in.

So as **You** comfortably attend college and contemplate your future dreams, **You** should pay respectful homage to these Professional Dreamers who sacrificed their fortunes, their reputations and in some cases, their lives, just so **You** could have the privilege, the honor, the freedom, the liberty to **freely Dream**. They paid the ultimate price for your freedom. It wasn't FREE.

Abraham Lincoln—
Why did Abraham Lincoln draft and sign the Emancipation Proclamation and *eventually* free all the slaves? Historians want us to believe it was for one of two reasons: **military**—the Union army needed the extra manpower to defeat the South or **moral**—Abe Lincoln cared so much about the plight of the tortured, kidnapped, constituently deprived slaves that he was morally bound to redress this grave miscarriage of justice. My old man believed both those reasons were wrong. Lincoln didn't do it for military or moral reasons; he did it for personal reasons. He did it to be remembered and revered. Lincoln was mentally malnutritioned from the lack of respect he received from his peers. Lets look at his track record:

<u>Abraham Lincoln Track Record</u>
1. **Failed in business—Age 22**
2. **Ran for Legislature and was defeated—Age 23**
3. **Failed in business—Age 24**
4. Elected to Legislature—Age 25
5. **Sweetheart Dies (Ann Rutledge)—Age 26**
6. **Lincoln has 1st Nervous Breakdown—Age 26**

According to Joshua Wolf Shenk, in his book "Lincoln's Melancholy: How Depression Challenged a President and Fueled His Greatness" as cited in a *New Yorker* article called *The Critics: A Critic At Large*, and I quote, "At twenty-six, Lincoln had what seems to have been a nervous breakdown, the first of two." Shenk notes that unipolar depression typically emerges in the mid to late twenties. He reckons that, since Lincoln had two breakdowns, psychiatrists today would classify his case as a, "major depressive disorder, <u>recurrent.</u>" And he finds a family history of mental illness. A paranoid uncle, Mordecai Lincoln, lived alone and tinkered with pigeon coops: visiting family members, he would play the violin and weep in lieu of conversation. Mary Jane Lincoln, the daughter of a cousin, was committed to the State Hospital for the Insane, Jacksonville, Illinois, in 1867 and Shenk has found the entry in the hospital's admissions book: **"Insane thirteen years—Cause Unknown/Not thought to be hereditary—Not suicidal/Her father was cousin to Abraham Lincoln and she has features much like his.**"

Abraham Lincoln must have been alarmed; he knew his uncle Mordecai was nuts, and it must not have been a secret that the daughter of his cousin, who had an uncanny resemblance to him, was certifiable. He was probably hoping this was an isolated episode in his life and that he wouldn't ruin his fledgling political career by winding up like one of these two cuckoos.

7. **Defeated for Speaker—Age 29**
8. **Lincoln has 2ⁿᵈ Nervous Breakdown—Age 32**

According to the *New Yorker* article, "Lincoln's second collapse occurred in the winter of 1840 and 1841…In December, during a meeting of the Illinois legislature, he jumped out a second story window in an **unsuccessful** attempt to deny the democrats a quorum. (He wasn't hurt, and the Democrats joked that it was because the legs of the six-foot-four representative nearly reached to the ground.) In January of 1841, he missed roll call votes for several days and then for a full week because he had, in the words of Mary Todd's brother-in-law, gone **"Crazy as a Loon."**

Now Abraham Lincoln is really worried: second episode in six years. He is afraid people would find out about his family history and infer he was unsuitable for his elected office because he was nuts; you know the old, "The apple doesn't fall far from the tree syndrome." He didn't help matters any by jumping out a second story window and then going AWOL for a week, shirking his elected responsibilities. He must have been afraid that this illness would eventually get him, like it got two of his close family members. Especially since he looked just like one of them. According to the same article, "Late in life, Speed recalled that Lincoln had wished to die in 1841 but had lamented that he, **"Had done nothing to make any human being remember that he had lived."**

Translation; he didn't want to succumb to his losing battle with mental illness before he had an opportunity to do something that he could be respected and remembered for.

9. Elected to Congress—Age 37
10. **Defeated for Congress—Age 39**
11. **Defeated for Senate—Age 46**
12. **Defeated for Vice-president—Age 47**
13. **Defeated for Senate—Age 49**
14. Elected President of the United States Of America—Age 51

Abraham Lincoln was a virtual nobody until somehow, someway in 1860 he stumbled into the highest office in the land, like a lucky lottery winner. Prior to his ascent to the Presidency, his track record was clear and well known to his peers: failed in business twice, two nervous breakdowns, and defeated in six out of eight elections. Most notably, the twelve years prior to his becoming President, age 39–51, he was a professional losing-candidate. He was on a twelve-year losing streak. He had the Midas touch in reverse; every election he entered turned to shit instead of gold. When he got elected, the other politicians were stunned. They couldn't believe Abraham Lincoln, who had a career of being the losing candidate, ascended to the highest sought after political position in the land: President. How could they or any other onlooker respect Lincoln? Since he wasn't elected to any position in the legislative branch of our government for the past twelve years, he drafted absolutely zero bills that became law and in effect had absolutely no say in how the country was run and now, by happenstance, he had the final say in how our great country was governed. Abe had a twelve-year drought where he was powerless and then POOF!!, he was omnipotent; he was the President—the most powerful political position in America. The only problem was most people viewed him as a fluke and refused to extend the proper respect due a man of his new power and stature.

Abe was so disrespected that according to Doris Kearns Goodwin in her book, "Team of Rivals: The Political Genius of Abraham Lincoln," a Houston newspaper complained in 1860 that Lincoln, **"has most unwarrantably abused the privilege which all politicians have of being ugly."** Abe wins the election, and instead of being respected for his major accomplishment, he is basically called the ugliest of all the politicians of his time. I know the historians say Lincoln was a prankster, who probably laughed it off, but deep down inside this disrespect must have saddened his psyche immensely. He was the President, for goodness sake, and this was an insulting slap in his face. Did Lincoln want to be remembered as the ugliest president in history? I doubt that's how he wanted his presidential legacy to play out. This is not a very respectful memory that he wanted to leave behind for human beings to remember that he existed.

Goodwin in her book, "Team of Rivals: The Political Genius of Abraham Lincoln," says she thinks it was a stroke of managerial genius for Lincoln to appoint to his first Cabinet three rivals he had beaten for the Republican presidential nomination in 1860. The old man felt differently, he said it was a well-devised ploy by Lincoln aimed at garnering respect from his fellow politicians. Lincoln wanted to show them he was a winner, not a loser like his past track record showed. He was trying to show his peers he was the victor, not a defeated beaten man that they were accustomed to in past elections. By parading these three beaten rivals around, it was a constant reminder to all who observed that they should respect Lincoln for his new status of "Elected Winner." It took him twelve patient years to get to the coveted "winners circle" and he didn't want anybody to forget it. Granted, it was a good will gesture for unity in the newly formed Republican Party, but it also served to boost the disrespected image of Lincoln.

Lincoln's deficient respect took an even bigger hit once the war began. Major Northern newspaper editorials lambasted what little of his ego and respect was left by blaming him for choosing his party over his country, causing the Civil war and destroying the experiment called democracy.

"If this result follows—and follow civil war it must—the memory of ABRAHAM LINCOLN and his infatuated advisors will only be preserved with that of other destroyers to the scorned and execrated...And if the historian who preserves the record of his fatal administration needs any motto descriptive of the president who destroyed the institutions which he swore to protect, it will probably be some such as this: Here is the record of one who feared more to have it said that he deserted his party than that he ruined the country, who had a greater solicitude for his consistency as a partisan than for his wisdom as a Statesman or his courage and virtue as a patriot, and who destroyed by his weakness the fairest experiment of man in self-government that the world ever witnessed."—Editorial that appeared in *The American Standard,* New Jersey on April 12, 1861, the same day the Civil War started at Fort Sumter.

"We are to have civil war, if at all, because Abraham Lincoln loves a (the Republican) party better than he loves his country... (He) clings to his party creed, and allows the nation to drift into the whirlpool of destruction." Editorial that appeared in *The Providence Daily Post* on April 13, 1861, one day after Civil War unofficially began.

This was a public relations nightmare for Lincoln. (He became president on March 4th. A little more than a month later, he is being blamed for starting one of the bloodiest wars in history). This war could jeopardize any chance he had to redeem his tarnished character and earn the respect he deserved as the winning political candidate of the highest office in America's political forum,

President. Did he want to be remembered as the President who started a Civil War that could destroy America? This was not a very respectable memory that he wanted to leave behind for posterity, so future human beings could remember that he lived.

According to Shenk's book, the popular joke about Lincoln at the time of war was:

"One lady confides to another that she thinks the Confederates will win the war because their President, Jefferson Davis, prays. The second points out that Lincoln also prays. "Yes," replies the first, "but when Abraham prays, the Lord will think he's joking." If you pray for forgiveness with no hope of receiving it, is that what you are doing—joking?"

This humor shows that people of his time were elevating his disrespect by extending it all the way to the heavens; even God wouldn't respect him enough to believe the validity of his own prayers. Therefore they would remain unanswered, summarily dismissed, like Lincoln, as a joke.

As the war lingered on, the Union troops were taking a beating, and then something wonderful happened for our respect-starved Abraham Lincoln; he finally found his **something**—the one thing that he could do that he could be respected and remembered for by any human being that ever lived. Lincoln would win the war by freeing the slaves and be revered by all humanity for performing an act so memorable, so indisputably respectful, so presidential, so great, that all mankind would remember his magnanimous gesture. He concocted the Emancipation Proclamation, basically an official edict that freed all slaves who were willing to join the Northern army in their quest to defeat the South.

According to the *Smithsonian* magazine article of January 2006, when Lincoln is signing this document he says, **"I never, in my life, felt more certain that I was doing right, than I do in signing this paper,"** and he also says, **"If my name ever goes into history it will be for this act, and my whole soul is in it."** Lincoln says, **"If my hand trembles when I sign the Proclamation, all who examine** the document hereafter will say, 'He hesitated.'" According to the *Smithsonian* article, "...the president waited a moment and then took up the pen once more, **slowly and carefully** writing his name. **The signature proved to be unusually bold, clear and firm, even for him.**" Fred Seward recalled: Lincoln wasn't talking about the merits of extra troops or the plight of black people when he slowly, methodically, quite clearly, and without hesitation penned his name on this paper. He talked about only one thing, how well he would be remembered in future history for performing such a great act. He wanted to make sure his signature was pronounced so any future historian would not doubt the authenticator of this great act. He knew the value of what he was signing. He was willing to liberate an entire race of people, people that he didn't even like, just so he could earn his respect and guarantee that people in history would remember that he lived. He knew from that day forth, he was history in the making; if his ploy won the war, he would be known as the president who freed the slaves and saved the country. A well respected memory.

After he signed the document, again according to the *Smithsonian* article, "Ohio congressman-elect James Garfield... though he retained a low opinion of Lincoln...states, **'Strange phenomenon in the world's history...when a second-rate Illinois lawyer is the instrument to utter words which shall form an epoch memorable in all future ages.'**" According to the same article, **"When his old friend Joshua Speed next came to visit, Lincoln reminded him of the suicidal depression he had suffered two decades earlier, and of his disclosure that he would gladly die but that he 'had done nothing to make any human being remember that he had lived.' Now indicating his Emancipation Proclamation, he declared: 'I believe that in this measure....my fondest hopes will be realized.'"**

The Emancipation Proclamation was signed on September 22, 1862. Below are some quotes from Abraham Lincoln after he signed this act.

"Root, hog, or die."—Lincoln's comments to poor and illiterate ex-slaves unprepared for freedom—February 3, 1865.

Translation: Provide for yourself or do without and die.

"They had better be set to digging their subsistence out of the ground." —Lincoln, War Department memo dated April 16, 1863

"I cannot make it better known than it already is, that I favor colonization."—Lincoln supporting deportation of all blacks from America in a memo to Congress—December 1, 1862.

As is painfully obvious, Lincoln was no big fan of black people. He liberated them for his own agenda, and it wasn't just to win a war, granted they helped immeasurably; it was his one great act to be remembered for. And for that he would get to live his dream of finally being respected.

The old man said, **"One man's zeal for self respect eventually destroyed an industry that captivated an entire race of people, and launched our country in a whole new direction of thinking."**

I asked the old man, "Who killed Abraham Lincoln?"

The old man said maybe he hired someone to kill him. Maybe he was afraid he would succumb in his older days and lose his battle with insanity. He had already experienced two nervous breakdowns in his life that were so severe he actually contemplated suicide. Maybe he was afraid the third and final nervous breakdown, the one that would debilitate all his mental faculties, was forthcoming. You know three strikes and you're out. Maybe he didn't want to be remembered as the ugly lunatic who freed the slaves. Maybe he didn't want his great act to be perceived as the whim of an insane person. Maybe he didn't want to face the prospect of being locked up, forcibly detained, and in most cases, illegally kidnapped (like the slaves he freed), and put in an insane asylum. He was acutely aware of his family history; the insanity bug caught at least two members of his family—Mordecai and Mary. And maybe since he had two major breakdowns already, he felt the doctors were wrong about insanity not being hereditary. Maybe he felt he was next in line to catch the family plight of insanity. He experienced the hopeless horror of losing his mind at least twice that we know of. Maybe he had more episodes that we were not privy to. Maybe, because he was president, these episodes were shielded from public eyes. Maybe his advisors didn't want anyone to know how fragile his mental state really was. Maybe it would have been a national security risk to leak such a devastating realization about the man in charge of our domestic and foreign policies. Maybe it would have deleteriously affected our negotiating position in all political spectrums.

Maybe he was afraid of losing the respect that he worked so hard to attain. Maybe he didn't want his insanity to mar his winning ploy (Emancipation Proclamation). Maybe Lincoln knew he was losing his grip on reality and took matters into his own hands and arranged his own demise. Maybe he wanted to beat insanity to the punch and check out on his own terms. Maybe he wanted to go out a winner, a well respected winner. Maybe he didn't want to see it coming. Maybe it was all well planned. Maybe he figured he might as well hedge all bets and have someone he trusted kill him, so if suicide gets you the hell whammy, at least he had a shot at entering the pearly gates. Maybe he set his sights much higher than just getting some respect by drafting an Emancipation Proclamation. Maybe he wanted to elevate his status from finally well respected to worshipped and remembered forever by becoming a Full Fledged Martyr, at his timely death. Forever remembered as THE MAN who died so the slaves could be free and live. If he could only see how far his dream of being remembered played itself out. He is remembered like a King. Only a King gets his birth date declared a national holiday. On February 12, Lincoln's birthday, the entire population takes off from work just to respectfully remember the man. He is remembered like a Hero. Only a Hero gets his face plastered on millions of coins and bills that circulate through the general population. Every time you get a penny or five dollar bill, how can you not remember and respect the King of the average guy, the Hero of the underdogs, Abraham Lincoln? What a legacy to leave behind!

Do you think he would have gotten the same royal treatment if he had another nervous breakdown and finished out his golden years "crazy as a loon" in a nut house? I don't think so, and I don't think Lincoln thought so either. The old man said Abraham Lincoln believed enough in his **dream** that he was willing to die for it, and he did.

Tom Edison—

His dream was to invent. He was a prolific inventor; he was the only person in America to ever have a patent granted every year for sixty-five consecutive years, 1868-1933. He was *Life Magazine's* "Number One Man of the Millennium," credited with 1,093 patents to his name. He was so blinded by his ambition to invent, he didn't care about the group opinion; he steadfastly held his course and suffered through thousands of failed attempts, until his racked brain harnessed the power of electricity and produced a workable light bulb with a long lasting filament. An invention is a realized dream. Each failure inches you closer and closer to success until Poof!! The dream comes to life and reality is forever changed. True failure is conforming your mind to the thought pattern that the dream is unattainable. Once you internalize that thought process, dreams are suppressed by the restrictions of rational thoughts. Edison wasn't afraid to fall on his face and lose to make his dream come true. He knew the loser can gain more knowledge than the winner, for it is the greater act of the effort of losing that leads to the breakthroughs of thinking required to eventually win. Edison was quoted as saying:

" **I have not failed. I've just found 10,000 ways that won't work.**"

Edison was proof positive that if your imagination can produce it, your dream to succeed at it can create it. His dreams changed our reality. Where would we be without his dogged determination to light up our lives? His fantasy of inventing a workable source of light became the reality of our illuminated lives. Thank goodness, he was **"Too stupid to quit."** In Edison's own words, **"Genius is 1% inspiration and 99% perspiration."**

Walt Disney—

Walt's dream was *animation*; to animate our lives, to show us there is a place that exists inside each and every one of us—a Dream World, so to speak, where the impossible is possible. As Disney himself said, "It's kind of fun to do the impossible." A Dream world was created with no limitations or boundaries where ducks, mice, and dogs talk, elephants fly, giants and dwarves exist, broomsticks and witches and sorcerers exist, a veritable wonderland, where anything goes. Walt did not want to keep his dream world to himself; he manifested the **dream world** into our **real world**, so it took on a physical form, and we can **believe** it can really exist. So we can walk around in it (Dream World) and get lost in its allure for three or four days. Disney Land was created in his rich mind first, a mind full of limitless "sparks" that ignited his energy and guided the merciless dreamer in his quest, a mind filled with endless possibilities and wild, childlike, uninhibited ideas, before it manifested into the sane, sedate *real* world and came to life before our incredulous eyes. Disney Land is a real place that parents can escape the harsh realities of life into the infinitely comfortable world of *dreams*. He believed it before he saw it, so we could see it and believe it. He brought the **dream world** to **life**. It was willed to life by the vision or dream of one relentless professional dreamer, Walt Disney.

Walt wasn't in it for the money; he was following his dream. Walt was reared on a farm in Marceline, Missouri, where he became interested in drawing at a young age. He sold his first sketches to neighbors when he was only seven years old. At sixteen, Walt joined the Red Cross as an ambulance driver, but never lost focus on his dream; his ambulance was the only one in WW1 that was covered from stem to stern, not with stock camouflage, but with drawings and cartoons. In August, 1923, Walt left Kansas City with only a dream and $40 in his pocket. He went to Hollywood to live his dream of animating the world with his drawings conjured up in his dream world. We all know his **dream** came true; we are still **living** in it.

In 1965, after the tireless dreamer conquered his dream of animating the world through his drawings and movies, he turned his attention and money toward another dream, improving the quality of urban life in America. He personally designed an Experimental Prototype Community of Tomorrow or as we know it—**EPCOT.** In Disney's own words,

"I don't believe there is a challenge anywhere in the world that is more important to people everywhere than finding the solution to the problems of our cities. But where do we begin? Well, we're convinced we must start with the public need. And the need is not just for curing the old ills of old cities. We think the need is for starting from scratch on virgin land and building a community that will become a prototype for the future."

Disney's new dream was to build it. He bought 43 miles of virgin land, double the size of New York's Manhattan. He master planned his new dream, but unfortunately he died in December of 1966, before his dream could be realized. But this was the dream of a professional dreamer, not an amateur dreamer; it was a **real dream. Real** *dreams* never die; they survive physical death. Case in point—On October 1, 1971, five years after his death, his **dream** became our **reality**, and Walt Disney World in Florida was opened to the public. Mankind thanks you, Walt, for showing us what you always **believed,**

"If <u>You</u> Can Dream it, <u>You</u> can do it"
Walt Disney

Howard Stern—

Howard got his spark for broadcasting at a young age; he would tag along with his father Ben who worked at a local radio station. When he got older, he didn't lose this interest; it led him to pursue broadcasting as a career at Boston University. Howard chose to get a **real** education in broadcasting so he could pursue his **dream** of being a radio broadcaster with conviction and knowledge. His dream wasn't about making a half a billion dollars in radio, it was about getting the training required to earn an honest living as a free spirited DJ in the broadcasting business. If he told his mother,

Raye, "Mom I want to follow in Dad's shoes and go to Boston University and learn broadcasting, so I can make half a billion dollars from the radio industry," what do you think his mother would have said? I am just speculating, but it might go something like this;

Raye—Ben, Howard is smoking the funny cigarettes again!! He is having severe delusions of grandeur. I think he needs a shrink. He has lost his grip on **reality**. He's **dreaming** of making big bucks from the radio business. Ben, please explain to Howard the stark economic **realities** of broadcasting.

Ben—Howard, you will never be **rich** from radio; only the owners of the station get **rich**. You're **dreaming**, Son.

If Howard had made this bold proclamation to his parents at a young age, he would have been perceived as a lunatic, a disturbed bipolar, a madman, a wacko, or an unrealistic pipe dreamer living in a fantasy world. Because this **dream** is so far removed from the safe confines of the **reality** that they were accustomed to, they would naturally think he was a joke. Little did anyone know how **serious** this **joke** could be.

When he went to college at BU, I am pretty sure they didn't have a broadcasting course that outlined how to become the "King of all Media" and make half a billion dollars from radio. I could see his instructor telling him, "Howard, finish all your books and then use your vivid imagination to revolutionize the broadcasting business and make a half a billion dollars." I am sure that is not what happened. They couldn't have had such a course. It wasn't completed yet; it was still festering around inside the mind of its creator, the professional dreamer, Howard Stern. As a matter of fact, it is still being developed as we speak in Howard Stern's imaginative dreams. The only difference is they aren't dreams anymore; they're our reality.

What did happen was: Howard Stern followed his passion for broadcasting instead of following his passion for money and it led him to a jackpot of up to $500,000,000 and counting.

When Howard Stern was eighteen years old, could he have imagined in his **wildest dreams**, that his **dream** of being a radio broadcaster could land him a **real** job that pays him up to $100,000,000 a year (one hundred million)? Probably not; he was too busy having fun conquering his dream of being the best broadcaster in the world to worry about trite matters like money. The truth is he came perilously close to getting nothing. When the FCC and other factions of society tried to muzzle his voice and destroy his dream of being a broadcaster with usurious fines and picket signs, his story could have ended there. He could have been out of a job and broke. When management started losing advertisers and pressured Howard to tame the show's content or get fired, he didn't abandon the integrity of his work by watering down his dream. Not him. You couldn't buy his silence or subordination for any amount of money, the credibility of his FREE SPEECH was a big part of his **dream** and it wasn't for sale. He wasn't afraid to be hated for speaking his mind; he was **real,** and his growing audience knew that and loved him for his brutal honesty. He wasn't an amateur dreamer; he was a consummate professional. He was willing to sacrifice his current job for his more important dream of being the best broadcaster in the free world. A lesser grade DJ would have caved in and relented. These amateur dreamers only **dream** of living like the stars they interview. The disc jockeys that morph into professional dreamers, like Howard Stern, **live** the dream of living like the stars they interview, and then some.

His dream to be a broadcaster wasn't stifled by the critics or regulators; he doggedly persisted until a new medium of broadcasting welcomed this pioneer of human communication—the censor free satellite airwaves. His dream wasn't destroyed when he was fired numerous times and almost fined out of existence. NO!! It was heightened to a fever pitch; it gave him an opportunity to have an even greater voice, an unlimited voice, not syndicated around the country, but around the WORLD. His dreams carried him the whole way or maybe he just answered the help wanted ad.

<u>Help wanted</u>
Fledgling Industry Requires
Communications Expert
To Mastermind Expansion
Of New Technology
Into Burgeoning Marketplace
Salary Based on Performance
Earn Up to $500,000,000 or more in 5 years
Only <u>REAL DREAMER'S</u> Need Apply

Translation: that's $1,923,076.92 per week.
Following your dream pays big dividends
(Guess he won't need to bag lunch anymore)

Mike Tyson-

Born June 30th, 1966, in Cumberland Hospital, in the Bedford-Stuyvesant section of Brooklyn NYC, Michael was the *19th* child fathered by the prolific Jimmy Kirkpatrick, a portly, vociferous laborer. Michael was the bastard son of Jimmy Kirkpatrick and Lorna Tyson. Prior to Michael's birth, Lorna smith married and divorced a man named Percel Tyson. Lorna never remarried, but after falling in love with Jimmy, Lorna respectfully assumed his surname, and addressed people as Lorna Kirkpatrick. When Michael was only two years old, Jimmy moved out, and Lorna reverted back to her legally changed marriage name, TYSON. Thus Michael Gererd was unleashed into our world as a Tyson not a Kirkpatrick.

Michael wasn't like the other kids who lived in Brownsville, the poorest section of one of America's roughest cities, Brooklyn. He was born with a unique tone of diction, a high, lisping, almost squeaky voice. The other kids would taunt him for this and call him "little fairy boy" and then Mike would fight them, usually knocking them out. This speech defect actually became one of Mike Tyson's greatest assets in life. It forced him to hone the skills of his eventual trade, fighting, at an early age. Mike wasn't fighting for money, he was street fighting for something way more important; his respect. When Mike was nine years old, a fifteen-year-old bully made the mistake of disrespecting him by stealing one of his pigeons and killing it by pulling its head off. Tyson flew into a furious rage and publicly humiliated this well respected gang member by throwing him a much deserved beating. After that day, Mike was the Man, no other kids would dare call him "little fairy boy" anymore. Mike only knew one way to get respect from people—beating it into them with his rock hard "iron" fists. In another incident, Michael recalls in his own words, "One morning I woke up and found my favorite pigeon, Julius, had died. I was devastated and was gonna use his crate as my stickball bat to honor him. I left the crate on my stoop and went in to get something, and I returned to see the sanitation man put the crate into the crusher. I rushed him and caught him flush on the temple with a titanic right hand. He was out cold, convulsing on the floor like a infantile retard." Tyson's early habit of punching first and asking questions later, led him to become one of Brownsville's most respected and feared street fighters. Tyson used this new respect to launch his criminal career. At ten years old, Tyson was the youngest recruited member of a notorious gang called the Jolly Stompers. Mike was involved in muggings, armed robberies, burglaries, assaults, and lots of arrests. Tyson was arrested dozens of times before he was twelve years old.

This is where the story of Mike Tyson should have ended. He should have been a lost statistic in the penal system, or dead from his nefarious activities, but his age, and his status as a juvenile, prevented that reality. Instead, Tyson was sent to a New York correction center called the Tyron School for Boys. This is where the dream that saved Michael Gererd Tyson's life began. It is here that Mike Tyson met Bobby Stewart, an ex-heavyweight boxer who was the school's athletic coach. Bobby took Tyson's raw talent for street fighting and started molding him into an aspiring boxer. Suddenly, all of Mike's pent up rage had an outlet, a well focused direction, a reason to exist. Mike took to boxing like a virgin in a brothel; he couldn't get enough. He became obsessed with the sport of boxing. There wasn't enough time in the day to satisfy his unquenchable desire to learn boxing. He consumed the hours of each day practicing boxing techniques and training hard. He would devour books and absorb countless tapes on the great fighters of the past. The staff at Tyron were quoted as saying, "…it was possible to hear grunts and groans coming from Tyson's room at 3, 4 o'clock in the morning-It was Mike working on his defensive moves." Mike found his passion, his calling in life and he was only thirteen years old. At thirteen, he weighed 200 lbs and was bench pressing 220 lbs for $10 bets with the staff at Tyron. At Tyron, Mike ironically found legitimacy and love for his seemingly aberrant behavior of beating people up. It was OK to beat people up in a ring. They don't send you to jail; they pat you on the head instead. It was respected. It was a job he liked learning. It was fun. All the fights he ever had in his short life were now all justified; they were informal sparring matches for his new career as a fighter. He was a fighter, and he was starting to dream of being the best fighter in the world.

Bobby Stewart was so impressed with young Mike's new affinity for boxing that he felt Tyson was ready for advanced training and arranged for him to meet an old contact of his, the legendary trainer Cus D'amato. Cus had tremendous credentials; he trained legendary fighters Floyd Patterson and Jose Torres to their respective championships. After sparring a few rounds for Cus, Stewart asked Cus, " Well Cus what do you think?"

"I think that is the next heavyweight champion of the world, if he wants it."

Mike was hooked. He now had a new reason to live, the dream of being heavyweight champ. How convinced was Cus that Mike could successfully pull off this dream? Constantine "Cus" D'amato was so impressed with Mike's boxing potential that he persuaded the authorities to allow Tyson to live in the Catskills house he shared with his partner of forty years, Camille Edward. Under Cus's tutelage, Tyson started the physical and mental training required to make this dream come true. Tyson had a father figure for the first time in his life and a new mission or objective in life—sacrificing whatever time and energy it took to become a boxing champion.

Eventually, Cus paired Mike Tyson with two top boxing managers, Jim Jacobs and Bill Cayton.

Mike was in his glory, Jacobs and Cayton not only supplied financial support for realizing his dream but training material as well; they owned the largest collection of film fights available. In 1961, Jacobs and Cayton combined their boxing films and organized the film library, Big Fights, Inc., and now young Mike had access to this wealth of boxing knowledge. While we were all watching the boob tube till the wee hours of the morning, this warrior in training was watching, digesting, and learning the moves and styles of every great fighter there was. Tyson became a veritable walking and talking encyclopedia of boxing methodologies. Tyson read the books, watched the tapes, did the training; it is no wonder he tore up the amateur boxing circuit. As an amateur, he was virtually unstoppable. He compiled a record of 24-3. Nothing was going to stand in the way of Tyson and his dream, not even the loss of his mother Lorna at sixteen years young. Tyson relentlessly persevered toward his prize—heavyweight champ. Now he was ready to pursue his dream further; his dream wasn't amateur heavyweight champ; it was professional heavyweight champ. It took five long, hard years of strenuous work to reach this apex and he knew the journey was just now beginning.

The eighteen-year-old Tyson, now legally adopted by Cus, turned pro on March 6, 1985. He was well positioned for this adjustment in skill level. The confidence he obtained in the amateurs gave him the belief he needed to enter the pros with only one thing on his mind, living the dream of being the heavyweight champ that his dad promised could be his if he wanted it. He wanted it. It was the only thing he dreamed of. After he demolished his first pro opponent, Hector Mercedes in only 107 seconds, he could taste that dream in his hungry heart. He finished the year by destroying fourteen more obstacles in the way of his dream. He finished the year 15-0, all by knockout. Twelve more consecutive wins and he was ready to assume his position atop the heavyweight division and claim his sought-after prize—the unfathomable dream of being the Heavyweight Champ. Only one obstacle stood in his way now, Trevor Berbick. Nothing was going to stop this professional dreamer from accomplishing his mission, not even the untimely death of his new dad and mentor, Cus D'amato, on November 4, 1985. As he entered the ring on November 22, 1986, the culmination of seven years of dedicated conditioning, studying, and training entered that ring with him as twenty- year-old Mike Tyson annihilated the last obstacle standing before him and his dream. Mike made history that night, becoming the youngest heavyweight champion in boxing history at twenty years and 144 days young. Tyson was crowned the WBC heavyweight champion by defeating Trevor Berbick with a second round knockout.

You know the rest of the story:

Tyson amassed over $400,000,000 in his career, yet was $34,000,000 in debt and legally bankrupt before his 2005 fight with Kevin McBride, for which he earned $5,000,000 compared to McBride's paltry $150,000.

A lot of people think Mike Tyson was a loser for pissing away all that money. He wasn't. He was a winner. He was living the life you could only dream of living, only difference was he wasn't sleeping through his dream, he was fully awake and enjoying the ride. He wasn't in it just for the money. He burned through that money with wanton disregard. Once he conquered his dream of being heavyweight champ, he was lost. Everything he had lived for, he just accomplished. The only problem was he was only 20 years old and motherless, fatherless twice, and friendless. When the reporters hounded him on his financial irresponsibility's, he responded:

"I'm the most irresponsible person, in the world. The reason, I'm like that is because, at twenty-one, you all gave me $50 or $100 million, and I didn't know what to do. I'm from the ghetto. I don't know how to act. One day I'm in a dope house robbing somebody.

The next thing I know, 'You're the heavyweight champion of the world'...Who am I? What am I? I don't even know who I am. I'm just a dumb child. I'm being abused. I'm being robbed by lawyers. I think I have more money than I do. I'm just a dumb, pugnacious fool. I'm just a fool who thinks I'm someone. And you tell me I should be responsible?"

Tyson didn't do the irresponsible thing and read books and watch tapes on how to properly invest money, he did the responsible thing and read books, watched tapes, and trained for only one thing, his focal point, the one reason to live, his **dream,** being heavyweight champion. Make no mistake about it, he was a professional dreamer. He read the books. He studied the tapes. He knew the past and present of boxing as he shaped the future of this sport with his realized dream of being the youngest Heavyweight Champion in boxing history. He could care less about the money. In his own words:

"Real freedom is having nothing. I was freer when I didn't have a cent. Do you know what I do sometimes? Put on a ski mask and dress in old clothes, go out on the streets, and beg for quarters."

When Tyson had three valuable years of life to kill in prison, did he spend it reading books on how to properly invest millions of potential earnings he might garner upon his release? No, In his own words, **"When I was in prison, I was wrapped up in all those deep books. That Tolstoy crap—people shouldn't read that stuff."** He read philosophical books to make his mind rich not his wallet.

After Tyson was incarcerated and stripped of his coveted heavy weight crown, who did he seek upon his release? Don King. The man who purportedly mismanaged his money. Why? Because he wasn't concerned about money, he wanted to be heavyweight champ again and Don King had a track record with Mike of making that dream a reality. A powerful dream has that irrational effect on a man.

As boxing promoter Dan Duva said on Mike Tyson hooking up again with promoter Don King: **"Why would anyone expect**

him to come out smarter? He went to prison for three years, not Princeton."

In retrospect, Tyson was a professional dreamer living his dream of being Heavyweight Champ, the only problem was he met two other professional dreamers on his way into the ring; Don King and Robin Givens who were both living an entirely different dream, the great American dream of getting rich. There were no winners or losers. They all won. All three helped each other reach their respective dreams together. In Tyson's own words he was, **"Smart too late and old too soon...."**

Hey, money comes and goes, but living the dream of being the baddest mother f*#$er on the planet is a once in a lifetime experience; that is worth way more than any money Mike could have pissed away. He didn't make all that money by being a financial wizard, he made it by following his dream and wherever it led him. It led him to $20,000,000 in 91 seconds on June 27th, 1988 in a fight against Mike Spinks, that's $219,780.22 per second. Overall It led him to a jackpot of over $400,000,000 (four hundred million), not bad for a high school dropout with limited prospects. So he wasn't sophisticated enough to keep all the money, so what? When you are finally knocked out of life you won't be taking your money with you either, but at least his kids will know the unlimited value of dreams.

Bill Gates—

In 1975, twenty-year-old Bill Gates made what would prove to be the biggest financial decision of his life. He walked away from the guaranteed future that he would have had as a Harvard educated graduate and chose to follow his childhood dream instead, to whatever uncertain future it would lead him. Bill couldn't help himself, he was driven by a passion; a passion created at Lakeside Prep School, where at thirteen-years-old he and his future business partner, Paul Allen, a fellow classmate, were first exposed to and fell in love with computers. A passion so great that they would hibernate in the computer room all day and night, writing programs, reading computer literature and experimenting on the computer. A passion so intense that they started skipping classes and homework just to play with their new toy. These wild-eyed kids were so enamored with the computer, they gobbled up a year's worth of computer time (which Lakeside leased from GE) in just a few weeks.

By following this early passion, they got a taste of what it felt like to make money in the obscure unexploited new world of computers. At fourteen, they combined their energy and enthusiasm and got paid $4,200 from their prep school to write a scheduling program. Now these inquisitive fourteen-year-old kids had 4,200 reasons to be hooked on computers and started the adventure of devouring any and all conventional information and knowledge that was readily available about this new cutting edge technology. This childhood adventure eventually landed this tag team, at ages fifteen, another paying gig at the University of Washington campus where Bill's sister Kristi, who was in student government at UW helped Bill and Paul land a $500 contract to help computerize class enrollments. At UW they gained access to "C-Cubed" (a computer center corporation formed by four UW faculty members) and its coveted PDP-10. (The same time-sharing computer that they experimented on at Lakeside). They had, in their childhood fervor, exhausted all the conventional resources and information available concerning this emerging field of study. At UW, they welcomed the opportunity to quench their thirst for even greater computer knowledge by experimenting on computers with some like-minded college scholars. Now they were learning at an accelerated, frantic pace, driven by their insatiable desire to learn and earn. Computers were a game to them, and they got so good at the game that quite naturally their childhood curiosity drifted them too far from protocol. You know "kids will be kids," and they were banned from the computer for a summer for hacking into the system without authorization.

But that didn't stop these dreamers. They had the computer bug and nothing was going to stop them from learning. Paul Allen was so determined to continue his education on the PDP-10, he hacked into the electrical engineering department's free account at "C-cubed" and continued his computer training throughout the banned summer. Bill followed suit shortly thereafter. They were now learning at a hectic speed. The old adage, "Two heads are better than one," applied to these dreamers as they bounced ideas and knowledge off of each other.

This burning, yearning for learning was eventually rewarded by the computer center when they recognized the merits of their childhood antics and hired them to hack into and plug any defective flaws that could crash their computer system. Bill and Paul were in their computer glories, they had unlimited access to the greatest toy ever invented, the computer. Gates was quoted as saying, **"It was when we got free time at C-Cubed that we really got into computers. I mean, then I became hardcore. It was day and night."** Now, they were unstoppable, but alas the computer center went belly up in 1970, and they were back to square one. They were still in high school, and someone just took away their favorite toy. These two determined dreamers would have none of that. They were not going to stop their education midstream because of the glitch of a defunct company. They were avid riders now, and they wanted to get back on their horse.

Paul Allen, in his juvenile zeal, decided to take matters into his own hands, and quite simply walked into the computer center at UW one day and started using the computers. When he was approached by the professor and asked, "Are you a student here?" Paul responded NO, but he was so helpful answering other students' questions regarding computers, he was allowed to stay. Bill followed suit thereafter. When his craving for more computer learning exceeded the normal hours of the computer center, Bill's passion for computers compelled him to sneak out of his home in the middle of the night, to take advantage of an unused PDP-10 in the Old Physics Building at UW. Bill was quoted as saying, **"I also found that the Old Physics building at the UW had a PDP-10 computer that was busy about 20 hours…I felt a duty to do something about those remaining four hours."** That is the dedication **You** need to be a **real dreamer**.

By age seventeen, Bill and Paul 's unrelenting passion for computers led them to form a corporation called Traf-O-Data, where they honed their computer skills and together created a small computer that measured traffic flow. They grossed $20,000 from this business. This was their first real taste of the amount of money they could make together in the virtually untapped lucrative new world of computers. They disbanded this company when Bill abandoned his childhood dream and sought refuge in the real world of Harvard University. Bill was going to make his dad proud and follow in his footsteps and become a lawyer. That sentiment didn't last long. Bill's childhood fascination kept gnawing at his soul and driving his actions, and he naturally migrated from pre-law studies to Harvard's computer center, where he instinctively resumed his love for computers. Once again, Bill's passion for computers got in the way of his studies. He couldn't help himself. He would spend tireless nights camped in front of the school's computer and sleep during the day usually in classes.

Bill realized at Harvard that he was still uncontrollably excited about computers. He couldn't shake the bug. It was like a virus that was gaining momentum and would soon consume all his intellect and energy. To make matters worse, his former business partner and good friend Paul Allen, who Bill kept in constant contact with during his Harvard experience couldn't shake the bug either. They were still both hooked on computers, and during the summer, they both furthered their computer skills by getting jobs together at Honeywell. They plotted the possibility of one day rekindling their partnership and forming a business together again. Then it happened. Paul Allen saw a *Popular Electronics* magazine article touting the new Altair 8800, the precursor to the personal computer, and showed it to Bill and they saw their opening, their way into the magical world of computers. They were so convinced of their computer abilities from their past successes together, they did the unthinkable. They contacted MITS, the maker of the Altair 8800, and told them they had a workable Basic program for this computer before they even created it. It took them eight weeks to turn this lie into the truth of a workable program. This experience opened their eyes to the possibilities and profit potential of personal home computers.

A Dream was born. They would design and mass market an affordable computer for personal use. The problem was they needed a workable operating system to facilitate this dream. The other problem was there were a lot of other dreamers who were sharing the same dream. They both knew the fledgling computer industry was a volcano looking to erupt, and timing was everything. Whoever had the right technology at the right time would explode into the stratosphere like a runaway profit rocket. These professional dreamers were so convinced that they were going to be pilot and co-pilot of that rocket that they threw their futures away and risked everything and dropped out of college just to chase their dream of finding that right technology. They were going to find that right technology, the disk operating system (DOS) they needed, even if they had to develop it themselves.

Bill was too intelligent to be a dilettante. He wasn't going to give his dream half commitment—it was full commitment or no commitment. He couldn't continue his studies in college when his heart was in computers. He was a programmer; and he wanted to write the program on his own life. He wanted to create his own future, his own design for life, his own fate. He knew what he wanted, his destiny to be, and it wasn't pre-law; it was computers. He would have felt like he was missing his calling in life if he didn't pursue the challenge of the computer industry. No mortal man wants to risk missing his destiny. Leaving college was more than a whim, he had concrete reasons to leave college; it was defective for his purposes. The computer industry was still being molded and shaped when he matriculated. It was impossible to get a **real** education in computers in a school setting. They didn't have DOS 101 in Harvard, it was still circulating around in someone's unfinished dreams. In order to pursue his career objective, Bill had no choice but to leave the safe confines of the traditional educational experience and enter the unknown world of dreams, where the computer industry was taking root. He wanted to be a part of this growing trend before it took off without him.

Bill Gates was willing to go for broke. He was willing to throw away a bright, prosperous, well-charted future as a prominent, well-connected Harvard lawyer just to follow an inane, wild childhood dream—computers. He was ready to go for it, and he knew, like Lincoln knew, he couldn't hesitate. It was now or never. He stepped out of the secure **real** world and like a true pioneer stepped into the uncharted realm of his dream world. He wasn't worried about the real world anymore; his new priority in life was conquering the new reality taking shape in his dreams. He left his guaranteed future to discover and create a whole new future for himself. They loved computers so much, they both dropped out of college—society's barometer for success—and joined the race to spearhead the design of this fledgling industry by together forming a company called Microsoft.

It wasn't an easy road. The road to your conquered dreams is littered with the reality of major disappointments, minor setbacks, and untimely failures. In their first year in business, these two college dropouts and their newly formed company, Microsoft, earned a meager $16,005. A chilling realization must have gripped these two dreamers—"Did we both leave college and screw up our **real** future to get paid $8,000 a piece for a future based on a **dream**?" Amateur "non-committal" dreamers would have labeled this dream a nightmare and would have high-tailed it back to the safety of the real world in college. Not these professional dreamers. They were on a mission, and nothing, not even lack of initial monetary success, was going to prevent them from riding that rocket. They knew this was the ride they were meant to be on. What kept them going? The passion to win the hunt of finding that right technology, the disk operating system that could make their dream of personal home computers a viable reality. They suffered through five more years of poverty, trying to develop their own disk operating system, and then in 1980, they found this right technology at a company called Seattle Computer Products and promptly pooled their resources and acquired it for $50,000. Now they had the keys to that rocket ride, and they blasted off into a dream world of colossal profits. They chose the thrill of dreams over the sedation of reality. How big of a financial decision was this? How big did their dreams pay off?

Their <u>Dreams</u> made them Billionaires in our real world.

Bill Gates—billionaire (his dream earned him the moniker "richest man on the planet")

Paul Allen-billionaire

If everyone was meant to be rich, it would be a meaningless endeavor to conquer; it would lose all value if everyone got this grand prize. That special honor is exclusively reserved for people like Bill Gates and Paul Allen who dare to dream beyond the confines of reality. The uniqueness of making large sums of money is unparalleled to any other achievement in life. With lots of money you can change the world the rest of us live in, if that's your dream. As Bill and Paul have already proved to us, anything is possible in your dreams. Maybe Bill will have the pleasure of teaching us this very valuable lesson twice, when he, wife Melinda and fellow dreamer Bono conquer the impossible dream of solving world hunger.

As a side note, I wanted to make mention that some misinformed souls actually believe Bill and Paul were disingenuous when they acquired a disk operating system for $50,000 that they used to board that profit rocket. This is not the case; they were just adroit enough to realize the potentiality of this technology and its proper application. They did not steal it, they did the admirable thing; they justly compensated the proprietor, who was obviously a **realistic non-dreamer.** This is not the first time or the only time that this has happened. In 1961 Ray Kroc, another professional dreamer, saw the potential of franchising and bought a string of hamburger joints from two brothers named Richard and Maurice McDonald for $2.7 million dollars and franchised it into a multibillion dollar corporation. McDonalds may have been Richard and Maurice's' stark reality, just a string of impersonal restaurants, but for 2.7 million dollars, it became Ray Kroc's billion dollar realized dream.

Here are some interesting quotes you should engrain in the memory banks of your vast mind as you traverse through the hallowed halls of your fine, educational entity dreaming about your future.

"Example isn't another way to teach, it is the only way to teach."
Albert Einstein

"The biggest risk in life is not knowing what your future life could have been like had you taken that risk."
Tim Larkin

"There's many a bestseller that could have been prevented by a good teacher."
Flannery O'Connor (1925-1964)—a person with the conviction to judge the merits of her own work and follow her dream of being a writer.

"The concept is interesting and well-formed, but in order to earn better than a 'C', the idea must be feasible."
—A Yale university management professor responding to student Fred Smith's paper on the feasibility of an reliable overnight delivery service. Fred followed his dreams instead and founded Federal Express Corp.

"Everything that can be invented has been invented."
Charles H. Duell, Commissioner U. S. Patent office
I guess Charles didn't get the Post it; Inventions are as limitless as the imaginations that create them—Infinite.

"If I had thought about it, I wouldn't have done the experiment. The literature was full of examples that said you can't do this."
Spencer Silver on the research that led to 3M "Post-it" notepads.—When you follow your dreams you never know where it leads you.

"Who the hell wants to hear actors talk"

Warner Bros 1927—rejecting the virtues of sound in motion pictures. Now they wouldn't dream of making a movie without it. Go Figure.

"Heavier-than-air flying machines are impossible." "
1895—Lord Kelvin, President Royal Society—That's what they have professional dreamers for, to make the impossible possible. Case in point.

"This 'telephone' has too many shortcomings to be seriously considered as a means of communication. The device is inherently of no value to us."
1876—Western Union internal memo ——How big a Dream did they miss?

"The wireless music box has no imaginable commercial value. Who would pay for a message sent to nobody in particular?"

1920's—David Sarnoff's office when asked to invest in new communication medium called a radio. Where would Hip-Hop be today if Sir Oliver's and Marconi's dream was allowed to die?

"We don't like their sound, and guitar music is on the way out"
Decca Recording—1962 (rejecting the Beatles) Where would rock and roll be if the Beatles hadn't followed their dreams?

"I think there is a world market for maybe five computers"
1943 IBM Chairman Tom Watson—
He was right, the only difference was it was five computers per home, a little larger market.

"There is no reason anyone would want a computer in their home"
Ken Olson—1977 Digital Corp.—How poor of a rational thought was this?

"So we went to Atari and said, 'Hey, we've got this amazing thing, even built with some of your parts, and what do you think about funding us? Or we'll give it to you. We just want to do it. Pay our salary, we'll come work for you.' And they said, 'No.' So then we went to Hewlett-Packard, and they said, 'Hey, we don't need you; you haven't got through college yet."

Steve Jobs—trying to get Atari and HP interested in investing in his dream called Apple Computer. Boy, were they asleep!! No, No they were fully awake that was the problem, they should have been dreaming like Steve was.

The only way you will be truly rich, is if you loosen your mind and do like Steve jobs does

"Stay Hungry, Stay Foolish," enough to enjoy following your dreams wherever it takes you, like a billion dollars.

Translation: Loosen up and let your dreams flow and then you will prosper.

"Don't sleep through your dreams in life, Wake up and Live them."
Tim Larkin

<u>The Lesson to be Learned</u>

The next time someone you love and respect calls you psychotic for having the *right* frame of mind to *dream* of being rich, maybe you should ignore their well intentioned advice and have enough love and respect for your own judgment to forge ahead with your grand plans; only then will you become truly rich in the conviction that makes that wild fantasy a reality. *Translation:* being rich isn't about the money; it's a change in attitude created by the conviction of rich thoughts.

Maybe you should tell the ones you love to expand their mental horizons to include the possibility that **Dreamers** like YOU can make the most money in the *real* world by forgetting about the money and instead pursuing their dreams conjured in the fantasy world of their imaginatively creative minds. There is no limit to the riches created in the mind. Maybe it is time for you to tap into this wealth-building logic and be a foolish dreamer.

Dreamers are impervious to the "real world" time we live in. They are not bound by this limitation; it does not impede, slow or retard their mission. The mission of accomplishing their goals slices through the conventional boundaries of our time system. Have you ever sat down and played a video game; you were so hell bent on beating the game, you lost track of time, not realizing you were at it for three hours. You were so absorbed in the game, you didn't want to stop playing until you won. Time freezes for the dreamer pursuing his/her dream. Albert Einstein put it best, **"Put your hand on a hot stove for a minute, and it seems like an hour. Sit with a pretty girl for an hour, and it seems like a minute. THAT'S relativity."** That's the dedication of the dreamer; it's the glory of winning, the thrill of the kill that drives a true dreamer. The dreamer is pre-occupied in one singular direction, totally focused like a laser beam on conquering the dream; monetary gains are secondary to attaining the dream.

Some people in my family think I am abnormal for writing this book. They want me to seek professional help. They think the book is part of a psychotic episode; I am having the delusions of grandeur of the troubled bi-polar soul. They think I haven't gotten over the old man's death, that I somehow cling to his philosophy and methodologies because I can't face his death like a *normal* person. What they fail to realize is the old man was far removed from your customary standard of normal. The old man raised the bar on what's normal and showed me I was half living in the confines of the body, a body borrowed at that. The old man was beyond being a non-conformist; he was like our founding fathers, a revolutionary thinker. Because of his noncompliance to your standard of normal, he was rich in thought and money.

When I dropped everything in life and blindly pursued my dream, I never got mad at my family for thinking I was abnormal.

It was a compliment, because I knew I was abnormal. It was testament to the fact that the old man trained me well. The old man said to be a Professional Dreamer you have to have an abnormally trained mind. He said, **"The normal human mind is oblivious to the power of dreams because it is untrained to think beyond society's self-imposed limits of rationality."** The old man used to tell me, it is the person who spends the right time to retrain the brain that elevates his being to the status of professional dreamer. He instructed, **"The normal human mind, once trained, becomes abnormal enough to discard society's normal boundaries of reality and has the knowledge and confidence to trust the imagination that creates the new reality of its unlimited dreams."** The amateur dreamers' untrained minds only allow them access to one world, the rational world, where only the possible is possible. The professional dreamers' highly evolved aura allows them to exist in both worlds simultaneously—the rational world of the possible and the irrational world of the impossible—the dream world. The amateur dreamer is trapped in the limitations of the rational world; the professional dreamer is free to roam the universe in both worlds with no limitations. I am honored that my family loves me enough to acknowledge that I possess the same abnormality of thinking required to be like the professional dreamers I profiled in this book. I am privileged to be held in such high regard. It is company that I am honored to keep.

The old man used to tell me, **"The rest of your life is a blank page; fill it with your wildest dreams,** but be vigilante. There is a dark side to dreams; the power of dreams can be used to create evil, sinister results. As powerful as dreams are in creating beneficial results in life, they are just as powerful at creating destructive results in life. That is why **You** have to be careful and make sure what you wish for is what you wish, because if **you** can dream it and believe it, **you** can see it, no matter how majestic or horrific it is. Dreams do not discriminate between good and evil because there is no limit to the possibilities of the imagination that creates them. Dreams used for the right purposes can make the world a better place to live in. Conversely, the power of dreams in the wrong hands can make society, as a whole, a worse place to live in."

Dark dreams? I stopped the old man in his tracks and said, "I thought you instructed me that metaphysical dreams can only be carried over into our physical reality with love. In your own words, love is the bridge, the cosmic glue that makes a metaphysical dream come to life in our physical world. You didn't mention anything about hate. Aren't dark dreams the product of hate, the antithesis of love?"

The old man said, "Absolutely not. If you hate something so much that you want to kill it, the love possessed in your metaphysical soul to successfully carry out that heinous dream is what makes it a physical reality."

Translation: You hate the person, but only the love in your soul can really make the dream of killing that person a physical possibility. You can commit horrible acts in life when you love a hateful dream.

The old man said, **"True evil is only carried out with love."** History teaches us this solemn lesson.

John Lennon—

Contrary to popular opinion, your government didn't conspire to kill this peace icon; a runaway professional dreamer from the darkside did it for them. Dreams are powerful like that. With the right thoughts, they can turn a jealous fan into a twisted, psychopathic killer. At a recent parole board hearing, John Lennon's killer admitted shooting the former Beatle because he wanted to "steal" his fame. This dark dream began one day in his Hawaiian apartment as he scanned the cover of the Beatles album, Sgt. Pepper's Lonely Hearts Club band and became violently antagonistic toward Lennon's stature and status in life. In his own words, **"There was a successful man who kind of had the world on a chain, so to speak, and there I was, not even a link of that chain, just a person who had no personality. And then something in me just broke."** All morality flew out the window of his soul, as the force of a dark dream consumed him.

His dream was to gain a personality by becoming just as famous as John Lennon by killing him and gaining all the notoriety attached to the dubious title of "John Lennon's Killer." Unfortunately, he wasn't an amateur dreamer. He was a professional dreamer with the right dedication of effort and thought pattern to successfully carry out such an evil dream.

In his own words, **"Nothing could have stopped"** him in his quest to track down and assassinate our beloved ex-Beatle. He was so focused on his dream of eliminating John Lennon from the mortal world that, **"It was like a train, a runaway train; there was no stopping it."** He was as he said, **"…under total compulsion."**

Even though he killed John Lennon, this nefarious dreamer's attempt to "steal" the fame of John Lennon backfired on him. Yes, he gained instant celebrity status for conquering his evil dream of killing such a popular living legend, but instead of stealing Lennon's fame, he raised Lennon's fame and stature to a higher level, a level usually reserved for a king, a saint, or an angel. After his brutal slaying, John Lennon became even more famous by morphing into a martyr, a sacrificial lamb for his cause of PEACE.

"All we are saaaaaaaaying is Give Peace a Chance."

Incidently, I won't give the killer the satisfaction of mentioning his name in this book because I refuse to be implicit in helping him further conquer his dream of unwarranted fame.

Ronald Reagan—

In April 1976, John W. Hinckley Jr. dropped out of college and jetted to California to pursue his dream of becoming a songwriter. While in his apartment in Hollywood, he became entranced by the movie *Taxi Driver*, digesting the movie fifteen times in one summer. Slowly, viewing-by-viewing, his good dream, his old dream, the dream of being a songwriter was overpowered by a new dream, a dark dream. He became enraptured with the star attraction of the movie, the prolific actress and professional dreamer in her own right, Jodie foster. His "new found" love for Jodie Foster was so strong it wiped out his old dream and fueled the creation of a new dark dream. His new dream was to court Jodie Foster. Every rational desire in his mind was eradicated; replaced by the permanently seared image of Jodie Foster and him together. John knew he was way out of her league; he knew he was a virtual nobody, and the only way a person of Foster's stature and looks would date him is if he got her attention by becoming a "noticed" somebody. He knew Jodie Foster was famous, and he figured he had to elevate his status to that same level if he had any chance to win her affections. He instinctively knew his lackluster songwriting abilities weren't going to garner the fame he needed to date such a high profile actress, so like any other professional dreamer he dropped this ill-advised, "un-doable" path to Jodie Foster and replaced it with what he considered a "do-able" path to win her heart.

His new plan to conquer his dream of courting Jodie Foster was to gain instant fame and get noticed instantly by committing a "historical deed," a deed so dastardly, she couldn't help but to notice it. The whole world would notice it. He figured the only way to conquer a dream of this magnitude was to kill someone world renown, someone with immense stature and popularity. He chose: the Chairman of the Board of the greatest economic superpower in this world, the Commander in Chief of the greatest armed forces since Roman times, the proselytizer of democracy, the single most powerful person, in the world at the time, the President of the United States of America. He wasn't picky, any current president would do. When he tried and failed in 1980 in Nashville to get Jimmy Carter, he didn't quit his dream like an amateur; he learned from the experience and trudged on like a professional. When his psychiatrist convinced his wealthy parents to cut him off financially in a rational attempt to quash his dream, he didn't flounder. He carried on. His dream was a real dream and was going to be accomplished with or without money. He had no choice. In his mind, Jodie was eagerly waiting for him to become a "noticed somebody" so she could justify dating him.

There was no stopping John Hinckley Jr.; he was determined to win the love of his life—Jody Foster. And if it meant killing a president to make that dream a reality then so be it. Nobody's life was worth more than his professional dream, not even the mighty President. On Monday March 30, 1981, Hinckley, driven by his dream to win Jodie Foster's admiration, love, and respect attempted to do that monumental something that would finally get him noticed, he attempted to assassinate the exulted leader of our great nation, our President Ronald Reagan. Reagan survived with a wound to the left chest; Jodie Foster repulsively rebuffed him; and now John Hinckley Jr. has the pleasure of living with his unfulfilled dream at St Elizabeth's Mental Hospital in Washington DC. A Nightmare like this only happens when a Professional Dreamer blatantly misuses the power of dreams for a sinister, evil purpose.

Robert F. Kennedy—

On June 5, 1968, Robert F. Kennedy's professional dream of being our next President of the United States of America was abruptly shattered by the senseless actions of another professional dreamer. Kennedy was well on his way to living his dream of being our next president. He had just won the California democratic presidential primary election and was well positioned to make his wild dream our calm reality. But while he was dreaming of all the good he could do for our country by attaining this position of power, an equally determined dark dreamer was dreaming of all the good he could do for his country (Palestine) by blocking this dream from becoming our reality. On this fateful day, two professional dreams clashed, and the end result: Kennedy's aspirations of being our president were nullified in a hail of bullets that destroyed his dream and wiped out his reality. The dark dreamer lived his dream of killing our presidential hopeful and forever changed the future course of our history.

The killer ostensibly annihilated our beloved Robert's dream out of blind loyalty to his country. It was supposedly retribution for Kennedy supporting Israel against Palestine in the Six-Day Holy War. But upon further circumspection, the real motive for this heinous atrocity reared its ugly head. This dark dream was really committed for the same reason that Lennon's killer murdered him: unwarranted fame and notoriety. He wasn't a true religious zealot. He was a publicity hound seeking the "fame" ascribed to killing such a potentially high profile, powerful person of the world. Unfortunately, Robert Kennedy's life stood between him and the attainment of his highly powerful dream of gaining instant fame. Kennedy died so this killer's dream could live. He acknowledges this in his own words, **"They can gas me, but I am famous. I have achieved in one day what it took Robert Kennedy all his life to do."**

Once again, I refuse to aid this violator of the power of dreams by mentioning his name and furthering his unjustified fame. His dream will not live on in this book.

Tupac Shakur—

All the rational cards were stacked against him:

- No biological father to guide his journey in life (no role model at all).
- No stepfather to mold him in life—His stepfather, Dr. Mutulo Shakur, a drug dealer who was put away for sixty years for armed robbery (not a very good role model to follow).
- His loving mother, Afeni Shakur, who served jail time for a bombing charge and was a member of the notorious Black Panthers, was busy battling her drug addiction.
- No real friends to guide him in life—he lived in squalor, bouncing from homeless shelters to cheap accommodations around the country; NYC, Baltimore, California. It is hard to maintain and keep any meaningful friendships when you are always on the move.

The only thing he had to guide him in life was his dreams; he had to mold his character from deep inside himself, devoid of reality's limitations. He created a new reality in his imagination, because the rational world he lived in was too oppressive to accept as his reality. He militantly disregarded the structured confines of our <u>real </u>world and comfortably escaped into the unlimited reality of a more acceptable world, an alternate reality within our reality, the <u>dream</u> world. Tupac knew this dream world really existed. He was quoted as saying, **"Reality is wrong. Dreams are for real."** He understood the awe-inspiring power that dreams had to shape his current reality. In his own words, **"During your life, never stop dreaming. No one can take away your dreams."**

While in the dream world, he kept laborious notes as is evidenced by his poetry writings and diary entries. He used these notes to launch his dream into our real world. These notes in rational hands were defiant diatribes, but in retrained hands, the hands of a seasoned dreamer like Tupac, they were the basis for the lyrics that jump-started his real dream of being a rap star. We all know how that dream turned out; we lived through it; unfortunately he didn't.

Tupac was quoted as saying, "My mama always used to tell me: **'If you can't find somethin' to live for, you best find somethin' to die for.'"** Some professional dreamers will do whatever it takes to conquer their dream, even if it means killing other people or faking their own death. Physical life is meaningless compared to the attainment of the professional dreamer's dream. Its purpose transcends human life. Do I believe Tupac faked his own death to further conquer his dream? I think he was a professional dreamer with the commitment level and imagination required to do anything within his power to carry out such a Machiavellian act, but then again, maybe another professional dreamer crossed his path and eliminated his physical life to realize his own dream of being monetarily wealthy. Tupac was owed almost $10,000,000 prior to his untimely death. Anything is possible, once **you** realize there is no limit to the possibilities of the imagination that creates the powerful force of a dream. Either way, it didn't stop his dream. His dream was a **real dream**. It survived. Even after physical death, he is still living his dream.

Tupac Shakur—Born June 16,1971
Tupac Shakur—Died September 13, 1996

The Dream Lives on:

Album—Makavelli-Don Killuminati Seven Day Theory— released March 31, 1997 (Post Physical death)

Album—2Pac's Greatest Hits—released August 20, 2002 (Post physical death)

Kurt Cobain—

He not only believed in the dream world, he visited it so often in his childhood, he made a friend—a best friend, an imaginary friend named Boddah. Boddah was with Kurt, as he conquered his childhood dream. Dreams are conquered in the imagination first, before you can manifest them into the physical realm. Boddah must have helped young Kurt conquer that dream in his imagination first, before it **really happened** and became our new reality. Once you conquer a dream in your imagination, it gives you the confidence, the belief, the faith, the conviction, the work ethic, to make that conquered imaginary dream a conquered real dream.

CASE IN POINT

Nirvana Rocked, and Cobain gained so much money and fame at such an unprecedented speed, in effect going from zero to hero, that he became an adored idol to millions of adulating fans. Kurt rocketed out of our real world and scorched into the limelight of the dream world, where he was, what he dreamed of becoming, a full fledged worshipped like a superhero, ROCK STAR.

He entered the world of dreams. The only difference was it wasn't an imaginary dream world anymore; it was the reality of our real world. He wasn't dreaming of being a rock star anymore, he was a real rock star in our real world. In effect, our real world was his dream world. All rock stars live in the dream world within our real world. The world unrestricted by the confines of reality. Anything is possible in the dream world. Skies the limit. Now everyone is kissing your ass and sucking up to your ego. It is a sycophantic orgy. A frenzy of fawning, phony, plastic people, that cling to your being like a famished swirl of parasitic leeches.

Everyone wants to be your new best friend and they will give you anything you want, anytime you want it, as much as you want of it. No limits. Excess is expected. Anticipated. Ordained. Socially acceptable. Required of the position. Decadence is the norm. It comes with the title. Its part of the turf, the image. A Rock Star is supposed to have: unlimited money and fame, unlimited access to the "A" list parties, unlimited access to any food liquor or drug, and unlimited groupies that please them on command. Conquering the dream of being a Rock star has its perks.

The only problem is, now that you accomplished your dream, your sole purpose in life, what do you do when you realize you aren't dreaming anymore? You are fully awake and now have no meaningful dream to guide your life? You are lost outside of the dream world that made you a Rock Star in the real world. You were more comfortable dreaming about being a Rock Star, than actually being a real Rock Star. This is a whole new world to you. You never actually experienced living in the dream world of being a real Rock Star, you only fantasized about it in your wildest dreams. Now that WILD DREAM is your WILD REALITY. You are who everyone else wishes, dreams, they could be. You are who they aspire to be. Your real life is their dream life. You have it made. You are set in life. You have the good life. The glamorous lifestyle they could only dream of. They are all stuck in the confines of the real world, while you get to bask in the unlimited glory of a world they could only imagine in their wildest dreams. You are living their wildest dreams, and they respect you by paying you handsomely for achieving a dream so elusive to millions of aspiring musicians. You are Revered. You are Royalty. You are a REAL ROCK STAR. They would trade places with you in a heartbeat; because they love you and what you represent to them. You are living proof that wild dreams can come true; you did it and now they are safe to dream of doing it as well.

The only problem was, now that you did it (became a real rock star), you discovered after you got there that you didn't want to be who you actually became. You didn't want to be a phony commercial sell-out. You were still dreaming that you had total artistic control over the creation of your rock star dream. You didn't want any realistic people screwing up or altering your creation, your dream, your rock star dream come true. They wanted you to be untrue to yourself. A sacrifice you felt in good conscience was contrary to your real dream. As you put it, **"The worst crime is faking it."** You rebelled. In your own words, **"I would rather be hated for who I am, than loved for who I am not."** Again in Kurt's words, **"Wanting to be someone else is a waste of the person you really are."**

You weren't really content the way this dream turned out. So naturally, you escaped back into the comfort and sanity of the dream world, where only you were in charge, and used the same dream making skills that made you a real rock star to launch a new dream to conquer. Your new dream was scoring heroine.

At first it wasn't a dream; it was just a recreational hobby, something you experimented with in your past to sooth your uneasy stomach. But like any good hobby, it became a passion, an obsession that consumed your time and money. The new you had the bankroll and conviction level to expand that recreational use to a full time habitual addiction. After a while it was all you want to do. Music was secondary. Career was secondary. Family was secondary. Friends were secondary. The real You was secondary. Hit by hit it slowly massaged your ego and became your friend. Hit by hit, it slowly masturbated your mind and became your best friend. Hit by hit, it slowly isolated you from the real world until it became your only real friend. Hit by hit, it slowly convinces you that you can't live a normal life without it. Hit by hit, you slowly yielded to the belief that the drug was the most important thing in your life. Hit by hit, it slowly seduced your soul into believing it was the love of your life. Hit by hit, the temptation to be with it grew until it reached a fever pitch and you were hooked; a full-blown strung-out, insanely in love with a drug, Junkie. Hit by hit, it slowly became your sole purpose in life; your dream. And now all you could **dream** of was getting high, so you could forget the real person you were when you were straight. Now, scoring drugs was your dream, and it blocked out your rationality and morality and altered the code inside you, the universal code that guided you; it made you a different person from whom you were really meant to be. It gave you a false euphoria that encapsulated and numbed your soul, and tricked you into believing that you were somebody that you really weren't. Scoring drugs is a powerful dream. It possesses the mind of its host. All reasonable thoughts are exorcized from your rational mind as it consumes your intellect and guides your will. You can't tolerate the pain of being who you really are without it. You seek the joy of being who you become under its intoxicating guise. You get antsy without it. You can't sleep without it. You get cold flashes with goose bumps without it. Your legs twitch uncontrollably without it. Your whole body is painfully sick without it. You cower in a corner like a love sick baby without it. You need it more than the air you freely breathe. You fiend for its loving attention. The craving is so powerful, it can make people so numb they can prostitute the sanctity of their bodies by bartering for it. It can make people so cruel they can rob, cheat, and lie for it. It can make people so weak that they can beg people like a starving dog for it. It can make people so desperate that they will be willing to risk their lives by breaking into a stranger's home for it. It can make people so despicable that they will be willing to murder the soul of someone by raping their physical body for it. It can make people so paranoid that they will be willing to assault, stab, or shoot for it. It can make people so evil-hearted, they can destroy someone else's dreams by killing them for it. It is so powerful, it can make an idolized, world famous, rich rock star with a devoted wife and adoring child and millions of loyal fans, who has every rational reason in the world to live, kill himself for it.

On April 5, 1994, Kurt Cobain's imaginary friend became deadly real when Kurt addressed his suicide note to him as he left our real world to accompany Boddah in the unlimited potentiality of the dream world. Like many Rock stars before him, Kurt Cobain's dream of being a real Rock star was eventually overpowered by, engulfed by, eclipsed by, destroyed by, the most potent dream known to mortal mankind; the lust for drugs; the dream that can destroy its host if used improperly. If he wasn't such an experienced conqueror of dreams, he would probably still be alive somewhere, most likely in a rehab clinic with the rest of the amateur dreamers who quit their drug addictions prematurely, before they experienced the full ride of killing themselves. Unfortunately, Kurt was an experienced professional dreamer that committed himself to drugs as fervently as he committed himself to being a Rock Star. There was no stopping him; he was determined to live the full drug dream, until he **"Broke on through to the other side,"** at the end of the ride, like fellow rocker Jim Morrison did.

That is why **You** have to be careful and make sure what you wish for is what you wish, because if **you** can dream it and believe it, **you** can see it, no matter how majestic or horrific it is.

The best way to learn something is to experience it, because as we all know experience is the best teacher. Maybe if You **see** one dream come true, unfold right in front of your incredulous eyes, you will be receptive to **believe** the possibility that other wild dreams or fantasies can come true as well. This book was that dream. By reading this book, you have given me the opportunity, the pleasure, the privilege of conquering my dream of preserving the memory of my old man's life and teachings, and for that I graciously thank you. Your reward for helping me conquer my dream is enlightenment. Maybe now you won't think other wild dreams are so far-fetched.

Maybe now you can stop being **poor** in the **rational real world**, by using the power of your **rich** thoughts in the **irrational dream world** of your imagination, to make your **impossible dream** of being **rich** in the real world a **possible reality**. This book is a perfect example of that concept. I am the Dummy light that goes on in your head to remind you not to forget something very important in your **physical** life, the unlimited potential of the power of your dreams in your **metaphysical** life. Now take Steve Tyler's cue and DREAM ON; your future is eagerly waiting for **You.**

Part 3—Change the way you invest

T he old man said, "Now that you have opened up and expanded the portals of your mind and changed the way you think, you are ready for the final stage in your transformation to becoming a bona fide King of the Middle Class." The final step in your quest to be a King of the Middle Class is to change the way you invest.

To be a King of the Middle Class you need:

A) A simple, easy to follow, time-tested, and proven *system* of investing that can generate enormous amounts of wealth in a relatively short span of time. An automatic system, no strenuous thinking or heavy negotiating involved, no tricky sales jargon or complicated formulas or strategies to learn. A rudimentary plan of action that anyone and everyone can follow; no MBA required, basic literacy will suffice. A universal *system* of wealth-building. In short a "Meat and Potatoes investing System for the average Joe/Jane."

B) To successfully invest using this *no nonsense, no-brainer system* and create the wealth you need to retire like a King.

C) To hide the wealth (in plain sight) created by the system and live the regal life.

D) To be a future millionaire by investing your money like 90% of the other multimillionaires—safely and securely in Real Estate.

Here's how the old man became a "King of the Middle Class" and conquered his **dream** of being rich in real estate, detail by detail, I know it works because I made it *my* **dream** and conquered it too; and if you make this your **dream,** I am sure you can duplicate this great success, because as **you** should have proved to yourself already, if you can **dream** it, you can be it.

The old man said there are four reasons why you should invest in Real Estate:
1) Forced Equity
2) Market Equity
3) Tax write-offs
4) Positive cash flow

1)" Forced Equity"—Automatic monthly windfall

The old man said, before you can fully appreciate the concept of forced equity you must have a general understanding of how a mortgage loan works and what amortization is. He cited a typical example: You find a house for sale for $260,000, you put 20% down which is $52,000 and now you are looking for money to pay for the balance of the purchase price remaining that is due the seller of this house, in this case $208,000. The best way to get this money ($208,000) is to borrow it. You go to your local mortgage broker or a bank, and they check out your credit, income, and assets, and if everything checks out okay; you meet their underwriting guidelines, and they agree to lend you money, Bingo You are Approved!! You are now entitled to rent their money for a specific amount of time and at a predetermined rate of rent called interest. You then have the privilege of going to a closing where you will pay the lender any fees associated with renting this money, commonly called closing costs. At the closing, you will be given a HUD-1 statement: basically a itemized receipt for all the money it cost you to rent the money you needed to pay the seller for the privilege of buying his house.

At the closing, you will sign hundreds of legal documents— banks take lending their money out pretty seriously. It's not like the old days where you shook hands and blindly trusted each other.

The old man snapped, "Corruption killed that honesty game." Now everything in real estate, according to the Statue of Frauds, has to be in writing. The most consequential of these written documents are the Mortgage and the Mortgage Note. These documents clearly lay out in writing the terms and conditions of borrowing this money.

Contrary to popular opinion, the bank or licensed mortgage banker does not give you a mortgage on a property; he gives you rented money. You give the lender a mortgage—it's like a pledge, an IOU. You pledge to pay back the lender based on the terms and conditions of a mortgage note that you also signed at the closing. If you do not live up to this pledge, the documents you signed give the lender the legal right to force you, by court order if necessary, to abide by the terms and conditions you agreed to, as evidenced by your signature, or lose your home. Simply put, you don't pay; you don't stay. The mortgage that the lender records in the County Clerk's Office (so it is public information) is collateral for the repayment of the rented money. If you do not pay the rent per month (the mortgage payment), the lender can foreclose on the house.

Translation: the lenders can sell the house through a legal process called foreclosure to recover rent monies (interest) due them under the terms of the Mortgage Note.

The mortgage note, on the other hand, is the actual evidence of the debt owed. The mortgage note spells out in no uncertain terms how much money you rented or borrowed and how much you will pay back, usually on a monthly basis and for how long a term (10,15, 20, 25, 30, 40 years). The note is never recorded, only its cousin, the mortgage gets that privilege. I guess the concept is why should the whole world know what rent you pay for the honor of borrowing money? The old man said, the lenders like this privacy policy as well; it makes it harder for competitors to steal their yields through refinancing. If Dum Dum Lending Corp. recorded the mortgage note, all their competitors would know exactly what price to charge to steal their business—the business of renting money. If Dum Dum, in its infinite wisdom, recorded a mortgage note showing that it was charging the borrower 8% interest (rent) to borrow its money, it would not take long for a competitor, willing to take less rent (interest) say 7% to steal it by refinancing the debt and paying off Dum Dum Lending Corp. The lenders don't like to lose their customers; they spend a lot of money on advertising and other marketing expenses to get these customers. The note, not being recorded, protects the lenders from easily stealing each other's business. If the interest rates or rent people paid to borrow money was public information then the bankers would be forced (due to competition) to work on leaner and meaner profit margins—not good for their bottom line. It is better for the entire banking industry that the interest or rent people pay remain a guarded secret, like how today's Fair Isaac Company (FICO) scores that all lenders use is calculated. The old man wasn't around for FICO scores, but if he was, I am sure he would have demanded that his tenants, or as he would call them his *"Pension Walkers,"* pay him on time so as to preserve that high FICO score, guaranteeing the maximum borrowing power with the lowest rate.

The other natural reason for not divulging interest rate charges is that people would use this information to judge each other. If someone knew you paid a high interest rate (rent to borrow money) they would assume one of three things: a) you were stupid for paying a high rate when you could easily refinance, or b) you were paying a high rate because you were too lazy to do the paperwork required to lower it, or c) you had bad credit and this rate is the best you can get with your credit. High interest rate people would be outcasts; the bankers wouldn't want this to happen to their best paying customers; it's bad for business.

The note usually contains another protective clause that prevents the borrower from switching lenders for the first twelve months; it is called the pre-payment penalty. If you obtain a loan at 9% interest (rent to borrow) on April 1st and two months later another lender offers you a 8% rate—you can drop your first lender but they will charge you a departure fee for the privilege of paying off this debt earlier than they could make any real money off of you; this privilege usually runs around 5% of the unpaid principal balance owed. On a $208,000 loan, this privilege would cost you $10,400 (5% of $208,000). You could take the lower rate loan and pay the legal extortion ($10,400) or you can refrain from refinancing until the pre-pay period is over (usually one year, but certain California lenders have three and five year pre-pays) and hope rates are still low enough to justify switching companies. One strange advantage of an adjustable rate mortgage is that there is no pre-payment privilege attached to it. Go figure. I wonder why? I guess its because the lenders could keep raising your rate (the rent they charge you to borrow their money) through dubious indexes and keep you paying the rate by holding the pre-pay departure fee over your head. The customer would be forced to choose between two evils—a higher payment per month, when the rate adjusts, or a very high bail out fee called the pre-pay.

These notes are usually stored in very safe places, as they are the only proof of the IOU existing between mortgagor (borrower) and mortgagee (lender). The note is only valid with original signatures; copies are meaningless. If the lender loses the original note, theoretically the mortgagor (the person renting the money) can challenge the validity of the debt. The mortgagee (lender) uses the note as a back up to the recorded Mortgage. If the house is sold to recover the money owed (foreclosure) and the lender does not receive all monies due; they can sue you (the borrower/renter of money) personally for the money owed. This is called a deficiency judgment.

Translation: If you default on the loan and the lender sells your house based on the mortgage you gave to them at public auction through the foreclosure process and the lender does not net enough money to satisfy all the monies owed under the note you signed, they can and will personally sue you via a deficiency judgment for the balance remaining.

As a side note, mortgage companies/banks require escrow accounts for payments of property taxes and homeowners insurance because non-payment of these expenditures would endanger the collateral (the house) that you pledged as security for repayment of loan. For example, if the house burned down and there was no fire insurance on the property naming the lender as loss payee, the lender would have no protection from a default on the loan. They would be stuck with a burned out shell as collateral instead of a fixed up home. If the property taxes aren't paid on the property, the county could after, say three years, foreclose on the property and wipe out the mortgage loan so the lenders make damn sure your taxes are paid. (Property taxes are a superior lien they can wipe out a mortgage lien regardless of recordation date—if the mortgage was recorded prior to tax debt doesn't matter—taxes have to be paid—the county would record a tax deed and forcibly take property regardless of the mortgage loan on property). If you fail to pay the property taxes, smart lenders pay them (the mortgage documents you signed allow them to) and add payment to the principal's balance remaining on your loan.

Translation: A Mortgage / Mortgage Note is like any other contract—it is only as good as the quality and integrity of the people who sign these legally binding documents. In an ideal world the mortgage companies would never need protective documents like a Mortgage or Mortgage Note to insure they get paid; a handshake would do, but in the real world, unforeseen events like losing a job, death, divorce, relocation, and bankruptcy make these protective measures a necessity.

The Note that you signed at closing clearly spells out in plain English how much money you rented (borrowed), how much you will have to pay the lender per month to rent (borrow) the money (affectionately called interest), and for how many years you will pay this rent (interest) to the lender. For example: you borrow $208,000 @ 7% interest for 30 years (360 monthly installments). The Note you sign at closing would clearly state that you rented $208,000 from the lender, and that you will pay the lender $1,383.83 in equal monthly installments for the privilege of using their money, and you will pay this rent (interest) for 360 months (30 years) at which time the loan will be paid in full. This concept is known as amortization. Once the loan is paid in full, it is important to get a SAT (a legal document from the lender acknowledging that loan has been paid in full and your obligation to the lender is satisfied). Once you obtain the SAT, it is imperative that you spend the extra dough (100-200 bucks) to record the SAT in the County Clerk's office, so the whole world knows your debt is absolved, no questions asked. The old man said, "I can't tell you how many times I have saved a closing by picking up an original SAT haphazardly tossed in a drawer—the owner unaware of the legal importance of this document."

The SAT is the only official legal proof that the loan has been paid in full, so if you want to avoid a major title problem whenever you refinance or sell, make sure: a) if you paid off your loan you get a SAT from the lender (Some lenders take 2-3 months to forward papers, in a refinance the title company usually, for a fee, takes care of this) and b) after you get the SAT from the lender, you promptly invest a few bucks and record it. The old man was adamant on this point; he said if you lose the original SAT they sent you, it could take weeks to replace it, and if your lender went out of business (like some scammy fly-by-night home improvement lenders) or got bought out or merged with another lender it could take months or years to solve the problem. You could even be forced to spend thousands on an attorney to legally extinguish your obligation through the courts.

Translation: If you want to save lots of time and money and mental energy give your SAT the respect it deserves and record it. (PS—you always knew when the old man recorded his SAT—he always threw a party—only his closest friends and family knew it was a burn-the-mortgage party).

The old man said, now that you have a mortgage loan, you should become familiar with the concept of amortization. Basically, amortization means you make one equal payment to a lender on a monthly basis for a set number of years until the loan is paid in full. This equal payment is broken down into principal and interest payments. The interest payment column goes down each month and the principal column goes up each month.

Translation: Even though you are making the same constant equal payment month after month, the amount of each payment that goes toward principal payback of loan and interest charged to use the money changes every month. You owe less and less interest each month because the principal balance that is being used to calculate interest owed is being paid off.

The trick to this concept is to figure out what the equal payment per month should be based on how much you borrowed and how much interest you are being charged to borrow this money and for how long you need this borrowed money. For example if you need to borrow $208,000 @ 7% for 360 months (30 Yrs.) What would be the equal monthly payment you would have to pay, over a 30 year or 360 month period of time to pay back the loan plus all interest owed to lender? What would be the equal monthly payment if you wanted to pay back the loan over a 15 year or 180 month period of time? Well, thankfully some financial wizards got together and figured all this out for us. They created financial amortization charts. **Basically**, these charts are designed to tell you how much <u>per thousand</u> it would cost you per month to borrow (rent) money at different interest rates and different periods of time. To figure out your amortized payment, all you do is take your loan amount (which for our example will be $208,000) divide it by 1,000 (which is $208,000 divided by 1,000= 208) and then use the chart with this number (208) for any interest rate or term. If you were borrowing $208,000 @ 7% for 30 years, you would go to the left hand of chart and find the interest rate, which in our case is 7%, and then you would go across the 7% column and find the per thousand multiplier that corresponds to the term of the loan, (10, 15, 20, 25, 30) which in our case is 30 years or 6.65 per 1,000. Now take your 208, multiply it by 6.65, and voila you got your monthly principal and interest payment: $1,383.20 per month. This is the equal payment you would have to make each and every month for the next 30 years, in order to pay back the lender a 7% yield on the loan plus pay back the entire principal balance that you borrowed.

EQUAL MONTHLY PAYMENT TO
AMORTIZE A LOAN OF $1,000

TERM INTEREST RATE	10	15	20	25	30
6.0	11.10	8.44	7.16	6.44	6.00
6.500	11.35	8.71	7.46	6.75	6.32
7.0	11.61	8.99	7.75	7.07	6.65
7.125	11.68	9.06	7.83	7.15	6.74
7.250	11.75	9.13	7.91	7.23	6.83
7.375	11.81	9.20	7.98	7.31	6.91
7.500	11.87	9.27	8.06	7.39	6.99
7.625	11.94	9.35	8.14	7.48	7.08
7.750	12.01	9.42	8.21	7.56	7.17
7.875	12.07	9.49	8.29	7.64	7.26
8.0	12.13	9.56	8.36	7.72	7.34
8.125	12.20	9.63	8.45	7.81	7.43
8.250	12.27	9.71	8.53	7.89	7.52
8.375	12.34	9.78	8.60	7.97	7.61
8.500	12.40	9.85	8.68	8.05	7.69
8.625	12.47	9.93	8.76	8.14	7.78
8.750	12.54	10.00	8.84	8.23	7.87
8.875	12.61	10.07	8.92	8.31	7.96
9.0	12.67	10.14	9.00	8.39	8.05
9.125	12.74	10.22	9.08	8.48	8.14
9.250	12.81	10.30	9.16	8.57	8.23
9.375	12.88	10.37	9.24	8.66	8.32
9.500	12.94	10.44	9.32	8.74	8.41
9.625	13.01	10.52	9.41	8.83	8.50
9.750	13.08	10.60	9.49	8.92	8.60
9.875	13.15	10.67	9.57	9.00	8.69
10.0	13.22	10.75	9.65	9.09	8.78
10.500	13.50	11.06	9.99	9.45	9.15
11.0	13.78	11.45	10.41	9.90	9.62
11.500	14.06	11.69	10.67	10.17	9.91
12.0	14.35	12.01	11.02	10.54	10.29
12.5	14.64	12.33	11.37	10.91	10.68
13.0	14.94	12.66	11.72	11.28	11.07
13.500	15.23	12.99	12.08	11.66	11.46
14.0	15.53	13.32	12.44	12.04	11.85
14.500	15.83	13.66	12.80	12.43	12.25
15.0	16.14	14.00	13.17	12.81	12.65

**Note—The above figures are estimates only—exact figures are calculated by pre programmed computers—For example our $208,000 loan @ 7% for 30 years comes out to exactly $1,383.83 per month—but according to the chart 7% for 30 years is 6.65 per 1,000 or 6.65 X 208= $1,383.20. The computer is much more accurate—in our example, the per thousand multiplier is 6.653 X 208= $1,383.83

(www.freemortgageanalyzer.com—web site that can do calculations for you)

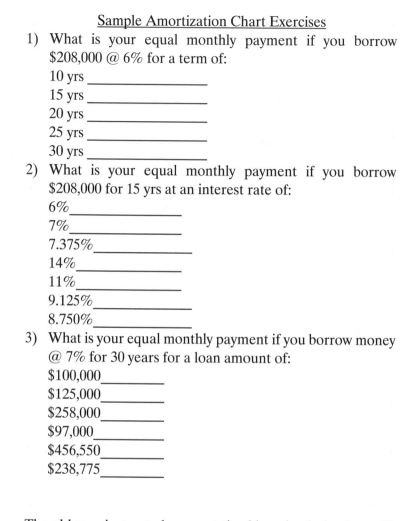

Sample Amortization Chart Exercises

1) What is your equal monthly payment if you borrow $208,000 @ 6% for a term of:

   10 yrs _____

   15 yrs _____

   20 yrs _____

   25 yrs _____

   30 yrs _____

2) What is your equal monthly payment if you borrow $208,000 for 15 yrs at an interest rate of:

   6%_____

   7%_____

   7.375%_____

   14%_____

   11%_____

   9.125%_____

   8.750%_____

3) What is your equal monthly payment if you borrow money @ 7% for 30 years for a loan amount of:

   $100,000_____

   $125,000_____

   $258,000_____

   $97,000_____

   $456,550_____

   $238,775_____

The old man instructed, an amortized loan by design is a self-liquidating loan, a loan designed to pay itself off, and that's why each equal monthly payment is divided into 2 parts—a) interest payment to the bank (the bank's profit per month) and b) principal payment to the bank (our profit per month—the equity caused by the monthly lowering of the principal balance remaining on our loan—the monthly windfall the old man affectionately called "Forced Equity," the Landlord's Forced savings plan). Your mortgage payment always remains the same (in our case $1,383.83 for 360 months (30 years)), how much of that payment goes toward principal and interest payments changes every month; because every month as you slowly chip away at the principal balance owed, you pay less and less interest because the principal balance that you use to calculate your interest payment is decreasing month by month.

The old man said, "Now get out your calculator and lets Go Figure," Forced equity is the by product of amortization and the only way you will understand amortization is to experience amortization. Lets do an amortization exercise, lets borrow $208,000 @ 7% for 10yrs /15 yrs / 20yrs / 25 yrs and 30 yrs—same rate of interest but different payback terms. We will manually, using our calculator, figure out the first 12 amortized payments of principal and interest on all 5 loans. We will do by hand, for purposes of learning and understanding, what a computer can do in seconds: create a one-year amortization schedule of payments for these loans. Lets begin.

You borrow $208,000 at 7% interest for 120 months (10yrs)— What is the monthly payment? You go to the chart and find the interest rate first, in this case it is 7.0, and then you find the multiplier per thousand for the term of loan, in this case 10 years is 11.61 per 1,000 dollars borrowed. Now it is simple math, 11.61 X 208=$*2,414.88* per month. This is the monthly payment you must tender to the lender to pay back this loan with interest in a 10-year time period. Total payments to lender in 10 years= $2,414.88 X 120 months = $*289,785.60.* Total profit to bank $289,785.60 minus $208,000 original principal owed = *$81,785.60* (this is how much money the bank would make if you kept the loan for the full 10 years). After 10 years, you would owe the bank nothing; the entire principal balance was eliminated month-by-month, year-by-year, through the process of amortization.

Now lets calculate our forced equity for the first month, by breaking down the amortized mortgage payment of $2,414.88 per month into principal and interest. (For our illustration we will use the more accurate computer-generated number for $208,000 @ 7% 10 yrs = $2,415.06 per month). How do we calculate what portion of this mortgage payment ($2,415.06) goes toward interest; the bank's profit and how much goes toward reducing the principal balance owed, our profit or "forced equity." It's simple math. You start with the principal balance. You only pay interest on what you owe, so for your first interest payment you would pay 7% on the full $208,000, which is $208,000 X 7% = 14,560 per year, 14,560 divided by 12= $1,213.33 interest for the month. This is the profit the bank makes the first month on the job. If the amortized payment per month is $2,415.06 (adjusted per computer accuracy), it's simple subtraction, $2,415.06 minus $1,213.33 = $1,201.73; this represents the portion of your payment that the lender uses to pay down your debt. You now owe your lender $208,000 minus $1,201.73. This $1,201.73 for this first month represents your forced equity profit. The first month of our loan, the $2,415.06 mortgage payment was broken down as follows:

$1213.33—interest to lender (bank's profit)

$1201.73—principal payment on loan to reduce debt (our forced equity profit)

By month #2 you do not owe $208,000 any more, you owe $208,000 minus $1,201.73 or $206,798.27. This is the new principal balance, and since you only pay interest on what you owe your 2nd interest payment will be 7% of 206,798.27 not $208,000.To calculate the 2nd month interest we multiply $206,798.27 by 7% equaling 14,475.88 per year divided by 12 equals $1,206.32 interest owed for month. This is the profit the bank makes the second month on the job. The first month we owed the lender $1,213.33 interest for the month because we owed the lender $208,000, the 2nd month we owed the lender $1,206.32 interest for the month (a little less) because the principal balance that we used to tabulate interest owed has been reduced from $208,000 to $206,798.27. Since the amortized monthly mortgage payment of $2,415.06 doesn't change, it's simple subtraction $2,415.06 minus $1,206.32 equals $1,208.74, this represents the portion of your payment that the lender uses to pay down your debt owed. You now owe your lender $206,798.27 minus $1,208.74. This $1,208.74 represents your 2nd month of forced equity profit. Each month our forced equity profits go up and the mortgage company's rent (profit) for using their money goes down because we owe them less and less as the months and years go by. The second month of our loan the $2,415.06 mortgage payment was broken down as follows:

$1,206.32—interest to lender (bank's profit)

$1,208.74—principal payment on loan to reduce debt (our forced equity profit)

By month # 3 you do not owe $206,798.27 any more, you owe $206,798.27 minus $1,208.74 or $205,589.54. This is the new principal balance, and since you only pay interest on what you owe, your 3rd interest payment will be 7% of $205,589.54 not $206,798.27. To calculate the 3rd month interest we multiply $205,589.54 by 7% equaling $14,391.27 per year divided by 12 equals $1,199.27 interest owed for the month. This is the profit the bank makes the third month on the job. The second month we owed the lender $1,206.32 interest for the month because we owed the lender $206,798.27, the third month we owed the lender $1199.27 interest for the month (a little less) because the principal balance that we used to tabulate interest owed has been reduced from $206,798.27 to $205,589.54. Since the amortized monthly mortgage payment of $2,415.06 doesn't change, it's simple subtraction $2,415.06 minus $1,199.27 equals $1,215.79; this represents the portion of your payment that the lender uses to pay down your debt owed. You now owe your lender $205,589.54 minus $1,215.79. This $1,215.79 represents your 3rd month of forced equity profit. The third month of our loan the $2,415.06 mortgage payment was broken down as follows:

$1,199.27—interest to lender (bank's profit)

$1,215.79—principal payment on loan to reduce debt (our forced equity profit)

By month #4 you do not owe $205,589.54 any more; you owe $205,589.54 minus $1,215.79 or $204,373.75. This is the new principal balance, and since you only pay interest on what you owe your 4th interest payment will be 7% of $204,373.75 not $205,589.54. To calculate the 4th month interest we multiply $204,373.75 by 7% equaling $14,306.16 per year divided by 12 equals $1,192.18 interest owed for the month. This is the profit the bank makes the fourth month on the job. The third month we owed the lender $1,199.27 interest for the month because we owed the lender $205,589.54, the 4th month we owed the lender $1,192.18 interest for the month (a little less) because the principal balance that we used to calculate interest owed has been reduced from $205,589.54 to $204,373.75. Once again the amortized monthly mortgage payment of $2,415.06 doesn't change, it's simple subtraction, $2,415.06 minus $1,192.18 equals $1,222.88, this represents the portion of your payment that the lender uses to pay down your debt owed. You now owe your lender $204,373.75 minus $1,222.88. This $1,222.88 represents your 4th month of forced equity profit. The fourth month of our loan the $2,415.06 mortgage payment was broken down as follows:

$1,192.18—interest to lender (bank's profit)

$1,222.88—principal payment on loan to reduce debt (our forced equity profit)

By month # 5 you do not owe $204,373.75 any more, you owe $204,373.75 minus $1,222.88 or $203,150.87. This is the new principal balance, and since you only pay interest on what you owe your 5th interest payment will be 7% of $203,150.87 not $204,373.75. To figure out the 5th month interest we multiply $203,150.87 by 7% equaling 14,220.56 per year divided by 12 equals $1,185.05 interest owed for the month. This is the profit the bank makes the 5th month on the job. The 4th month we owed the lender $1,192.18 interest for the month because we owed the lender $204,373.75, the 5th month we owed the lender $1,185.05 interest for the month (a little less) because the principal balance that we used to calculate interest owed has been reduced from $204,373.75 to $203,150.87.Since the amortized monthly mortgage payment of $2,415.06 doesn't change, it's simple subtraction $2,415.06 minus $1,185.05 equals $1,230.01; this represents the portion of your payment that the lender uses to pay down your debt owed. You now owe your lender $203,150.87 minus $1,230.01. This $1,230.01 represents your 5th month of forced equity profit. The 5th month of our loan the $2,415.06 mortgage payment was broken down as follows:

$1,185.05—interest to lender (bank's profit)

$1,230.01—principal payment on loan to reduce debt (our forced equity profit)

By month #6 you do not owe $203,150.87 any more, you owe $203,150.87 minus $1,230.01 or $201,920.86. This is the new principal balance, and since you only pay interest on what you owe your 6th interest payment will be 7% of $201,920.86 not $203,150.87. To figure out the 6th month interest we multiply $201,920.86 by 7% equaling $14,134.46 per year divided by 12 equals $1,177.87 interest owed for the month. This is the profit the bank makes the 6th month on the job. The 5th month we owed the lender $1185.05 interest for the month because we owed the lender $203,150.87, the 6th month we owed the lender $1,177.87 interest for the month (a little less) because the principal balance that we used to calculate interest owed has been reduced from $203,150.87 to $201,920.86. Since the amortized monthly mortgage payment of $2,415.06 doesn't change, it's simple subtraction, $2,415.06 minus $1,177.87 equals $1,237.19; this represents the portion of your payment that the lender uses to pay down your debt owed. You now owe your lender $201,920.86 minus $1,237.19. This $1,237.19 represents your 6th month of forced equity profit. The 6th month of our loan the $2,415.06 mortgage payment was broken down as follows:

$1,177.87—interest to lender (bank's profit)

$1,237.19—principal payment on loan to reduce debt (our forced equity profit)

By month #7, you do not owe $201,920.86 any more; you owe $201,920.86 minus $1,237.19 or $200,683.67. This is the new principal balance, and since you only pay interest on what you owe your 7th interest payment will be 7% of $200,683.67 not $201,920.86. To figure out the 7th month interest, we multiply $200,683.67 by 7% equaling $14,047.86 per year divided by 12 equals $1,170.65 interest owed for the month. This is the profit the bank makes the 7th month on the job. The 6th month we owed the lender $1,177.87 interest for the month because we owed the lender $201,920.86, the 7th month we owed the lender $1,170.65 interest for the month (a little less) because the principal balance that we used to calculate interest owed has been reduced from $201,920.86 to $200,683.67. Since the amortized monthly mortgage payment of $2,415.06 doesn't change, it's simple subtraction $2,415.06 minus $1,170.65 equals $1,244.41; this represents the portion of your payment that the lender uses to pay down your debt owed. You now owe your lender $200,683.67 minus $1,244.41. This $1,244.41 represents your 7th month of forced equity profit. The 7th month of our loan the $2,415.06 mortgage payment was broken down as follows:

$1,170.65—interest to lender (bank's profit)

$1,244.41—principal payment on loan to reduce debt (our forced equity profit)

By month #8, you do not owe $200,683.67 any more, you owe $200,683.67 minus $1,244.41 or $199,439.26. This is the new principal balance, and since you only pay interest on what you owe your 8th interest payment will be 7% of $199,439.26 not $200,683.67. To figure out the 8th month interest we multiply $199,439.26 by 7% equaling $13,960.75 per year divided by 12 equals $1,163.40 interest owed for the month. This is the profit the bank makes the 8th month on the job. The 7th month we owed the lender $1,170.65 interest for the month because we owed the lender $200,683.67, the 8th month we owed the lender $1,163.40 interest for the month (a little less) because the principal balance that we used to figure out interest owed has been reduced from $200,683.67 to $199,439.26. Since the amortized monthly mortgage payment of $2,415.06 doesn't change, it's simple subtraction $2,415.06 minus $1,163.40 equals $1,251.66; this represents the portion of your payment that the lender uses to pay down your debt owed. You now owe your lender $199,439.26 minus $1,251.66. This $1,251.66 represents your 8th month of forced equity profit. The 8th month of our loan the $2,415.06 mortgage payment is broken down as follows:

$1,163.40—interest to lender (bank's profit)

$1,251.66—principal payment on loan to reduce debt (our forced equity profit)

By month #9, you do not owe $199,439.26 any more; you owe $199,439.26 minus $1,251.66 or $198,187.60. This is the new principal balance, and since you only pay interest on what you owe your 9th interest payment will be 7% of $198,187.60 not $199,439.26. To figure out the 9th month interest we multiply $198,187.60 by 7% equaling $13,873.13 per year divided by 12 equals $1,156.09 interest owed for the month. This is the profit the bank makes the 9th month on the job. The 8th month we owed the lender $1,163.40 interest for the month because we owed the lender $199,439.26, the 9th month, we owed the lender $1,156.09 interest for the month (a little less) because the principal balance that we used to calculate the interest owed has been reduced from $199,439.26 to $198,187.60. Since the amortized monthly mortgage payment of $2,415.06 doesn't change, it's simple subtraction $2,415.06 minus $1,156.09 equals $1,258.97; this represents the portion of your payment that the lender uses to pay down your debt owed. You now owe your lender $198,187.60 minus $1,258.97. This $1,258.97 represents your 9th month of forced equity profit. The 9th month of our loan the $2,415.06 mortgage payment was broken down as follows:

$1,156.09—interest to lender (bank profit)

$1,258.97—principal payment on loan to reduce debt (our forced equity profit)

By month # 10, you do not owe $198,187.60 any more, you owe $198,187.60 minus $1,258.97 or $196,928.63. This is the new principal balance, and since you only pay interest on what you owe, your 10th month interest payment will be 7% of $196,928.63 not $198,187.60. To figure out the 10th month interest, we multiply $196,928.63 by 7% equaling $13,785 per year divided by 12 equals $1,148.75 interest owed for the month. This is the profit the bank makes the 10th month on the job. The 9th month we owed the lender $1,156.09 interest for the month because we owed the lender $198,187.60, the 10th month we owed the lender $1,148.75 interest for the month (a little less) because the principal balance that we used to calculate the interest owed has been reduced from $198,187.60 to $196,928.63. Since the amortized monthly mortgage payment of $2,415.06 doesn't change, it's simple subtraction $2,415.06 minus $1,148.75 equals $1,266.31; this represents the portion of your payment that the lender uses to pay down your debt owed. You now owe your lender $196,928.63 minus $1,266.31. This $1,266.31 represents your 10th month of forced equity profit. The 10th month of our loan the $2,415.06 mortgage payment was broken down as follows:

$1,148.75—interest to lender (bank profit)

$1,266.31—principal payment on loan to reduce debt (our forced equity profit)

By month #11, you do not owe $196,928.63 any more; you owe $196,928.63 minus $1,266.31 or $195,662.32. This is the new principal balance, and since you only pay interest on what you owe your 11th month interest payment will be 7% of $195,662.32 not $196,928.63. To figure out the 11th month interest, we multiply $195,662.32 by 7% equaling $13,696.36 divided by 12 equals $1,141.36 interest owed for the month. This is the profit the bank makes the 11th month on the job. The 10th month we owed the lender $1,148.75 interest for the month because we owed the lender $196,928.63, the 11th month we owed the lender $1,141.36 interest for the month (a little less) because the principal balance that we used to calculate the interest owed has been reduced from $196,928.63 to $195,662.32. Since the amortized monthly mortgage payment of $2,415.06 doesn't change, it's simple subtraction $2,415.06 minus $1,141.36 equals $1,273.70, this represents the portion of your payment that the lender uses to pay down your debt owed. You now owe your lender $195,662.32 minus $1,273.70. This $1,273.70 represents your 11th month of forced equity profit. The 11th month of our loan the $2,415.06 mortgage payment was broken down as follows:

$1,141.36—interest to lender (bank profit)

$1,273.70—principal payment on loan to reduce debt (our forced equity profit)

By month #12, you do not owe $195,662.32 any more; you owe $195,662.32 minus $1,273.70 or $194,388.62. This is the new principal balance, and since you only pay interest on what you owe, your 12th month interest payment will be 7% of $194,388.62

not $195,662.32. To figure out the 12th month interest, we multiply $194,388.62 by 7% equaling $13,607.20 divided by 12 equals $1,133.93 interest owed for the month. This is the profit the bank makes the 12th month on the job. The 11th month we owed the lender $1,141.36 interest for the month because we owed the lender $195,662.32, the 12th month we owed the lender $1,133.93 interest for the month (a little less) because the principal balance that we used to calculate the interest owed has been reduced from $195,662.32 to $194,388.62. Since the amortized monthly mortgage payment of $2,415.06 doesn't change, it's simple subtraction, $2,415.06 minus $1,133.93 equals $1,281.13. This $1,281.13 represents your 12th month of forced equity profit. The 12th and final month of our loan analysis the $2,415.06 mortgage payment was broken down as follows:

$1,133.93—interest to lender (bank profit)

$1,281.13—principal payment on loan to reduce debt (our forced equity profit)

Now, lets create a chart (see page 119), plug our figures in, and sum it up. As the chart shows, month by month the profit the bank makes gets lower because the principal balance owed that is being used to calculate interest owed is being lowered by the amount of our automatic monthly windfall forced equity. Month by month our forced equity profit gets higher because a larger portion of our pre-determined amortized monthly mortgage payment ($2,415.06) goes toward reducing the principal balance. The lower the principal balance, the lower the interest portion of our amortized mortgage payment.

Look at it this way; we pay rent to the lenders (in the form of deductible interest) to use their money and the tenants in turn pay us rent to use the house. The big difference is our rent for using the lender's money is going down month by month and year by year (due to the power of forced equity) and the tenants' rent they pay us usually goes up year by year. If the tenants' rent just covered our mortgage payment (principal, interest, property taxes, and insurance PITI) and we broke even each month, we would still win big because of forced equity. Lets say the tenant paid you $3,000 a month to rent your investment property and your mortgage payment was $2,415.06 and your property taxes were $6,000 a year or $500 a month and your homeowners insurance was another $85 per month, on the surface it looks like you are not making any money; you receive $3,000 a month and you pay out $3,000 a month ($2,415.06 plus 500 plus 85 equals $3,000), but now that you are familiar with the concept of amortization and its byproduct forced equity you know the truth. After only one year the tenant who invested $36,000 dollars ($3,000 rent per month for 12 months) has nothing to show for their efforts except a paid bill. On the flip side of the coin, the landlord who collects the rent and pays the mortgage has plenty to show for his monthly collection effort. If the tenant pays one year of rent, the balance owed on the loan is $193,107.50. (See amortization chart $208,000 @ 7% 10 yrs). The landlord just made $14,892.50 for the year. The old man said you make this $14,892.50 regardless of whether or not the property went up in value.

Translation: If the real estate market stood still—there was no such thing as appreciation; the asset you bought at $260,000 one year ago was still only worth $260,000 a year later, you just made $14,892.50, because you do not owe $208,000 on the property any more, you only owe $193,107.50 ($208,000 original principal balance minus $14,892.50—scheduled principal payments equals $193,107.50—new lower principal balance) If the real estate market stood still for another nine years; now your 10 year mortgage is paid off, and the asset you bought for $260,000 10 years ago was still only worth $260,000—you just made $208,000, because you do not owe $208,000 on the property any more—you owe nothing. The rents that the tenants paid the landlord over the years have paid the property off through the mechanism of "Forced Equity." You now have a free and clear asset thanks to your "royal subjects," your wonderful tenants. The old man looked me square in the eyes and proclaimed, "It's good to be the King."

Amount
Financed $208,000.00
Years   10
Interest
Rate   7

Monthly Payment $2,415.06		Bank Profit	Forced Equity Our Profit	
Month	Payment	Interest	Principal	Balance
1	$2,415.06	$1,213.33	$1,201.73	$206,798.27
2	$2,415.06	$1,206.32	$1,208.74	$205,589.54
3	$2,415.06	$1,199.27	$1,215.79	$204,373.75
4	$2,415.06	$1,192.18	$1,222.88	$203,150.87
5	$2,415.06	$1,185.05	$1,230.01	$201,920.86
6	$2,415.06	$1,177.87	$1,237.19	$200,683.67
7	$2,415.06	$1,170.65	$1,244.41	$199,439.26
8	$2,415.06	$1,163.40	$1,251.66	$198,187.60
9	$2,415.06	$1,156.09	$1,258.97	$196,928.63
10	$2,415.06	$1,148.75	$1,266.31	$195,662.32
11	$2,415.06	$1,141.36	$1,273.70	$194,388.63
12	$2,415.06	$1,133.93	$1,281.13	$193,107.50

$14,892.50

The old man said, the best way to learn something is to practice it until it becomes a knee-jerk reaction in your mind; an automatic no thinking involved activity, and then he instructed me to complete the remaining amortization exercises for $208,000 for 15 yrs/20 yrs/25 yrs and 30 yrs. He told me to use the first amortization exercise ($208,000 @ 7% for 10 years) as a template to figure out how to calculate the 1st year schedule on the four longer-term loans. The old man said, now it's your turn to GO FIGURE!!

Amortization Schedule Exercises

You borrow $208,000 @ 7% interest for 180 months (15 yrs)—What is the monthly payment? You go to the chart (page 107) and find the interest rate first, in this case it is 7.0, and then you find the multiplier per thousand for the term of the loan, in this case 15 years is 8.99 per 1,000 dollars borrowed. Now it is simple math, 8.99 X 208= *$1,869.92.* per month. Total payments to lender in 15 years = $1,869.92 X 180 months = *$336,585.60.* Total profit to bank $336,585.60 minus $208,000 original principal owed = *$128,585.60.*

(****As noted previously the amortization chart per thousand multipliers are estimates only—they are not as exact as the pre-programmed computers the lenders use. For your exercise, we will supply the more precise figure. In this example the $1,869.92 payment will be adjusted due to computer accuracy to $1,869.56)

When you have completed your mission, this is what your month-by-month chart should look like. After one year your forced equity profit is *$8,132.34.* ($208,000 original principal balance minus $199,867.66 new principal balance after scheduled principal loan payments)

Amount				
Financed	$208,000.00			
Years	15			
Interest				
Rate	7			
Monthly			Forced Equity	
Payment	$1,869.56	Bank Profit	Our Profit	
Month	Payment	Interest	Principal	Balance
1	$1,869.56	$1,213.33	$656.23	$207,343.77
2	$1,869.56	$1,209.51	$660.05	$206,683.72
3	$1,869.56	$1,205.66	$663.90	$206,019.81
4	$1,869.56	$1,201.78	$667.78	$205,352.04
5	$1,869.56	$1,197.89	$671.67	$204,680.36
6	$1,869.56	$1,193.97	$675.59	$204,004.77
7	$1,869.56	$1,190.03	$679.53	$203,325.24
8	$1,869.56	$1,186.06	$683.50	$202,641.74
9	$1,869.56	$1,182.08	$687.48	$201,954.26
10	$1,869.56	$1,178.07	$691.49	$201,262.77
11	$1,869.56	$1,174.03	$695.53	$200,567.24
12	$1,869.56	$1,169.98	$699.58	$199,867.66

$8,132.34

You borrow $208,000 @ 7% interest for 240 months (20yrs)—What is the monthly payment? Once again you go to the chart and find the interest rate first, in this case it is 7.0 and then you find the multiplier per thousand for the term of the loan, in this case 20 years is 7.75 per 1,000 dollars borrowed. Now it is simple math, 7.75 X 208= *$1,612* per month. Total payments to lender in 20 years = $1,612 x 240 months = *$386,880.* Total profit to bank $386,880 minus $208,000 original principal owed = *$178,880.*

(****In this example the $1,612 amortized monthly mortgage payment will be adjusted due to computer accuracy to $1,612.62)

When you have completed your mission this is what your month-by-month chart should look like. After one year your forced equity profit is *$4,948.19* ($208,000 original principal balance minus $203,051.81 new principal balance after scheduled principal loan payments)

Amount				
Financed	**$208,000.00**			
Years	20			
Interest				
Rate	7			
Monthly			**Forced Equity**	
Payment	**$1,612.62**	**Bank Profit**	**Our Profit**	
Month	**Payment**	**Interest**	**Principal**	**Balance**
1	$1,612.62	$1,213.33	$399.29	$207,600.71
2	$1,612.62	$1,211.00	$401.62	$207,199.10
3	$1,612.62	$1,208.66	$403.96	$206,795.14
4	$1,612.62	$1,206.30	$406.32	$206,388.82
5	$1,612.62	$1,203.93	$408.69	$205,980.14
6	$1,612.62	$1,201.55	$411.07	$205,569.07
7	$1,612.62	$1,199.15	$413.47	$205,155.60
8	$1,612.62	$1,196.74	$415.88	$204,739.72
9	$1,612.62	$1,194.32	$418.30	$204,321.42
10	$1,612.62	$1,191.87	$420.75	$203,900.67
11	$1,612.62	$1,189.42	$423.20	$203,477.47
12	$1,612.62	$1,186.95	$425.67	$203,051.81

$4,948.19

You borrow $208,000 @7% interest for 300 months (25 yrs)—What is the monthly payment? You go to the chart and find the interest rate first, in this case it is 7.0 and then you find the multiplier per thousand for the term of the loan, in this case 25 years is 7.07 per 1,000 dollars borrowed. Now it is simple math, 7.07 X 208 = *$1,470.56* per month. Total payments to lender in 25 years = $1,470.56 X 300 months = *$441,168.* Total profit to bank $441,168 minus $208,000 original principal owed = *$233,168.*

(**** In this example the $1,470.56 amortized monthly mortgage payment will be adjusted due to computer accuracy to $1,470.10).

When you have completed your mission, this is what your month-by-month chart should look like. After one year your forced equity profit is *$3,182* ($208,000 original principal balance minus $204,818 new principal balance after scheduled principal loan payments).

Tim Larkin

Amount				
Financed	$208,000.00			
Years	25			
Interest				
Rate	7			
Monthly			Forced Equity	
Payment	$1,470.10	Bank Profit	Our Profit	
Month	Payment	Interest	Principal	Balance
1	$1,470.10	$1,213.33	$256.77	$207,743.23
2	$1,470.10	$1,211.84	$258.26	$207,484.97
3	$1,470.10	$1,210.33	$259.77	$207,225.20
4	$1,470.10	$1,208.81	$261.29	$206,963.91
5	$1,470.10	$1,207.29	$262.81	$206,701.10
6	$1,470.10	$1,205.76	$264.34	$206,436.76
7	$1,470.10	$1,204.21	$265.89	$206,170.87
8	$1,470.10	$1,202.66	$267.44	$205,903.44
9	$1,470.10	$1,201.10	$269.00	$205,634.44
10	$1,470.10	$1,199.53	$270.57	$205,363.87
11	$1,470.10	$1,197.96	$272.14	$205,091.73
12	$1,470.10	$1,196.37	$273.73	$204,818.00

$3,182

The final analysis will be $208,000 @ 7% for 360 months (30 yrs). What is the monthly payment? You should know the routine by now, you go to the chart and find the interest rate first, in this case it is 7.0 and then you find the multiplier per thousand for the term of the loan; in this case 30 years is 6.65 per 1,000 dollars borrowed. Now it is simple math, 6.65 X 208 = *$1,383.20* per month. Total payments to lender in 30 years = $1,383.20 X 360 months = $497,952. Total profit to bank $497,952 minus $208,000 original principal owed = *$289,952.*

(****In this example the $1,383.20 amortized monthly mortgage payment will be adjusted due to computer accuracy to $1,383.83)

When you have completed this final mission, this is what your month-by-month chart should look like. After one year your forced equity' profit is $2,112.89. ($208,000 original principal balance minus $205,887.11 new principal balance after scheduled principal loan payments)

Amount

Financed $208,000.00

Years 30

Interest

Rate 7

Monthly

			Forced Equity	
		Bank Profit	Our Profit	
Payment $1,383.83				
Month	Payment	Interest	Principal	Balance
1	$1,383.83	$1,213.33	$170.50	$207,829.50
2	$1,383.83	$1,212.34	$171.49	$207,658.01
3	$1,383.83	$1,211.34	$172.49	$207,485.52
4	$1,383.83	$1,210.33	$173.50	$207,312.02
5	$1,383.83	$1,209.32	$174.51	$207,137.51
6	$1,383.83	$1,208.30	$175.53	$206,961.99
7	$1,383.83	$1,207.28	$176.55	$206,785.43
8	$1,383.83	$1,206.25	$177.58	$206,607.85
9	$1,383.83	$1,205.21	$178.62	$206,429.23
10	$1,383.83	$1,204.17	$179.66	$206,249.57
11	$1,383.83	$1,203.12	$180.71	$206,068.87
12	$1,383.83	$1,202.07	$181.76	$205,887.11

$2,112.89

After successfully completing these four amortization missions, you should be a master at this concept. If not, go back to the exercises and practice some more until you are. The old man said real estate investing is a simple business, "The more you learn, the more you earn," and you need to be an expert at amortization and the concept of forced equity in order to realize your maximum profit as a real estate investor.

The "numbers don't lie," the old man said. The longer you owe the money, the more money the vulture bankers make off of you. If you sacrifice and scrimp and scrounge and go for the shorter 15 year fully amortized loan payment of $1,869.92 instead of the more affordable 30 year fully amortized loan payment of $1,383.83 you pay $128,585.60 in interest to lender instead of $289,952 in interest, a savings of $161,366.40. You legally get to beat the bank out of over $161,000 dollars in profit just by making the simple decision of adjusting the payback timetable from 30 yrs to 15 yrs. The old man said, "Interest is tabulated based on principal balance reduction," so the quicker you reduce your debt owed to the lender, the more money you save. There are essentially two ways to defeat the bank's money making interest machine:

a) reduce principal balance owed quicker by raising your mortgage payment and amortizing loan over a shorter period of time (in our case $208k @ 7% 30 yr = $1,383.83 versus $208K @7% 15 yr= $1,869.92 a $486.72 per month difference) and

b) keep the mortgage payment low by amortizing loan over longer period of time (keep the affordable 30 yr payment $1,383.83) and make unscheduled principal payments on loan thereby reducing interest owed and shortening time required to payback monies. The old man said there is a third way to defeat the banks at their own game; make enough money from your investments to pay no interest by paying all cash for your home, but since most people are not in that position, learning the ins and outs of the mortgage process and borrowing the money makes the most sense. I asked the old man what do you do if you really can't afford the higher payment now but maybe in the future you might be able to swing it? Do you refinance the loan from the 30 year down to the 15 year? Absolutely not; you should save the money you would have spent on closing costs and make unscheduled principal payments instead. You would be surprised what a one-time $5,000 unscheduled principal payment on a $208,000 loan @7% 30 yr actually does. Lets do the calculations and see.

Before you get started, you will need a *reference tool*; the month-by-month amortization schedule for $208,000 @ 7% for

30 years. (For illustration purposes we will show the first 10 yrs of the schedule)

Unscheduled Principal Payments:
- Save money—less interest paid
- Save time—less years to pay back
- Lowers effective rate of interest
- Truth of the bi-weekly mortgage

REFERENCE TOOL—10 yrs of 30 yr Amortization Schedule

$208,000 @ 7%

Home Price	$260,000.00
Down Payment	$52,000.00
Amount Financed	$208,000.00
Years	30
Interest Rate	7
Monthly Payment	$1,383.83

Month	Payment	Interest	Principal	Balance
1	$1,383.83	$1,213.33	$170.50	$207,829.50
2	$1,383.83	$1,212.34	$171.49	$207,658.01
3	$1,383.83	$1,211.34	$172.49	$207,485.52
4	$1,383.83	$1,210.33	$173.50	$207,312.02
5	$1,383.83	$1,209.32	$174.51	$207,137.51
6	$1,383.83	$1,208.30	$175.53	$206,961.99
7	$1,383.83	$1,207.28	$176.55	$206,785.43
8	$1,383.83	$1,206.25	$177.58	$206,607.85
9	$1,383.83	$1,205.21	$178.62	$206,429.23
10	$1,383.83	$1,204.17	$179.66	$206,249.57
11	$1,383.83	$1,203.12	$180.71	$206,068.87
12	$1,383.83	$1,202.07	$181.76	$205,887.11
13	$1,383.83	$1,201.01	$182.82	$205,704.28
14	$1,383.83	$1,199.94	$183.89	$205,520.40
15	$1,383.83	$1,198.87	$184.96	$205,335.43
16	$1,383.83	$1,197.79	$186.04	$205,149.39
17	$1,383.83	$1,196.70	$187.13	$204,962.27
18	$1,383.83	$1,195.61	$188.22	$204,774.05
19	$1,383.83	$1,194.52	$189.31	$204,584.74
20	$1,383.83	$1,193.41	$190.42	$204,394.32
21	$1,383.83	$1,192.30	$191.53	$204,202.79
22	$1,383.83	$1,191.18	$192.65	$204,010.14
23	$1,383.83	$1,190.06	$193.77	$203,816.37
24	$1,383.83	$1,188.93	$194.90	$203,621.47
25	$1,383.83	$1,187.79	$196.04	$203,425.43
26	$1,383.83	$1,186.65	$197.18	$203,228.25
27	$1,383.83	$1,185.50	$198.33	$203,029.92
28	$1,383.83	$1,184.34	$199.49	$202,830.43
29	$1,383.83	$1,183.18	$200.65	$202,629.78
30	$1,383.83	$1,182.01	$201.82	$202,427.95
31	$1,383.83	$1,180.83	$203.00	$202,224.95
32	$1,383.83	$1,179.65	$204.18	$202,020.77
33	$1,383.83	$1,178.45	$205.38	$201,815.39
34	$1,383.83	$1,177.26	$206.57	$201,608.82
35	$1,383.83	$1,176.05	$207.78	$201,401.04
36	$1,383.83	$1,174.84	$208.99	$201,192.05
37	$1,383.83	$1,173.62	$210.21	$200,981.84
38	$1,383.83	$1,172.39	$211.44	$200,770.41
39	$1,383.83	$1,171.16	$212.67	$200,557.74
40	$1,383.83	$1,169.92	$213.91	$200,343.83
41	$1,383.83	$1,168.67	$215.16	$200,128.67
42	$1,383.83	$1,167.42	$216.41	$199,912.26
43	$1,383.83	$1,166.15	$217.68	$199,694.58
44	$1,383.83	$1,164.89	$218.94	$199,475.64
45	$1,383.83	$1,163.61	$220.22	$199,255.41
46	$1,383.83	$1,162.32	$221.51	$199,033.91
47	$1,383.83	$1,161.03	$222.80	$198,811.11
48	$1,383.83	$1,159.73	$224.10	$198,587.01
49	$1,383.83	$1,158.42	$225.41	$198,361.60
50	$1,383.83	$1,157.11	$226.72	$198,134.88
51	$1,383.83	$1,155.79	$228.04	$197,906.84
52	$1,383.83	$1,154.46	$229.37	$197,677.47
53	$1,383.83	$1,153.12	$230.71	$197,446.75
54	$1,383.83	$1,151.77	$232.06	$197,214.70
55	$1,383.83	$1,150.42	$233.41	$196,981.29
56	$1,383.83	$1,149.06	$234.77	$196,746.51
57	$1,383.83	$1,147.69	$236.14	$196,510.37
58	$1,383.83	$1,146.31	$237.52	$196,272.85

59	$1,383.83	$1,144.92	$238.91	$196,033.95
60	$1,383.83	$1,143.53	$240.30	$195,793.65
61	$1,383.83	$1,142.13	$241.70	$195,551.95
62	$1,383.83	$1,140.72	$243.11	$195,308.84
63	$1,383.83	$1,139.30	$244.53	$195,064.31
64	$1,383.83	$1,137.88	$245.95	$194,818.35
65	$1,383.83	$1,136.44	$247.39	$194,570.97
66	$1,383.83	$1,135.00	$248.83	$194,322.13
67	$1,383.83	$1,133.55	$250.28	$194,071.85
68	$1,383.83	$1,132.09	$251.74	$193,820.10
69	$1,383.83	$1,130.62	$253.21	$193,566.89
70	$1,383.83	$1,129.14	$254.69	$193,312.20
71	$1,383.83	$1,127.65	$256.18	$193,056.03
72	$1,383.83	$1,126.16	$257.67	$192,798.36
73	$1,383.83	$1,124.66	$259.17	$192,539.18
74	$1,383.83	$1,123.15	$260.68	$192,278.50
75	$1,383.83	$1,121.62	$262.21	$192,016.29
76	$1,383.83	$1,120.10	$263.73	$191,752.56
77	$1,383.83	$1,118.56	$265.27	$191,487.28
78	$1,383.83	$1,117.01	$266.82	$191,220.46
79	$1,383.83	$1,115.45	$268.38	$190,952.09
80	$1,383.83	$1,113.89	$269.94	$190,682.14
81	$1,383.83	$1,112.31	$271.52	$190,410.63
82	$1,383.83	$1,110.73	$273.10	$190,137.53
83	$1,383.83	$1,109.14	$274.69	$189,862.83
84	$1,383.83	$1,107.53	$276.30	$189,586.53
85	$1,383.83	$1,105.92	$277.91	$189,308.63
86	$1,383.83	$1,104.30	$279.53	$189,029.10
87	$1,383.83	$1,102.67	$281.16	$188,747.94
88	$1,383.83	$1,101.03	$282.80	$188,465.13
89	$1,383.83	$1,099.38	$284.45	$188,180.68
90	$1,383.83	$1,097.72	$286.11	$187,894.58
91	$1,383.83	$1,096.05	$287.78	$187,606.80
92	$1,383.83	$1,094.37	$289.46	$187,317.34
93	$1,383.83	$1,092.68	$291.15	$187,026.19
94	$1,383.83	$1,090.99	$292.84	$186,733.35
95	$1,383.83	$1,089.28	$294.55	$186,438.80
96	$1,383.83	$1,087.56	$296.27	$186,142.53
97	$1,383.83	$1,085.83	$298.00	$185,844.53
98	$1,383.83	$1,084.09	$299.74	$185,544.79
99	$1,383.83	$1,082.34	$301.49	$185,243.31
100	$1,383.83	$1,080.59	$303.24	$184,940.06
101	$1,383.83	$1,078.82	$305.01	$184,635.05
102	$1,383.83	$1,077.04	$306.79	$184,328.26
103	$1,383.83	$1,075.25	$308.58	$184,019.68
104	$1,383.83	$1,073.45	$310.38	$183,709.29
105	$1,383.83	$1,071.64	$312.19	$183,397.10
106	$1,383.83	$1,069.82	$314.01	$183,083.09
107	$1,383.83	$1,067.98	$315.85	$182,767.24
108	$1,383.83	$1,066.14	$317.69	$182,449.56
109	$1,383.83	$1,064.29	$319.54	$182,130.01
110	$1,383.83	$1,062.43	$321.40	$181,808.61
111	$1,383.83	$1,060.55	$323.28	$181,485.33
112	$1,383.83	$1,058.66	$325.17	$181,160.16
113	$1,383.83	$1,056.77	$327.06	$180,833.10
114	$1,383.83	$1,054.86	$328.97	$180,504.13
115	$1,383.83	$1,052.94	$330.89	$180,173.24
116	$1,383.83	$1,051.01	$332.82	$179,840.42
117	$1,383.83	$1,049.07	$334.76	$179,505.66

118	$1,383.83	$1,047.12	$336.71	$179,168.95
119	$1,383.83	$1,045.15	$338.68	$178,830.27
120	$1,383.83	$1,043.18	$340.65	$178,489.62

In a traditional mortgage loan of $208,000 @ 7% interest for 30 years, we would have 360 equal payments of $1,383.83. That's $1,383.83 times 360 equals $498,178.80 total payments to lender. If we subtract the original principal balance that we borrowed $208,000 from the total payment of $498,178.80 we get $290,178.80; the bank's profit; the interest that we paid over a 30 year period of time to borrow this money at a 7% annual yield to lender. In a traditional "meat and potatoes loan" with no unscheduled principal payments we would pay our lender a whopping $290,178.80 profit.

Most traditional mortgage loans have a standard one year pre payment penalty clause (usually 5% of unpaid principal balance) in the mortgage documents if you pay any or all of the loan off in the first 12 months, so in order to avoid incurring this fee (in our case 5% of $208,000 or $10,400) it is beneficial to wait a year or so before you embark on your money saving, time saving unscheduled principal payment investment strategy. The first 12 months of the loan you will pay the same interest as a traditional meat and potatoes loan; $14,493.06 (add up all 12 columns).

Amount				
Financed	$208,000.00			
Years	30			
Interest				
Rate	7			
			Forced	
			Equity	
Monthly			Our	
Payment	$1,383.83	Bank Profit	Profit	
Month	Payment	Interest	Principal	Balance
1	$1,383.83	$1,213.33	$170.50	$207,829.50
2	$1,383.83	$1,212.34	$171.49	$207,658.01
3	$1,383.83	$1,211.34	$172.49	$207,485.52
4	$1,383.83	$1,210.33	$173.50	$207,312.02
5	$1,383.83	$1,209.32	$174.51	$207,137.51
6	$1,383.83	$1,208.30	$175.53	$206,961.99
7	$1,383.83	$1,207.28	$176.55	$206,785.43
8	$1,383.83	$1,206.25	$177.58	$206,607.85
9	$1,383.83	$1,205.21	$178.62	$206,429.23
10	$1,383.83	$1,204.17	$179.66	$206,249.57
11	$1,383.83	$1,203.12	$180.71	$206,068.87
12	$1,383.83	$1,202.07	$181.76	$205,887.11

$14,493.06

After 12 months, the principal balance remaining on loan is $205,887.11. If on the 13th month you made an unscheduled principal payment (a pre-payment) to the lender in the amount of $5,000 you would have to consult the reference tool (see page 127); (the amortization table for $208,000 @7% for 30 yrs) to figure out how much interest you saved and how much time you chopped off your loan.

The $5,000 unscheduled principal payment comes directly off the principal balance remaining on the loan; none of this money is profit to the bank; it is all used to reduce the balance owed.

(This is not costing you any extra money; you rightfully owe this money anyway; you are just giving them a portion of their money a little earlier than expected, and in return, you are accelerating the payback schedule and saving the interest you would have paid had you kept their money longer) The payment of $1,383.83 remains the same, but the amount of overall interest that we pay and time that we have to pay it has changed substantially.

By month #13 we do not owe $205,887.11 any more, we owe $205,887.11 minus $5,000 or $200,887.11. Now we have to consult our reference tool (pg # 127) and find out which month of our loan schedule comes closes to our new principal balance of $200,887.11. We find our answer at month #37. The principal balance remaining after 37 months of scheduled mortgage payments is $200,981.84. If we paid our loan as per our old schedule of payments we would have owed our bank their profit from month #13 thru month #36, but the pre-pay jumps us over these 24 payments and places us in the 37th amortized payment position. In essence our 13th payment becomes our 37th payment in our schedule. It would have taken us an extra 2 years of normal principal payments to get to the same point in our amortization schedule that one lump sum of $5,000 does in one day. This unscheduled principal payment has moved us from month #13 to month #37, chopping off 2 years of mortgage payments and saving the interest we would have owed from month #13 to month # 37 or $28,516.87.

You now have a loan with the same monthly payment of $1,383.83 but you only have 27 years remaining not 29. The bank is not making the full $290,178.80 that a 7% yield would have given them had you kept to the original schedule of payments; the bank is making $290,178.80 minus $28,516.87 or $261,661.93. The pre-payment actually lowers the profit the bank makes, effectively lowering the rate of interest that you were charged for renting this money.

I looked at my old man incredulously and said, "You mean I don't have to refinance to lower my rate of interest; I can just make unscheduled principal payments and accomplish the same thing?"

The old man said absolutely, now lets prove it. In our example the bank would have to make $290,178.80 profit over a 30 year period to make an annual 7% profit, so obviously if our bank made only $261,661.93 in profit over the same 30 year period, the annual % has to be lower. The question you have to solve is what effective rate of interest would generate a profit of $261,661.93 on a loan amount of $208,000? The easiest way to do it is to go to your computer and plug different interest rate variables in until you get to the one closest to the profit generated. In our case, that would be 6.426%. The first year of the loan you would pay the same 7% yield to the bank; the moment you prepay your meat and potato loan, you change the effective yield of the loan from that point on. In our case, we paid 7% the first year and 6.426% for subsequent years. If we made a $5,000 unscheduled pre-pay after say 10 years; the first 10 years of the loan we would pay a 7% yield to the bank, and then we would pay a 6.426% effective rate of interest on any remaining payments to lender. (Years 1-10 you paid 7%, years 11, 12, 13, 14 and so on you are effectively paying a rate of 6.426%, If you were to make more unscheduled principal payments you would reduce the effective rate of interest even lower, because you would legally beat the lender out of more of its profit).

Without Pre-Pay   With Pre-Pay

Meat and Potato Fixed Rate Loan   **Meat and Potato Fixed Rate Loan w/ Gravy**

Without Pre-Pay	With Pre-Pay
Home Price —$260,000	Home Price —$260,000
Down Payment —$52,000 (20%)	Down Payment—$52,000 (20%)
% Rate 7%	% Rate 6.426%
Period (Years) 30	Period (Years) 30
Amount Financed—$208,000	Amount Financed—$208,000
Total Number of Payments—360	Total Number of Payments—360-24
Total Payments—$498,178.51	Total Payments—$469,654.31
Total Interest Payments$290,178.51	Total Interest Payments $261,654.31

Translation: By making a one-time, unscheduled $5,000 principal payment on our loan, we have saved over twenty-eight thousand dollars in interest, shaved almost 2 years off of our scheduled payments and lowered the effective interest rate that we were initially charged to borrow the money from 7% to approximately 6.426%. The old man called this pre-payment investing strategy the *gravy* on the standard "meat and potato fixed rate" loan. The money and time you save by employing this tactic makes the loan much more palatable.

I asked the old man; if I don't have the extra $5,000 lying around, can't I accomplish the same thing by just calling up those companies that arrange bi-weekly mortgages? You know, keep the same mortgage payment but pay every 2 weeks instead of once a month. The old man responded, the bi-weekly mortgage is nothing more than a masqueraded unscheduled principal payment, basically it's 13 payments a year, not 12. The numbers don't lie, Son, Do the Math!! Use our loan as an Example:

$208,000 @ 7% 30 years= $1,383.83 per month for 12 months = $16,605.96 for year.

Add one extra unscheduled principal payment (13th payment): $1,383.83 for year

Total monies tendered to bank for the year:*$17,989.79*

Bi-weekly: Take the $1,383.83 per month and divide it by 2 = $691.92 every 2 weeks

(There are 52 weeks in a year, so we will pay this $691.92 for 26 weeks)

$208,000 @ 7% 30 years = $691.92 X 26 weeks = *$17,989.92*

Total monies tendered to bank for the year: *$17,989.92*

As the numbers clearly show, there is no monetary difference between a bi-weekly mortgage product and an unscheduled principal payment. Both options require the same expenditure: $17,989 give or take the cents. Basically, with a bi-weekly mortgage, you are making an unscheduled principal payment of one full monthly mortgage payment per year. In our case, you are making an unscheduled principal payment of $1,383.83 per year minus the fees these companies may charge for their service. (Typical fees: one time setup fee of about $200-$500, plus a service fee of $2.50 to $4.50 for each biweekly payment. A typical 30-year loan can be wiped out in approximately 22 years, and you would wind up paying $1,600—$2,000 in fees)

The old man said, "Why pay thousands when you can do it yourself? It's easy; no specialized software or fancy accounting are needed. All you are really doing with a bi-weekly mortgage is paying someone else $1,600—$2,000 for knowledge of something

I have just taught you, and you should know by now, namely the money-saving, time-saving knowledge of how forced equity works. It's easy; all you have to do is save up some extra money; make an unscheduled principal payment, and use your amortization schedule (your reference tool for this investing strategy) to keep your lender honest and to verify with exact figures how much interest you saved and years you chopped off your loan, and bingo, you eliminate the services of a middle man by doing it yourself. The old man said instead of wasting your hard earned dollars on this bogus service, you would be better served investing that same $1,600—$2,000 as your first unscheduled principal payment. As I showed previously, a one time $5,000 pre-pay nets you over $28,000 in savings, you can and should do the calculations for how much a $1,600 or $2,000 pre-pay would net you before you invest; you wouldn't be able to justify the expense otherwise. You should also figure out how much time and interest you save by making that extra unscheduled 13th payment of $1,383.83 every year.

I asked the old man, "If I don't have any extra money to invest in unscheduled principal payments, shouldn't I lower my mortgage payments each month by getting involved with the ever popular interest-only mortgage loan?" The old man gave me a quizzical look and stated interest-only loans are not a separate type of mortgage, interest-only is an *option* that can be attached to any type of mortgage loan. Basically, you choose not to: a) employ the powerful concept of amortization and forced equity (that you just learned) and b) pay any principal payments per month on loan. The monthly payment is for interest-only. Using our reference tool as a guide (page 127, amortization schedule $208,000 @ 7% 30 yrs) we can clearly show the difference between the standard "meat and potato fixed rate loan" and the interest-only *option*. In the case of an *interest-only-loan* the monthly payments would be $1,213.33 versus $1,383.83, which would "save" you $170 per month in the short-term, but in the long-term you would lose the *power of forced equity* By going for the small buck you lose out on the big buck.

"Meat and Potato fixed rate amortized loan payment—$1,383.83"

Amount
Financed $208,000.00
Years   30
Interest
Rate   7
Monthly   Forced Equity
Payment $1,383.83   Bank Profit   Our Profit

Month	Payment	Interest	Principal	Balance
1	$1,383.83	$1,213.33	$170.50	$207,829.50
2	$1,383.83	$1,212.34	$171.49	$207,658.01
3	$1,383.83	$1,211.34	$172.49	$207,485.52
4	$1,383.83	$1,210.33	$173.50	$207,312.02
5	$1,383.83	$1,209.32	$174.51	$207,137.51
6	$1,383.83	$1,208.30	$175.53	$206,961.99
7	$1,383.83	$1,207.28	$176.55	$206,785.43
8	$1,383.83	$1,206.25	$177.58	$206,607.85
9	$1,383.83	$1,205.21	$178.62	$206,429.23
10	$1,383.83	$1,204.17	$179.66	$206,249.57
11	$1,383.83	$1,203.12	$180.71	$206,068.87
12	$1,383.83	$1,202.07	$181.76	$205,887.11

$2,112.89

"Interest-only Non-amortized loan payment —$1,213.33"

Amount				
Financed	$208,000.00			
Years	30			
Interest				
Rate	7			
Monthly			Forced Equity	
Payment	$1,213.33	Bank Profit	Our Profit	
Month	Payment	Interest	Principal	Balance
1	$1,213.33	$1,213.33	0	$208,000.00
2	$1,213.33	$1,213.33	0	$208,000.00
3	$1,213.33	$1,213.33	0	$208,000.00
4	$1,213.33	$1,213.33	0	$208,000.00
5	$1,213.33	$1,213.33	0	$208,000.00
6	$1,213.33	$1,213.33	0	$208,000.00
7	$1,213.33	$1,213.33	0	$208,000.00
8	$1,213.33	$1,213.33	0	$208,000.00
9	$1,213.33	$1,213.33	0	$208,000.00
10	$1,213.33	$1,213.33	0	$208,000.00
11	$1,213.33	$1,213.33	0	$208,000.00
12	$1,213.33	$1,213.33	0	$208,000.00

The logic of the bankers hawking these interest-only loans to investors is as follows:

The interest-only loan has a lower monthly payment than the standard amortized loan and therefore the investor's positive cash flow (the money the investor has left in his pocket after the tenant pays all his bills on the rental property) is higher. If the investor had a tenant paying say $2,000 a month and the standard amortized loan repayment was $1,383.83, the investor would gross $616.17 a month. If the same investor had an interest-only loan, the repayment would be $1,213.33 a month and the investor would gross $786.67 a month. Lets see, do I the investor want to pocket $786 a month or $616 a month to borrow the same amount of money? It seems on the surface that the banker is being uncharacteristically kind to the investor; like the money the banker is lending you is on sale. In the above example, the investor would safely assume since her payments are $170 dollars per month less that she was in a better position with this loan than the standard meat and potato-amortized loan. The thing is the bankers do not really care about the investor's bottom-line; they are in the business of peddling loans and making money by renting out money. The more people they can qualify to rent their money, the more profits they realize. The real logic of the bankers pushing these loans is simple: the interest-only loan is a lower payment than the standard amortized loan and will allow the bankers to lend the investor more money and, therefore, the bankers make more money. The bankers are not concerned about the investor's bottom-line; they are concerned about their own bottom-line. Lets not take my word for it—lets do the homework. Lets crunch the numbers. **The Numbers Don't Lie. Lets compare apples to apples.** Lets make believe **Investor A** bought a rental for $260,000 with a 20% down payment ($52,000) and financed the balance of the purchase price with a $208,000 interest-only loan. **Investor B** bought a similar rental for $260,000 with a 20% down payment ($52,000) and financed the balance owed with a standard meat and potato, no frills amortized loan of $208,000. Lets go ten years into the future and see how each investor did.

Investor A spent $145,599.60 in mortgage payments versus $166,059.60 for investor B. On the surface it looks like investor A was the big winner because they spent $20,460 less than investor B (166,059.60-145,599.60). But investor B has a bonus plan attached to its payments, almost like a rebate program, it's called Forced Equity and for the $166,059.60 spent on mortgage payments, this investor gets back $29,510.38 meaning they only spent $136,549.22, $9050.38 less ($145,599.60-$136,549.22) than investor A. After 10 years, Investor B is ahead by $9,050.38 and growing. Each month the mortgage payment is made, investor B, with the power of forced equity, is pulling further and further ahead of Investor A. Furthermore, Investor A has a poison pill attached to its loan; its called the balloon payment. A balloon payment is the agreed upon time that the lender wants the investor (5, 10, 15 years), who was only paying interest on the loan, to pay back the entire principal balance owed on the loan (the balloon payment is due and payable) which means the investor must refinance the house and incur at least $10,400 (5%) in closing costs to do so.

Translation: if you have a $208,000 interest-only loan that is due and payable in full in 10 years, you will owe $208,000 in 10 years because you chose not to make any principal payments; it was your *option*. You will be forced to waste money on a refinance or bail out of the investment and sell the house to pay the lender back. That means investor B is now ahead $9,050.38 plus $10,400 for a grand 10-year total of $19,450.38.

$208,000 @ 7% Interest-only Option versus Self Amortizing Finance Comparison

Investor A	Investor B	Investor B bonus
INTEREST-ONLY	**SELF -AMORTIZING**	**FORCED -EQUITY***
Year 1: 1,213.33 x 12 = 14,559.96 for the year	Year 1: 1,383.83 x 12 = 16,605.96 for the year	$208,000.00 —$205,887.11 = $2,112.89
Year 2: 1,213.33 x 12 = 14,559.96 for the year	Year 2: 1,383.83 x 12 = 16,605.96 For the year	$205,887.11 —$203,621.47 = $2,265.64
Year 3: 1,2113.33 x 12 = 14,559.96 for the year	Year 3: 1,383.83 x 12 = 16,605.96 for the year	$203,621.47- $201,192.05=$2,429.42
Year 4: 1,2113.33 x 12 = 14,559.96 for the year	Year 4: 1,383.83 x 12 = 16,605.96 for the year	$201,192.05- $198,587.01=$2,605.04
Year 5: 1,2113.33 x 12 = 14,559.96 for the year	Year 5: 1,383.83 x 12 = 16,605.96 for the year	$198,587.01- $195,793.65=$2,793.36
Year 6: 1,2113.33 x 12 = 14,559.96 for the year	Year 6: 1,383.83 x 12 = 16,605.96 for the year	$195,793.65- $192,798.36=$2,995.29
Year 7: 1,2113.33 x 12 = 14,559.96 for the year	Year 7: 1,383.83 x 12 = 16,605.96 for the year	$192,798.36- $189,586.53=$3,211.83
Year 8: 1,2113.33 x 12 = 14,559.96 for the year	Year 8: 1,383.83 x 12 = 16,605.96 for the year	$189,586.53- $186,142.53=$3,444
Year 9: 1,2113.33 x 12 = 14,559.96 for the year	Year 9: 1,383.83 x 12 = 16,605.96 for the year	$186,142.53- $182,449.56=$3,692.97

Year 10:	Year 10:	$182,449.56-
1,2113.33 x 12 = 14,559.96 for the year	1,383.83 x 12 = 16,605.96 for the year	$178,489.62=$3,692.97
Balance owed after 10 years $208,000 Balloon Payment due— (*Poison Pill *) $208,000— two choices 1) Refinance and pay off balloon. cost estimate 5%—of $208,000= 10,400 2) Forced to sell		Balance owed after 10 years= $178,489.62
Total money spent in 10 Years = 14,559.96 x 10 = $145,599.60 plus $10,400 to pay off balloon= $155,999.60	Total money spent in 10 Years = 16,605.96 x 10= $166,059.60	Landlord Rebate Program **Forced monthly equity. (120 months) $208,000- $178,489.62= $29,510.38

* Forced equity is a by product of self amortizing loan
** Refer to Reference tool—amortization schedule $208,000 @ 7% 30 years (page 127)

Total Money spent in 10 years:

Investor A—$155,999.60
Investor B—$136,549.22 ($166,059.60 minus $29,510.38)

Investor B is $19,450.38 richer because of the concept of forced equity. In 20 more years, Investor B will have an asset paid for in full by using tenants rent money coupled with the powerful investing mechanism of Forced Equity.

An investor should Never Ever take out an interest-only loan unless:

1. FLIPS—Short-term hold position (3months–1 year)—Buy low, fix up, sell high. Interest-only loan keeps holding costs down. (Remember our example—$1,213.33 versus $1,383.83) While the investor is waiting to resell the property at a profit, the expenses are lower. Less holding costs = more profit
    OR

2. Appreciation only investing in red hot seller's market—The interest-only loan keeps holding costs down while the forces of the market drive the price up and the investor unloads the property at a tidy profit—usually within 3-5 years. (RISKY—this investor only wins if real estate market is going up—if real estate market is stagnant or in a down spiral—investor could be forced to sell at a loss—These investors are equivalent to speculators—they are short-term opportunists—They do not enjoy the protection of forced equity that the long-term investors have built into their system of investing.)
    OR

3. Long-term investing for the Disciplined Saver—a disciplined saver can win big with an interest-only loan. They can increase their Positive cash flow month-by-month or semiannually by making unscheduled principal payments on loan. The investor can pre-pay this loan from day one, unlike the meat and potato amortized loan that usually has a one-year pre-payment penalty attached to it.

Remember these payments will actually lower the overall monthly mortgage payment per month. The one big advantage of a non-amortized loan is that the payment per month actually goes down when you make an unscheduled principal payment unlike the meat and potato amortized loan where the payment stays constant but the time to repay the loan decreases.

In an interest-only loan if you owed say $208,000 @ 7% your interest-only payment would be $1,213.33, (208,000 times 7% = 14,560 divided by 12 = $1,213.33) but if you gave the lender a 10,000 payment towards principal you would owe $208,000 minus 10,000 or 198,000. Your new payment would be 198,000 times 7%, which is $13,860 per year divided by 12 would be $1,155 per month. The investor just increased his positive cash flow by $58.33 per month ($1,213.33 minus $1,155 = $58.33). If this investor is disciplined enough to pay off the entire principal balance on loan prior to the balloon payment, (usually 10 years) he wins big. Every unscheduled payment he made lowered his monthly nut (P&I), putting more money in his pocket to use to pay off debt and realize his dream of owning the asset FREE and CLEAR. Now the disciplined saver can milk this CASH COW every month for the maximum amount of positive cash flow in his pocket.

I then asked the old man, "If I don't have any extra money to invest in unscheduled principal payments, shouldn't I lower my mortgage payments every month by getting involved with an adjustable rate mortgage loan?"

The old man smiled at me and said, "If you were gambling who would you rather be—the player or the house?"

Naturally I said the house, historically over time the house always wins. The old man said no matter what you call it, an ARM(adjustable rate mortgage) an AML (adjustable mortgage loan) or a VRM (variable rate mortgage), the adjustable rate mortgage is a mortgage loan that was designed by bankers aka "the house," for bankers to guarantee one thing—that they win the game of yield. Many years ago, the lending industry had a problem; they lent out trillions of dollars at low, fixed rates of interest and when the rates shot up, the bankers wound up losing billions of dollars of profit, because a lot of their money was tied up in these lower yielding loans. In order to combat this problem, the bankers came up with a creative solution; they created the adjustable rate mortgage. Let me show you what I am talking about. If Dum Dum Lending Corp. lent out $208,000 @ 7% 30 yr, they would gain in 30 yrs a profit of $290,178.80 ($1,383.83 times 360 months= $498,178.80 minus $208,000= $290,178.80). If prevailing interest rates shot to 10% by the end of the year and Dum Dum Lending Corp. lent out the same $208,000 @ 10% 30 yr, they would realize in 30 yrs a profit of $449,446.40 ($1,826.24 times 360 months= $657,446.40 minus $208,000= $449,446.40) The bank would wind up losing $159,267.60 ($449,446.40 minus $290,178.80= $159,267.60) on only one loan because there was no mechanism in place to grab those extra yield dollars by increasing the interest rate on the loan until the coveted and much respected ARM rolled into town. It took the guesswork out of timing the market for the bankers. The bankers could now regulate their profits in a high or low interest rate market. The bankers no longer needed a psychic with a crystal ball to predict when rates would change. All they needed with the ARM was a mathematician with a pen. The ARM loan is a *fixed* game; all the cards are stacked in the house's favor. When the rates go up so do you, when the rates go down so do you *or do you?*

The old man said, "For the average Joe or Jane, the bankers made the ARM a very complicated loan to understand." The bankers deliberately did this because as my father said, "In confusion, there is lots of profit." The bankers purposely designed a system so fundamentally difficult that the average person would have no clue whether or not their lender was cheating them. There are so many variables involved in figuring out this loan:

1) **Initial interest rate**—is this the actual rate of interest or was this a "Teaser rate"—a below average interest rate to lure customers in, but not used to make interest rate adjustments. This "Discount rate" pretty much guarantees your monthly payment at adjustment will go up regardless of the market; you paid an artificially low rate to begin with; you owe the lender for their generosity. What is the "prevailing " or actual rate of interest at the start of the loan?

2) **Adjustment period**—the period between one rate change and the next is called the adjustment period; with ARM's the interest rate and monthly payment can change every three months, every six months, every year, every three years or every five years or some variation in between. The old man said, "You better keep your calendar and pen handy so you do not miss your period." In a 3-year ARM, the rate can change once every three years. In a 3-month ARM, the adjustment period is every three months and the rate can change once every three months.

3) **Caps on monthly payment**—The maximum amount of money per adjustment period that the lender can adjust the mortgage payment. Basically, a limit on how much your monthly payment can be increased or decreased at each adjustment interval. Payment Caps do not limit the amount of interest the lender can earn, so they may cause negative amortization.

3b) **Lifetime cap on monthly payment**—The maximum amount of money, for the life of the loan that the lender can legally adjust the mortgage payment. Basically, a limit on how much your monthly payment can be increased or decreased for as long as you have the loan. These lifetime caps do not limit the amount of interest the lender can earn, so if rates shoot to the moon you may owe negative amortization.

4) **Caps on interest rate**—A limit on how much the interest rate can go up or down at each prescribed adjustment period.

4b) **Lifetime cap on interest rate**—A limit on how much the interest rate can go up or down for the entire life of the loan.

5) **Negative amortization**—Positive amortization is when your monthly payments are large enough to pay the interest owed and reduce the principal on your mortgage. Negative amortization is when your monthly payments are *not* large enough (usually due to caps on monthly payments) to cover the interest owed to the lender. The lender will not forgive this profit; instead, the lender will conveniently add this interest cost to the unpaid principal balance.

Translation: Even after making many payments on the loan, you could wind up owing more money than you originally borrowed. You could borrow $208,000 and in 6 years you could owe $215,000 or more.

6) **Index**—The index is the tool or the gauge that the lender uses at the adjustment period to increase or decrease the interest rate on your ARM. The index is like a compiled average of interest rate charges for a given financial sector. The index is a physical number published daily or weekly in most prominent newspapers. Your interest rate is "tied" to your index, which means when the index rate goes up, your interest rate, at adjustment time, goes up with it.
   The most common indexes are:
   - Constant Maturity Treasury (CMT)
   - 11th District Cost of Funds Index (COFI)
   - London Inter Bank Offering Rates (LIBOR)
   - Treasury Bill (T-Bill)
   - 12-Month Treasury Average (MTA)
   - Certificate of Deposit Index (CODI)
   - Cost of Savings Index (COSI)
   - Certificates of Deposit (CD) Indexes

- Bank Prime Loan (Prime Rate)
- Fannie Mae's Required Net Yield(RNY)
- National Average Contract Mortgage Rate

Which one of the above indexes do you want attached to your ARM? Is one index historically better than another one? Some financial wonders suggest a loan tied to a *lagging index (like COFI)* is better when rates are rising, while others suggest that loans tied to an index like CMT is best during periods of declining rates. Who is right? Who is wrong? Do I specifically target a loan based on the past history of the index? Is the past history of an index indicative of its future performance? Do I pay less interest with certain indexes? The answers to these questions are not clear-cut; the only thing for sure is that nobody really knows; it's anybody's guess. Are there certain "bad" indexes that favor the lenders and certain "good" indexes that favor the borrowers? Who knows!! You can only go back in time and historically plot how the index already moved not how it will move in the future. All the educated scholars and financial analysts can do is professionally guess.

7) **Margin**—the number of percentage points the lender adds to the index at the adjustment period to increase or decrease the interest rate on your ARM. *Translation:* To calculate new interest rate you add a "spread" on top of the index called a margin.

8) **Conversion option**—The ability to pay an extra fee in certain ARM's to change the adjustable rate mortgage to a standard fixed rate loan, usually at the end of an adjustment period.

The old man said this loan is a paperwork nightmare; at every adjustment period, you would have to cross-reference multiple sources of information to accurately determine the validity of your new mortgage payment. If you had multiple properties with multiple loans and differing adjustment periods, you could have a real mess on your hands.

WOW!! Very confusing to say the least—you probably need an MBA, a NY times and a strong stomach to swallow all of that information in one sitting. The average investor will just assume the bankers know better and that the numbers and fancy calculations the banks use to determine monthly payments are accurate. Most investors will hide behind their egos and never admit lack of comprehension concerning the ARM. Most investors are oblivious to the unknown perils of the seemingly innocent ARM. For example, an annually adjusted ARM for $200,000 may start at 5%, but a 6% cap could allow it to go to 11% within four years. This would raise the payment from $1,073.64 to $1,904.65, an increase of $831.01 per month. (An unexpected increase of this magnitude would destroy the investment value of the rental property).

The old man said, "For the average investor, this loan is...."

- Too complicated
- Too much thinking involved
- Too much information to remember
- Too many layers of confusion to unravel
- Too stressful (constantly worrying about the changing terms of the loan)
- Too difficult to budget money and realistically figure out positive cash flow on rental property. (Fluctuating mortgage payment at adjustment)
- Too easy to get fleeced by greedy bankers

The old man liked an investing system that was simple to do, easy to duplicate, and not mentally draining; that's why he chose standard, no frills, straight-laced, easy to decipher vehicles to work with; namely the "meat and potato fixed rate amortized mortgage loan" or the "interest-only loan." There is absolutely no confusion at all with these loans. The "meat and potato" loan is as easy as 1, 2, and 3.

1) Loan amount
2) Term of loan
3) Fixed interest rate

The "interest-only" loan is as easy as 1, 2, 3, and 4.

1) Loan amount
2) Term of loan
3) Fixed interest rate
4) Balloon payment due

There is no "teaser rate," adjustment period, caps, index, margin or anything else that could cloud your investment mind, just "plain Jane," basic, easy to follow and profit from mortgage vehicles. The old man said he built a small empire on the backs of these powerfully simplistic mortgage vehicles, and so can you if you heed my advice. His final parting words on the ARM was "...the ARM was born out of the necessity to qualify otherwise unqualified, desperate, first-time home buyers for a home, *not* for the long-term hold position of the sophisticated investor's rental property.

2) **"<u>Market equity</u>"**—commonly known as Appreciation. The old man was very clear on his definition of Appreciation—**the gradual increase in value of real property through the natural course of events.** The old man said let me translate that for you: A property's value goes up naturally, due to market conditions, not due to external factors like spending money on improvements or additions. If your house is worth $300,000 and you invest $100,000 to do an extension and now the property's value has increased in value to say $360,000, this $60,000 increase in property value was *not* due to natural forces' it was caused by an unnatural event called a construction project and, therefore, it is not appreciation.

The old man said, the laws of supply and demand naturally move the real estate market into and out of a **Seller's Market** and a **Buyer's Market**.

- **Seller's Market**—Low supply of homes for sale in market and High demand from large supply of qualified buyers.

Translation: 10 buyers and only 2 houses for sale. The large pool of qualified buyers fight over scarce supply of homes to buy, raising values and causing High Appreciation rates in the real estate market. A market favoring sellers, the seller can command top dollar in this highly competitive market place. Bidding wars—pitting buyer vs buyer are common in this market. This is a great market for an investor looking to unload any undesirable rentals. The intense competition among realtors for listings makes the seller's market a great environment to sell in. The seller can guarantee a higher net sales price by negotiating hard with desperate realtors who need inventory (listings). In a seller's market, where listings are scarce, it is not uncommon for realtors to accept 4%, 3%, 2% and even 1% to sell your house. Some "flat fee" realtors will even work for less than 1%, just to score the listing. In a red hot seller's market, some sellers have successfully bypassed realtors altogether and opted to sell on their own and pay $0 commission.

In a seller's market, it's **all about the house**; whoever has the listing controls the game. The seller has the upper hand and all the leverage. The seller is not interested in creative deals or holding paper; they want all cash and they want to close yesterday if possible. The seller doesn't care what defects a licensed engineer or home inspector finds concerning the property; the price to the buyer is nonnegotiable or the seller will replace that buyer with a less discriminating buyer who will accept property as is. If the appraisal comes in too low, the seller won't reduce price; the seller will require you to make up the difference with cash or find another buyer who will.

In a highly appreciating seller's market, the most lucrative investment vehicle for investors is the no money down techniques. These investors tie up as many properties as possible and put as little as possible down, gaining maximum leverage, and ride the appreciation wave to big profits. The investors are not concerned about what the property is worth *today,* they will pay whatever it takes to gain control of a highly appreciating house in a hot seller's market. The investors are buying the house based on the future value of what the house can and will be worth *tomorrow.* This is a one-dimensional investing strategy that the old man called "appreciation only investing" or speculating. These investors could care less about **forced equity** or **positive cash flow** or **tax write offs;** they are only concerned with appreciation and short-term flip profits. These investors are shortchanging the return on their real estate investment by only investing short-term for one reason (market equity) instead of long-term, for four reasons, like the old man did: **1) forced equity, 2) market equity 3) positive cash flow and 4) tax write offs).** For example, the short buck, one-dimensional "appreciation only" investor buys a house for $260,000 and in 1 year of red hot appreciation, sells it for $290,000, making a short-term $30,000 dollar gross profit. The more experienced investor lazily stays in the investment longer and realizes much greater rewards by profiting from the benefits of all four dimensions of the real estate investment. The long-term, multi-dimensional investor buys the same house for $260,000, and holds it for say 10 years, realizing the long buck profit of approximately $214,621 (see real estate breakdown pg #205) The old man said, "It's simple math," the short-term quick buck investor makes money, the investor with his eye on the long-term becomes obscenely wealthy by investing for the long buck profits. The old man said, "Don't settle for the pennies of the short-term hold; go for the big dollars of the long-term hold." The old man said, "Don't get me wrong, there are exceptions to every rule and the profit potential of the 'Wreck' property with its inherited equity is one of them."

The "Wreck" property (usually a foreclosure) is unique because usually the house was bought years ago, and is now in such disrepair, it disallows years of long-term appreciation. In other words, while other similar homes in the area were naturally going up in value, this house maintained an artificially low value due to its poor condition. The smart investor gobbles up the dilapidated house, and activates the dormant long-term appreciation by renovating run down property and in effect inheriting equity that would have taken years to acquire. Unlike "appreciation only" investing, the investor does not have to wait for the market to go up in value prior to sale; the wreck already had the benefit of time to naturally increase its value. All you did was activate equity that was already there, but hidden by years of deferred maintenance by a neglectful owner. This is the only short buck game the old man liked to play. In essence, you buy property at *yesterday's* low price, fix it up, and resell it at *today's* higher price. A guaranteed winner for the investor that is familiar with the resale values of properties in their marketplace.

- **Buyer's Market**—High supply of homes for sale in market and low demand from small supply of qualified buyers. ***Translation:*** 10 houses for sale and only 2 buyers. The small pool of qualified buyers has an overabundance of homes to choose from. This glut causes sellers to adjust their prices downward to attract more offers, resulting in stagnant or low appreciation rates in the real estate market—a market favoring buyers. There are so many properties available that the buyer now has the upper hand when negotiating with the seller. The buyer is no longer locked in a bidding war with other buyers. This is a great market for an investor looking for a bargain priced property. The oversupply of listings makes the buyer's market a great environment to invest in. You can score deals and even steals in a ripe buyer's market. The sellers' over inflated concepts of value (what their houses are worth) have been stripped away by the reality of the buyer's market. The sellers know the tide has turned. The days of double-digit appreciation are over. The neighborhood is littered with real estate signs; every other house is adorned with the placard FOR SALE.

The buyer can guarantee the lowest buying price by negotiating hard with multiple sellers desperate for their money. The buyer routinely submits multiple low ball offers on various properties hoping to land the most negotiable and flexible seller. The only hope the seller has of getting Top Dollar in a buyer's market is to hope they have enough cash reserves and time to wait for the buyer's market to run its course and for a new seller's market to begin. In a buyer's market, the seller gets clobbered on price from the limited buyers and hammered on commission from the real estate industry. In a buyer's market, where listings are plentiful and it's tougher to sell a house, it is it is not uncommon for realtors to charge upwards of 6%, 7%, 8% and even 9% and over 10% to sell your house.

In a buyer's market, it's **all about the buyer**; whoever has the buyer, controls the game. The buyer has all the leverage to structure creative deals with sellers. The sellers are very receptive to negotiating favorable terms like holding paper or signing contracts subject to the buyers selling their old house. The sellers will do whatever it reasonably takes to liquidate the property. In a buyer's market, the engineers report or home inspection report is a powerful negotiating tool for the astute investor, because now the seller is actually willing to listen to and correct any defects or adjust the price accordingly. If the appraisal comes in lower than the contract price, the seller, fearful of losing the buyer, may reduce the price or offer some other incentive like a low interest seller held second to keep the deal alive.

In the low to no appreciating buyer's market, the most lucrative investment vehicle for investors is well-priced, long-term rentals with favorable terms and short-term flips using a short sale. The investor is looking to buy rental properties with a substantial down payment, creating instant equity in investment and allowing a healthy positive cash flow to ride out the down market. The investor is basically in a holding pattern, obtaining well-priced assets and waiting for those assets to appreciate in value when the current buyer's market eventually turns around and naturally flows into the seller's market. The smart investors are looking to acquire two to three bargain priced rentals in the buyer's market and then sell two of the three rentals in the higher priced seller's market and pay off the outstanding mortgage on remaining rental, leaving the investor with a paid-in-full, free and clear asset—a rental property with a positive cash flow that pays them every month. The rental is your own personal "cash cow" that you, the investor get to milk twelve times a year.

The high foreclosure rates associated with a buyer's market make it fertile ground for the "short sale" mortgage flip. Basically the short sale is when a mortgage company "discounts" or takes less than what is owed to them in order to avoid the costly expenditures of a foreclosure action. If a mortgage company is owed $400,000 on a property that was worth $440,000 in a seller's market and is now worth $380,000 in a buyer's market, the company may be willing to accept $320,000 cash from a buyer in order to cut any future losses. The investor can then fix up and flip property for a handsome profit. The short sale is a great vehicle for an investor to pick up a below priced rental property for a long-term hold or a well priced investment property for a short-term "quick profit" flip.

The **seller's market** and the **buyer's market** are indirectly controlled by what the old man euphemistically called the "**Greenspan Effect**" (affectionately named after Allan Greenspan). The **Greenspan Effect** is: interest rate changes indirectly control property values via affordability.

Translation: the lowering or raising of interest rates affect the affordability of housing, thereby raising or lowering value of property. Further *Translation:* Low interest rates make homes more affordable for more people, creating greater demand to buy homes, increasing the price people will pay to buy the home, leading to high appreciation rate in the area causing a **seller's market.**

Increasing interest rates make homes less affordable for more people, creating less demand to buy homes; decreasing price people can afford to pay to buy the home, leading to stagnant or low appreciation rate in the area, causing a **buyer's market**.

Affordability is the issue. The same house will be worth one price in a seller's market and another price in a buyer's market because the monthly mortgage payment per month will remain the same for both values. For example, if you bought a home in a buyer's market for **$300,000**, when interest rates were 10%, and you put down 5% ($15,000); you would borrow $285,000 and your 30 year monthly payment of principal and interest would be **$2,502**. The same home in a seller's market, where interest rates are at say 6%, could fetch **$438,950** because at 5% down ($21,947), you would wind up borrowing approximately $417,000 and your 30 year monthly payment of principal and interest would be the same: **$2,502** (**GO FIGURE!**).

As these figures clearly show the **Greenspan Effect** allows a house selling for $438,950 to be just as affordable as a house selling for $300,000; it just depends on the interest rate. In other words the same house worth $300,000 in a soft buyer's market with high interest rates is worth $438,950 in a red hot seller's market with lower interest rates. The $138,950 difference in price does not affect the monthly mortgage payment. The mortgage payment is the same affordable $2,502 regardless of what price you pay. Affordability makes the same $300,000 dollar house worth $438,950, because you need the same salary to comfortably pay a **$2,502** $417,000 mortgage as you do to pay a **$2,502** $285,000 mortgage. You need to know that there are two simultaneous values attached to one property, a buyer's market value and a seller's market value. These values are established by the Greenspan Effect. The property is actually worth two prices at the same time, depending on the interest rate. The first value is what the property is worth at *Today's* interest rate and mortgage payment, and the second value is what the property could be worth *tomorrow* when the Greenspan Effect kicks in when the interest rates are raised or lowered. In the above example, the property is worth $300,000 (buyer's market value) when interest rates are at 10% and $438,950 (seller's market value) when interest rates are reduced to 6%. The old man said, "You need to understand this correlation between interest rates and property values in order to maximize your return as a successful long-term real estate investor." There is never a good time or bad time to invest in real estate—only a **seller's market** or a **buyer's market**. You need to know the truth about real estate values. The old man said the value of real estate never stays constant, it is constantly changing based on the affordability of money in the marketplace. Every time the interest rate is adjusted, a new property value is created because the property has become less affordable (higher rate) or more affordable (lower rate) to the paying public. The Greenspan Effect shows:

As the interest rate swings up and down, so does property value:

Rates are low—Prices are high—SELL

Rates are high—Prices are low—BUY

You want to buy when people are selling **(buyer's market)** and sell when people are buying **(seller's market).**

Translation: You want to buy properties at the buyer's market price when there is a glut of people selling and high rates of interest (double digits) keep property values artificially low and sellers highly receptive to flexible and creative terms resulting in deals and steals from desperate sellers. When rates go back down in say, who knows, 3-7 years, sparking a seller's market, you refinance and get rid of that double digit loan or cash out and profit from increased property values of **seller's market**.

Further Translation:

Buy at buyer's market bargain price. Wait for Greenspan Effect to naturally convert market to seller's market, and sell same property at higher seller's market price or refinance at lower rate and hold for long-term monthly residual income.

The old man said, "Now that you know how interconnected property values and interest rates are, you should realize that there is never a wrong time to buy real estate." The price you pay is relative to the interest rates present at the time of your investment. A high price and a low price can be the same price depending on the affordability. For example, if you were comfortable paying a $2,502 mortgage for a $300,000 house you should be just as comfortable paying a $2,502 mortgage for a $438,950 house. Affordability-wise, both houses are the same value. You won't overpay by paying $438,950 in a seller's market for the same house you can buy for $300,000 in a buyer's market. You didn't underpay when you paid

$300,000 in a buyer's market for the same house you would pay $438,950 for in a seller's market. In essence, you paid the same affordable price.

Armed with this knowledge, you should now know that if you bought a $438,950 house and the interest rates shot from 6%-10%, you shouldn't panic if your house loses $138,950 in equity, and now is worth only $300,000. This is supposed to happen. This is a natural event caused by the affordability or non-affordability of money in the real estate market. (aka Greenspan Effect). Naturally, when rates go back down, however long that takes, the property will recoup its value and once again be worth $438,950 or more. The old man said, "Money flowing into the real estate marketplace keeps values of real property in a constant flux, and only long-term real estate investors can take full advantage of the high and low property values created by changing interest rates." The old man said don't try to figure out why or how interest rates go up or down, just know that when the powers to be adjust the rates the real property values in a given market are either raised or lowered, due to the cost of borrowing money.

Translation: Appreciation is indirectly controlled by the **Greenspan Effect.**

3) <u>Tax Write-offs</u>—Lucrative Tax Deductions / Legalized Loophole

The old man said investing in real estate is like investing in any other business, "It doesn't matter how much you make; it's how much you keep that matters." Real estate is a business well suited for legally avoiding paying heavy income taxes. The old man said cash is king. With real estate, you can **legally bury the green.** The tax laws and compliance requirements can be ambiguous and subject to different interpretations, so it is important to retain an accountant who can guide you through the ever-changing forest of IRS and State tax codes.

Translation: A good accountant armed with the lucrative tax deductions of a rental property can legally shield you from taxes and keep more of your money in your pocket.

You should become familiar with:

The Arsenal of deductions available to the rental property investor.

Operating Expenses of the rental are fully deductible
- Accounting fees
- Insurance premiums
- License fees
- Office supplies and expenses
- Exterminator
- Advertising costs
- Landscaper
- Janitorial service
- Property taxes
- Repair costs
- Legal fees
- Commissions paid
- Salaries (if any)
- Snow removal service
- Trash removal
- Utilities
- Telephone
- Property management fees (if any)
- Cost of credit reports, criminal checks
- Misc. supplies
- Etc…

Mortgage Interest—
The interest on the rental property is fully deductible

Tim Larkin

Amount Financed	$208,000.00			
Years	30			
Interest Rate	7			
Monthly Payment	$1,383.83	Bank Profit	Forced Equity Our Profit	
Month	Payment	Interest	Principal	Balance
1	$1,383.83	$1,213.33	$170.50	$207,829.50
2	$1,383.83	$1,212.34	$171.49	$207,658.01
3	$1,383.83	$1,211.34	$172.49	$207,485.52
4	$1,383.83	$1,210.33	$173.50	$207,312.02
5	$1,383.83	$1,209.32	$174.51	$207,137.51
6	$1,383.83	$1,208.30	$175.53	$206,961.99
7	$1,383.83	$1,207.28	$176.55	$206,785.43
8	$1,383.83	$1,206.25	$177.58	$206,607.85
9	$1,383.83	$1,205.21	$178.62	$206,429.23
10	$1,383.83	$1,204.17	$179.66	$206,249.57
11	$1,383.83	$1,203.12	$180.71	$206,068.87
12	$1,383.83	$1,202.07	$181.76	$205,887.11

$14,493.06

The bank profit portion of your monthly mortgage payment is fully deductible. In this example, the rental property investor gets to write off the full $14,493.06 on his annual tax return.

Points

Any points paid on any mortgage secured by the rental property are deductible over the life of the loan. For example, if you obtain a $208,000 loan with a 30 year term and you pay 1 point to obtain the loan, you can write off $69.33 a year over the 30-year period for a total of $2,080. If you sell a rental, and pay the mortgage off early, you can deduct all unused points in that year.

Closing costs—The closing costs associated with the **purchase** of the rental property are deductible in the year of the purchase.
   • Title insurance

- Title fees
- Appraisal
- Application fee
- Recording fees
- Etc....

The old man said you should check with your accountant because certain closing costs associated with a **refinance** on the rental property are deductible as well

Depreciation—Loss on Paper

The government determines how many useful years your rental property has before wear and tear, age, or obsolescence should force you to replace the structure. The IRS then allows you to depreciate or write off the rental property over its useful life by taking a "paper loss" for a set number of years. Currently, the IRS allows residential rental properties to be depreciated over 27.5 years and commercial rentals to be depreciated over 39 years. For example, if you purchase a residential rental property in mid January for $260,000 you have 27.5 years to write off the cost of the rental property structure minus the land it resides on. The land where the rental property is located is worth $52,000 (approximately 20% of purchase price). The building is worth $208,000. You have a $208,000 deduction over a 27.5 year period of time. The rental property structure is depreciated by equal amounts annually over the 27.5-year period. ($208,000 divided by 27.5 = $7,563.63 per year paper loss).

Since you purchased the rental property in January, the IRS rules allow you to write off 11 full months of depreciation in the first year or $7,248.48, and a partial month of depreciation for January. For the next 26.5 years you would deduct $7,563.63 per year, and in the 28th year, you would write off the remaining month of depreciation, $315.15, in the final year.

Translation—Even though your rental property can appreciate in value year by year, the government gives you a preset number of years to depreciate the rental property and take a "paper loss" on your taxes.

Capital Improvements—Major improvements to the rental property like a new roof, new siding, a dormer or extension, etc... are subject to the same depreciation schedule as above. Capital improvements to a residential rental property are depreciated over a 27.5-year period of time. Capital improvements to a commercial rental property are depreciated over 39 years.

Personal property—The rental property investor can write off some personal property items (items which are not permanently attached to the land or improvements) like a dishwasher, microwave, washer, dryer, furniture, lawn mower, snow removal equipment, etc. The depreciation schedule on personal property can vary, a recovery period of 5, 7, or 10 years could be used; you should check with your accountant to determine the proper recovery periods for personal property.

The old man said, don't fall in love with your tax deductions, they could be, "Here today, Gone tomorrow." That's why you should never invest in real estate just for tax purposes. The politicians are forever changing the real estate landscape by changing deductions or wiping out certain write offs or adding newer more complicated tax codes and compliance requirements. The old man cited credit card deductions and depreciation schedules as good examples. The old man said prior to 1986, the best way to buy a rental property was using credit cards as your primary source of down payment money, because the interest charges were fully deductible. This lucrative tax saving door was abruptly closed in 1986 with the passing of The Tax Reform Act of 1986, which among other things wiped out interest deductions on credit cards. The investors who borrowed heavily on credit cards and counted on this deduction to justify their investment in a rental property were rudely awakened when this write off was arbitrarily eliminated. The old man said, "That's why you should never invest in real estate based solely on the tax consequences." The other three reasons: forced equity, market equity, and positive cash flow are equally if not more important in justifying your rental property investment.

The old man said, when I first started investing in rental properties in the late 70's, early 80's, the depreciation schedules were very lucrative for the rental property investor:"

1-1-81 to 3-15-84 —15 year schedule
3-16-84 to 5-8-85 —18 year schedule
5-9-85 to 12-31-86—19 year schedule

In 1987, when the government decided in its infinite wisdom to double the time it took to depreciate rental property (from 15 years to 27.5 years effective 1-1-87 to present), the old man didn't stop investing in rentals because the tax laws suddenly changed. The old man knew full well the financial merits of investing in real estate for all four reasons, not just one.

The old man said, even if the government took away all the deductions and write offs associated with rentals there still existed a legalized loophole to avoid paying any income taxes (capital gains) on the profit generated from the sale of the rental property, the 1031 Tax Deferred Exchange. The 1031 is the sacred cow of the rich property owning politicians. The 1031 Exchange is the vehicle that legally allows the rich to get richer in the forum of real estate.

The Mechanics of a 1031
Tax Deferred Exchange

1) All monies to be exchanged must be deposited with a non-interested third party called a qualified intermediary (QI) or exchange accommodator. The key words here are non-interested; the QI cannot be your best friend or your lawyer or your accountant. In order to avoid any conflict with the IRS, a non-partial unbiased unrelated third party should be retained. The typical intermediary fee for an exchange is $5-$10,000 or more depending on the complexity of the transaction.

2) The QI can facilitate many different types of exchanges:

- **Build to suit / Improvement**—The QI holds title to the replacement property on behalf of the property seller, while improvements are done to the replacement property. Commonly known as an Improvement Exchange.
- **Delayed**—In a delayed exchange, typically known as a Starker Exchange, your relinquished property (your old property) is exchanged for a promise from someone (most likely a facilitator company) to acquire a replacement property for you at a later date.
- **Reverse**—an exchange where you buy the replacement property first and then you sell your relinquished property (your old property) afterwards.
- **Simultaneous**—the sale of the relinquished property (your old property) and the purchase of the identified replacement property takes places simultaneously.
- **1033 Tax Deferred Exchange**—a special exchange exists when eminent domain (the legal right of the government to seize your property for just compensation) is involved in the sale of your relinquished property (your old property). You have up to 2 years to find a suitable replacement property in this exchange.

3) 45-Day Identification Period—the investor has 45 days from the closing of the property to select and identify property or properties to purchase and 180 total days to close the purchase of the identified property /properties. Since this is a real estate transaction, this selection process has to be in writing (Statue of Fraud). The old man said to remember weekends and holidays count so in actuality this identification time period can be much sooner depending on the time of year you do the exchange. In fair warning the old man said, "You should protect your best interests and identify more than one property for your exchange,

just in case your deal for the replacement property falls through. By code you can identify up to three properties regardless of value and you don't have to buy all three."

4) **Like Kind**—the property/properties that you exchange must be of "like kind." Like kind is real estate or other tangible property that is similar in nature or classification. *Translation:* Can you exchange raw land for a 10-unit apartment building? Yes, you can. They are both classified as real estate and therefore are of "like kind." Like kind property cannot be a primary residence or a second home; it must be for business or investment purposes

5) **Boot**—any non-qualifying property (property that is not "like kind" received from a 1031 Exchange. "Cash boot" and "mortgage boot" are the most common types of "boot." Boot is fully taxable. For example, you exchange your $500,000 rental property for a $470,000 rental plus $30,000 cash. The $30,000 would be "cash boot" and subject to taxation.

The old man said the 1031 Exchange has been a part of the IRS tax code since the roaring 20's; the very beginning of income taxes in America. The 1031 applies only to property held for commercial, business or investment purposes, your primary residence is ineligible.

The old man said, don't despair, there also exists a legalized loophole for avoiding paying income taxes on your primary residence when you sell it; **the Internal Revenue Code 121 Principal Residence Exemption.** You can legally exclude up to $250,000 on the gain of the sale of your primary residence if you are single and up to $500,000 on the gain at sale if you are married if "during the 5-year period ending on the date of the sale, such property was owned and used by you as your principal residence for a period aggregating 2 years or more."

Translation: You do not have to actually live in house to get exemption, just prove you lived in it 2 years out of the last 5 years prior to sale. The IRS rules for this exemption are very clear, you must satisfy both the ownership test and the use test for the 2-year residency requirement.

The ownership test is easy; you must be on the deed to the property for at least 2 years. The residency requirement is a little more stringent: Too many investors tried to get in on the fun so the IRS established certain guidelines to determine eligibility.

For your house to qualify as your principal residence, the IRS must verify:
  a) This house is the place you always plan to return to when you are away
  b) This house is the address you used to register to vote
  c) This house is the address that appears on your driver license
  d) This house is the address you use when filing your official tax returns
  e) This house is the address of record where your kids attend school

On a case-by-case basis, the IRS could be flexible on the occupancy test if the sale of the house was induced by:
  a) Health reasons
  b) Change in place of employment
  c) Unforeseen circumstances
    1) Death
    2) Divorce or legal separation
    3) Multiple births
    4) Unemployment
    5) Change of employment
    6) Condemnation, seizure or other involuntary conversion of property
    7) Damage to property due to man made or natural disaster, terrorism or acts of war
    8) Any other circumstances the IRS commissioner determines are unforeseen.

The old man said rentals held in a corporate entity offer even greater tax deductions as well as legal protection from certain lawsuits. He said, "If you are looking to hide your wealth and grow silently rich under the radar of public scrutiny, you must find the business structure to accommodate this lofty endeavor. That structure is the corporation."

If the property is in a corporation name, technically you do not own it. The corporation, which is considered a separate individual from you, owns it. The corporation, like the individual, has its own unique identifying number that separates it from you and the rest of the world. You have a nine-digit social security number; the corporation has a nine digit Federal tax ID number. The corporation can serve as a legal and financial buffer between you and what all the litigious people in the world want—your assets. You can legally distance yourself from your assets (rentals aka "cash cows") and hide your wealth with a corporate entity. The old man said no one in this "sue crazy" society should have the right to know the extent of your accumulated assets (like how many rentals you own), they should all be safely parked in corporations. The old man said when you shed your ego and place your assets in a corporation, it allows you to have direct control of your assets without the financial and legal worries of personal ownership. The old man said, amateur investors who hold the rental property in their own personal name (probably for bragging rights) leave themselves open for a massive lawsuit. The corporation provides a veil of protection from avaricious lawyers looking to separate you from your money. The old man said, if your rental was in your own name and you got in a car accident and killed someone, you could possibly lose your asset in a wrongful death lawsuit. The rental held in a corporation name, especially with multiple owners, is a little more difficult to obtain in a lawsuit since legally you do not own this asset. The old man said, "Don't get me wrong, the corporation is not fool proof protection from lawsuits. The lawyers could sue for the shares of the corporation that you personally own and still get the asset, or if you committed a felonious act, the corporate veil could be pierced, and they could get your asset. The old man said the most important reason to hold rentals in the corporate structure is the added tax write offs, the legal protection is an added bonus.

The corporation is the perfect vehicle to hide your money and protect your wealth. The old man said, "If you have a Pension Walker, it is mandatory for liability purposes and financial reasons to let a holding corporation own this valuable source of passive income. " What type of corporation you use to shield your wealth from the roving eyes of the general public depends on you and your accountant. Some accountants swear that the Limited Liability Corp. is the best option to hold real estate, while others prefer an S Corp or a C Corp." The old man was partial to the S Corp; it didn't allow "double taxation" of his profits, if any profits somehow existed after the lucrative tax write offs of the rental property were figured in. The old man said, the corporation not only allows you to hide the asset, it also allows you to legally hide the income generated from the asset by funneling the revenues (positive cash flow) through a corporation replete with deductible expenses. With the aid of the corporation, you can legally deduct a host of your living expenses like: car repairs, car lease, cell phone, health insurance, fun business trips to exotic locations, meals and entertainment, gas, educational seminars etc.... The corporation affords you the anonymity you need to privately and surreptitiously build your real estate empire.

The old man said for the ultimate form of anonymity, some investors chose the C corp. Unlike other corp. structures, the C corp. pays its own taxes, there is no Schedule E on your personal tax return that can be traced back to your corporation and the assets it controls.

Translation: Even if some one had access to your personal tax return, they would have no clue you owned other assets (like rentals) in a C corp. because you are not required to divulge this information on your personal return. Your own wife or husband wouldn't even know unless you volunteered this information. Other corporations or business structures leave a paper trail directly back to you.

Your personal tax return is the key that unlocks the door. The IRS requires business owners of certain business structures to report profit and losses of their business on their personal tax return.

The sole proprietorship business structure has the Schedule C, the partnership business structure has Schedule E part 2, the K-1, and if you have a 25% or more interest in corp., the 1065, the S corp. has Schedule E Part 2, the K-1, and if you have a 25% or more interest in corp., the 1120 S. The C corp. doesn't invade the sanctity of your privacy by requiring disclosure of corp. activities on your personal tax return; it is invisible to untrained eyes.

As a side note, the old man said, "When you pay off your primary residence, you should further protect your financial privacy by obtaining a Line of Credit on it, so no one has to know the house is paid off ." If your house was paid off and worth $600,000 and you obtained a $300,000 Line of Credit on it, a $300,000 lien would be recorded on the property even if there was no balance on the loan.

Translation: The whole world would see a $300,000 debt registered against you even though you owe nothing.

A great way to masquerade the fact that a) the house is paid off and b) that you are not struggling with a heavy mortgage like the rest of the lively middle class. The old man said the added kicker is the Line of Credit, if used wisely can bankroll your short-term real estate investments, like the occasional quick flip.

4) Positive Cash Flow—"The Pension Walker"
The old man said positive cash flow is the money left over per month after paying out all monthly property expenses on investment property. Technically, the tenant pays you rent; you pay the mortgage (Principal and Interest) and the property taxes (T) and the homeowner's insurance (I) on the rental (PITI) and any

monies remaining after paying these expenses are your monthly positive cash flow.

Translation: Positive Cash Flow is Rent Roll minus Total Monthly Expenses. For example:

RENTAL PROPERTY

Home Price	**$260,000.00**
Down Payment	**$52,000.00**
Amount Financed	**$208,000.00**
Years	**30**
Interest Rate	**7**
Monthly Payment	**$1,383.83**

Mortgage Payment —$1,383.83
Property Taxes $500 ($6,000 / 12)
Homeowner's insurance—$60 ($720/12)
Total monthly expenses—$1,943.83
Rent Roll—(monthly rent)—$2,500
Positive Cash Flow—$556.17 Per Month

Translation: You rent out your investment property for $2,500 per month and after using this money to pay your mortgage, property taxes and insurance you have extra spendable money, namely $556.17. Mooooo Mooooo, every month you get to milk this "cash cow" for over five hundred and fifty six dollars. Whenever the old man had a rental with a positive cash flow (which was all the time) he used to call it a "cash cow," and every month when he collected rent he referred to it as milking the cow. The old man called this extra money per month that he milked from his "cash cow" rentals—the "King's slush fund," the reserve money that the old man used to finance his surreptitiously lavish lifestyle. The old man said, "The smarter you invest, the larger your slush fund becomes." An average investor could easily attain a $2,000-$5,000 per month slush fund within a 10-15 year investment period. The superior investor can retire early by collecting monthly what some people make annually. The old man knew what he was talking about; he was putting $10,000 clear a month in his pocket back in the late 80's. The old man quickly became addicted to a new habit, namely getting paid *not* to work hard by collecting rent. The old man discovered that collecting cold, hard cash can be even

King of the Middle Class

more addictive than his other vices: women, coffee, and cigarettes. **Positive Cash Flow** was the reason the old man was semi-retired at 43-years-old. The old man never liked people to openly know he had money; he always cried poverty, even on the first of the month when his pockets were bulging with wads of fresh cash from his recently milked "cash cows." If you were after his money, he always threw you off the scent by claiming massive bills and heavy expenses, "casualties," he would half-heartedly say of being a struggling landlord. He never liked strangers to know how lucrative being a landlord really was; he reserved that information for fellow investors and close friends. The only people that needed to know how much the old man made was the old man, his accountant, and his silent partner—the government.

The old man said, Increasing Positive Cash Flow is the end-all goal of real estate investing. It is the reason you learned about the other three areas of real estate (forced equity, market equity and tax write-offs). The mission from day one of real estate investing is to use this collective knowledge to increase your positive cash flow and allow yourself to live like a king off the passive stream of monthly income generated by your tenants.

Increasing Positive Cash Flow
a. Amortization/Forced Equity—the "Do Nothing" system of Guaranteed future Positive Cash Flow, just pay your standard Meat and Potato fully amortized fixed rate mortgage loan every month and let the natural process of amortization wipe out your loan and increase your positive cash flow.
For example:

RENTAL PROPERTY

Home Price	**$260,000.00**
Down Payment	**$52,000.00**
Amount Financed	**$208,000.00**
Years	**30**
Interest Rate	**7**
Monthly Payment	**$1,383.83**

Mortgage Payment —$1383.83
Property Taxes $500 ($6,000 / 12)
Homeowner's insurance—$60 ($720/12)

Total monthly expenses—$1,943.83
Rent Roll—(monthly rent)—$2,500
Positive Cash Flow—$556.17 Per Month

This rental property is generating a $556.17 per month positive cash flow. All you have to do to increase the positive cash flow is "Do Nothing," just make all your mortgage payments (360) and amortization will naturally wipe out loan in 30 years, increasing the positive cash flow per month by $1,383.83 by eliminating the mortgage expense per month. In 30 years, this property will generate a positive cash flow of $556.17 plus $1,383.83=$1,940 per month.

Mortgage Payment —$0
Property Taxes—$500 ($6,000 / 12)
Homeowner's insurance—$60 ($720/12)
Total monthly expenses—$560
Rent Roll—(monthly rent)—$2,500
Positive Cash Flow—$1,940 per month

The old man said the end result of Forced Equity is a paid-off house which represents a rental property's maximum monthly positive cash flow dollars.

b. Accelerated Amortization/Forced equity—the "Pre-pay" system of Guaranteed future Positive Cash Flow, all you do is accelerate the payoff of your standard amortized "Meat and Potato" loan by making unscheduled principal payments and wiping out loan sooner, increasing the positive cash flow, earlier than scheduled.

Translation: You don't have to wait 30 years for your increased positive cash flow; you can speed up the amortization timetable with pre-pays and get the same result sooner; a $1940 maximum positive cash flow.

In the above example, if we gave a $5,000 unscheduled principal payment on the loan, we could arrive at our goal of increased positive cash flow in 28 years instead of 30 years. (See page #133 Meat and Potato Fixed Rate Loan w/ Gravy). The more money you invest into your forced equity column of your amortization schedule, the quicker you get to enjoy the benefits of your increased positive cash flow. The old man said if you do not need the extra $556.17 a month now, reinvest it into pre-pays; pay off the rental sooner; and retire early.

c. Interest-Only Non-Amortized Loan Pre-Pays

Unlike amortized loans, when you make an unscheduled principal payment on a interest-only loan the monthly mortgage payment gets reduced immediately, you do not have to wait 30 years like the "Do Nothing" system. Your positive cash flow increases by the next month. You get instant satisfaction from your pre-payments in an interest-only loan.

For Example:

RENTAL PROPERTY

Home Price	**$260,000.00**
Down Payment	**$52,000.00**
Amount Financed	**$208,000.00**
Years	
Interest Rate	7
Monthly Payment	**$1,213.33**

Interest-only payment is $1,213.33 ($208,000 X 7%= $14,560/12 = 12,13.33 per month)

Mortgage Payment —$1,213.33
Property Taxes—$500 ($6,000/12)
Homeowner's insurance—$60 ($720/12)
Total monthly expenses—$1,773.33
Rent Roll—(monthly rent)—$2,500
Positive Cash Flow $726.67

You make a $5,000 unscheduled principal payment on the loan; it changes the monthly mortgage payment from

$1,213.33 to $1,184.16, instantly increasing your positive cash flow on rental by $29.17 per month.

RENTAL PROPERTY

Home Price	**$260,000.00**
Down Payment	**$52,000.00**
Amount Financed	**$203,000**
Years	
Interest Rate	7
Monthly Payment	**$1,184.16**

After $5,000 unscheduled principal payment Amount financed is now $203,000 and the newly calculated interest-only payment is $1,184.16 ($203,000 X 7% = $14,210/12 = $1,184.16)

Mortgage Payment —$1,184.16
    Property Taxes—$500 ($6,000/12)
    Homeowner's insurance—$60 ($720/12)
    Total monthly expenses—$1,744.16
    Rent Roll—(monthly rent)—$2,500
Positive cash flow—$755.84

By the next month, the $5,000 pre-pay has increased the positive cash flow from $726.67 to $755.84.

d. Refinance Your Way to Increased Positive Cash Flow—If you bought a rental property when prices were low but interest rates were high (usually a buyer's market), you could increase your positive cash flow by refinancing property when interest rates eventually go down.

For example;

RENTAL PROPERTY

Home Price	**$260,000.00**
Down Payment	**$52,000.00**
Amount Financed	**$208,000.00**
Years	**30**
Interest Rate	**10**
Monthly Payment	**$1,826.24**

Mortgage Payment —$1,826.24
Property Taxes—$500 ($6,000/12)
Homeowner's insurance—$60 ($720/12)
Total monthly expenses—$2,386.24
Rent Roll—(monthly rent)—$2,500
Positive Cash Flow—$113.76

When interest rates are at 10%, you have a meager positive cash flow of $113.76 for the month

RENTAL PROPERTY

Home Price	**$260,000.00**
Down Payment	**$52,000.00**
Amount Financed	**$208,000.00**
Years	**30**
Interest Rate	**7**
Monthly Payment	**$1,383.83**

Mortgage Payment —$1,383.83
Property Taxes—$500 ($6,000/12)
Homeowner's insurance—$60 ($720/12)
Total monthly expenses—$1,943.83
Rent Roll—(monthly rent)—$2,500
Positive Cash Flow—$556.17 Per Month

When you refinance your 10% loan down to a 7% loan you increase your positive cash flow from $113.76 per month to a $556.17 a month, an extra $442.41 per month.

e. Sell/Trade Your way to Increased Positive Cash Flow—If you bought a rental property when prices were high but interest rates were low (usually a seller's market) you could increase your positive cash flow by waiting for enough equity to build up and sell or trade your way to a higher positive cash flow.

RENTAL PROPERTY

Home Price	**$260,000.00**
Down Payment	**$52,000.00**
Amount Financed	**$208,000.00**
Years	**30**
Interest Rate	**7**
Monthly Payment	**$1,383.83**

Mortgage Payment—$1,383.83
Property Taxes—$500 ($6,000/12)
Homeowner's insurance—$60 ($720/12)
Total monthly expenses-$1,943.83
Rent Roll—(monthly rent)—$2500
Positive Cash Flow—$556.17 Per Month

If this $260,000 rental appreciated in value (in 10 yrs.) and was now worth $420,000, you could sell it for $420,000 and use the proceeds to put a larger down payment on another rental guaranteeing you a higher positive cash flow. OR If you owned two rentals, you could sell one to pay down the mortgage or payoff the mortgage on the other one.

Sales Price—$420,000
Mortgage balance remaining after 10 yrs of amortization $178,489.62
Closing costs associated with sale—4% broker fee—$16,800
Transfer tax, attorney fee, adjustments, recordation fees, etc...$4,200
Sub total Expenses $199,489.62
Proceeds $420,000 minus $199,489.62= $220,510.38

You now reinvest your proceeds into a $300,000 rental and put a 50% down payment ($150,000) and increase your positive cash flow.

RENTAL PROPERTY

Home Price	**$300,000**
Down Payment	**$150,000**
Amount Financed	**$150,000**
Years	**30**
Interest Rate	**7**
Monthly Payment	**$997.50**

* (Check Amortization Chart $150,000 @7% = 150 X 6.65 = $997.50, page 107)

Mortgage Payment —$997.50
Property Taxes $500 ($6,000/12)
Homeowner's insurance—$60 ($720/12)
Total monthly expenses—$1,557.50
Rent Roll—(monthly rent)—$2,500
Positive Cash Flow—$942.50 Per Month

You just increased your monthly positive cash flow from $556.17 a month to $942.50 a month a $386.33 per month increase and you have $70,000 left over ($220,000 minus $150,000) for buying closing costs, misc. repairs, or seed money for another rental property.

The old man said the best way to accomplish this feat was Tax Free via the 1031 Tax Deferred Exchange. If done properly, you can indefinitely avoid the expense of any tax liability (no capital gains) associated with the sale. In essence, you are perpetually deferring the tax on the gain by reinvesting the proceeds of sale back into another similar property or properties with a higher positive cash flow. Technically you are not *selling* your property; just <u>exchanging</u> the equity in one property for the equity of another property or properties.

f. Protest Property Tax/Comparison Shop Homeowner's Insurance to Increase Positive Cash Flow—By lowering expenses on rental you increase positive cash flow per month.

Property Tax—Every year you have the legal right to try to lower the amount of property taxes that you pay on your rental by protesting your property tax bill. The goal is to challenge the tax bill by finding similar properties to yours that are paying less property tax than you are. The old man strongly recommended that you use a professional tax reduction service. He said, they do all the legwork and only get paid if and when they save you money. It cost you absolutely nothing to explore this expense saving option. If they do not lower property taxes initially, you should make it a yearly habit to contact them; you never know when future circumstances could change in your favor and you are granted a property tax reduction.

For Example:

Mortgage Payment —$1,383.83
Property Taxes $500 ($6,000/12)
Homeowner's insurance—$60 ($720/12)
Total monthly expenses—$1,943.83
Rent Roll—(monthly rent)—$2,500
Positive Cash Flow—$556.17 Per Month

If you successfully reduce property tax bill down to $5,000 from $6,000 you gain an extra $83.00 per month of positive cash flow.

Mortgage Payment—$1,383.83
Property Taxes—$416.66 ($5,000/12)
Homeowner's insurance—$60 ($720/12)
Total monthly expenses—$1,860.49
Rent Roll—(monthly rent)—$2,500
Positive Cash Flow—$639.51 Per Month

You have increased your positive cash flow from $556.17 a month to $639.51 by successfully protesting your property taxes and lowering your property tax expense on rental.

Another way you could reduce your property taxes and subsequently increase your overall positive cash flow in life is through property tax exemptions on your primary residence (where you live). An exemption is a reduction in property taxes for qualified property owners. Most exemptions are for primary residences only, non-owner occupied rental properties usually are not eligible. The old man said even though property tax exemptions usually do not apply to rentals, they get an honorable mention, since most investors own their own homes and could use the savings to increase their overall positive cash flow in life.

The old man said, "Do the research, Son. If you own a home, you owe it to yourself to take full advantage of any and all property tax reducing exemptions that you are qualified for. (Researched 2003) Some common property tax exemptions:

- **STAR**—New York State School Tax Relief Program—provides reduction in school tax portion of property tax bill for all New Yorker's who own their own homes and use ithem as primary residences.

  Two parts to STAR Program:
  1) **Basic Star**—reduction in school taxes for general public—no age or income requirements. Average tax savings per year —$200
  2) **Enhanced Star**—reduction in school tax for seniors—age and income requirements apply—must be 65 or over and make $66,050 or less to qualify.

     Average tax savings per year—$350

- **Veterans Exemption**—provides reduction in property taxes for a qualified veteran, the unremarried surviving spouse of a qualified veteran or a Gold Star parent (the parent of a child who died in the line of duty while serving in the US Armed Forces during one of the periods below) Primary residence only. No income requirements. Need veteran's DD-214 (separation papers) or proof of discharge.

  You are a qualified veteran if you served your country during one or more of the following periods of war or conflict;

  Mexican Border Period (5/9/1916 —4/5/1917)

WWI (4/6/1917-11/11/1918)
WWII (12/7/1941—12/31/1946)
Korean War (6/27/1950-1/31/1955)
Vietnam War (12/22/1961-5/7/1975)
Persian Gulf Conflict (commencing 8/2/1990)

Average tax savings per year—3 levels of benefits
1) 15% of property's assessed value (or $3,600 whichever is less)
2) Additional 10% (or $2,400 whichever is less) if you were in actual combat
3) Additional exemption applies if you saw combat and got disabled. (The exemption can go as high as $12,000 for disabled vets)

- **Senior Citizen Homeowner's Exemption (SCHE)**— provides reduction in property taxes for senior citizens on limited income. Must be 65 and over. Primary residence only. Adjusted gross income must be less than $32,400. Must own house for the last 12 months prior to applying for exemption (exceptions to 12 month rule can be granted). The amount of exemption is determined by a sliding scale of income; the lower the income the higher the exemption. *Translation:* the less you make, the less property tax you pay. In NY, the sliding scale is as follows:

IF the Owners' Income is Between	SCHE will reduce The assessed value by
$0 and $23,999	50%
$24,000 and $24,999	45%
$25,000 and $25,999	40%
$26,000 and $26,999	35%
$27,000 and $27,899	30%
$27,900 and $28,799	25%
$28,800 and $29,699	20%
$29,700 and $30,599	15%
$30,600 and $31,499	10%
$31,500 and $32,399	5%

(WWW.nyc.gov)

As a side note, the old man said, the biggest complaint that seniors have with the current property tax system is the school tax. Most seniors feel that since they have no children matriculated in school, they shouldn't be unjustly burdened with a heavy tax for a service that they do not receive. The old man always took time out of his busy life to educate seniors about the folly of their thinking. He would tell them, "You are not the only group of people that pays taxes for services that are not received." There are two other notable groups of people who equally contribute to the school tax coffers and receive minimal or no benefit:

1) **Optional education group**—the ever-growing group of parents who forgo public education for at home schooling or religious education, like Catholic school. These parents pay school taxes and their children do not even attend the school that their taxes subsidize. In essence, these parents pay twice; they pay school tax for public education plus they have the financial burden of paying for their child's private education. Unlike the seniors, there exists no exemption to reduce this burden. The old man said the government has been toying with ways to correct this injustice, like implementing a tax credit but as of late, this group has no relief from their "double bill."

2) **Walkers**—the group of residents who live too close to the school to get public busing. They pay the same school tax bill as everyone else yet they have to spend their gas money and time to physically drop off and pick up their kids from school while other parents get the benefit of public busing. The walkers have to rearrange their schedule to accommodate the lack of convenience of a bus. The walker group and their children are subjected to fumes emitted by cars lined up at drop off points, frigid cold, rain, snow, sleet, ice, etc. The old man said there should be a tax exemption for walkers; they unfairly pay taxes for buses that they do not get to use.

- **Disabled Homeowner's Exemption (DHE)**—provides a reduction in property taxes to low income disabled homeowners. Primary residence only. Applicant must have provable disability. Adjusted gross income cannot exceed $32,400.

Average tax savings per year—5%-50% of property's assessed value depending on income.

- **Home Improvement Exemption**—the real property tax exemption for capital improvements to residential property (usually 1-2 family properties owned for more than 5 years). Major renovations increase assessed property value and raise property taxes. This exemption can prevent the payment shock associated with the massive property tax increase of a major capital improvement like a dormer or an extension. Instead of raising your property taxes all at once, the assessor slowly increases your tax bill over a set number of years. Each locality is different; you need to do your own research to determine eligibility requirements. In Suffolk County, if you qualify for the HI exemption. they give you 8 years to adjust to your newly increased property tax bill.

Year Exemption%

Year	Exemption%
1	100
2	87.5
3	75
4	62.5
5	50
6	37.5
7	25
8	12.5

Translation: Year # 1 -you pay 0% of your inevitable property tax increase because you are 100% exempt from paying your increased tax obligation, Year # 2—you only pay 12.5% of your inevitable property tax increase because you are 87.5% exempt from paying your increased tax obligation, Year # 3 you only pay

25% of your inevitable property tax increase because you are 75% exempt from paying your increased tax obligation, etc. And so on for subsequent years.

- **Fire Dept/EMT**—provides reduction in property taxes for volunteer firefighters and ambulance workers. Primary residence only. No income requirements. Do your research; the amount of exemption can vary from town to town and county to county. In Suffolk County where I live, the exemption is 10% of assessed value. The exemption is only available to volunteer firefighters and volunteer EMTs who have been certified enrolled members for a minimum of 5 years. After 20 years of dedicated volunteer service the 10% exemption is usually granted for life.

Homeowner's Insurance—Every year like clockwork, the old man would conduct an insurance check-up on his rentals. His mission every year was always the same: save money by shopping around for the best coverage with the lowest possible premium payments. He conducted this mission at the same time each year; renewal time, when the insurance bill is fresh in your mind and you are least likely to forget. The old man said that there are a number of ways to save money on homeowner's insurance:

1) **Lower Premiums**—Find a company that will give you the same coverage for less money.

Mortgage Payment—$1383.83
Property Taxes—$500 ($6,000/12)
Homeowner's insurance—$60 ($720/12)
Total monthly expenses—$1,943.83
Rent Roll (monthly rent)—$2,500
Positive Cash Flow—$556.17 Per Month

Through cost comparison-shopping you reduce insurance bill down to $600 a year from $720 per year. You gain an extra $10.00 per month of positive cash flow.

Mortgage Payment—$1,383.83
Property Taxes—$500 ($6,000/12)
Homeowner's insurance—$50 ($600/12)
Total monthly expenses—$1,933.83
Rent Roll—(monthly rent)—$2,500
Positive Cash Flow—$566.17 Per Month

You have increased your positive cash flow from $556.17 a month to $566.17 a month by successfully shopping and subsequently lowering your insurance expense on your rental.

The old man issued a stern warning regarding insurance, "Never jeopardize good coverage for a low premium; always compare apples to apples. Use your old declaration page as a guide when shopping coverage and getting new quotes." You never want to have cheap insurance because of inadequate coverage. The old man said, "If disaster strikes, you'll be more concerned about how good your insurance policy is, *not* how low the premium is," so shop wisely. The little pennies you save on insurance today, could cost you big dollars tomorrow in the event of a claim. The old man said never make the amateurish mistake of saving money by **underinsuring** your rental with a "fire only" insurance policy. This cheap insurance policy covers damage to the rental property but leaves you vulnerable to the more costly damages of bodily injury and property damage to others. The old man said, "In this litigious society, it is in your best interest to be *properly* insured to protect the financial soundness of your rental property investment. If a chunk of your building falls off and kills someone, you could be liable for millions in damages. You'll wish you spent the extra money now, instead of losing all your money **later.**"

2) **Raise Deductible**—a deductible is the amount of money you have to lay out first before your insurance kicks in. If you have a $200.00 deductible on your insurance policy, you agree to pay $200.00 to cover any losses, before the insurance company pays the rest of the claim. Deductible's can range from $100-$5,000 or more. The higher the deductible, the lower the

insurance premium. By increasing your current $200.00 deductible to a $1,000.00 deductible, you might save 20 to 30 percent on your premiums. You may not have to switch companies to accomplish this feat. Your present company can usually oblige you by amending your current policy and reducing your premium.

The old man cautioned, "Always check your policy; some insurance companies may have a separate deductible in areas prone to similar damage claims, like if you live near the coast in the East, you may have a separate windstorm deductible or if you live anywhere near the San Andreas fault line in California, you may have a separate earthquake deductible.

Translation: Some insurance policies have two deductibles; one for regular claims and another one for specific claims, like wind damage in the East or earthquake damage in the West.

The old man reassured me, "Don't worry about the size of your deductible," if tragedy ever struck you can usually recover your deductible expense by hiring your own adjuster, a public adjuster, to negotiate on your behalf (for a fee) with your insurance company. The old man said you should always use a **public adjuster** on any medium—large insurance claim.

3) **Do Not Over Insure**—do not include the value of land in deciding how much homeowners insurance to buy, otherwise you will pay a higher premium than you should. The price you paid for the house and the price it would take to rebuild the house in the event of a catastrophe are not the same. For example, if you bought a 3,000 square foot house for $800,000, and the average cost to rebuild in the area is $125.00 per square foot, you would only need coverage of $375,000 ($125 X $3000= $375,000) to rebuild its structure, not $800,000. The expensive land that this house sits on isn't at risk from windstorm, fire, theft, lightening and any of the other perils covered in your homeowner's policy.

The old man warned, "Don't let your mortgage company pressure you into getting more insurance on your property than you need." In the above example, if you had a $600,000 mortgage on the property, you don't need to get a $600,000 insurance policy to cover the lender's money, the cost of rebuilding the structure hasn't changed it would still cost the same $375,000 to completely rebuild the house and protect the lender's collateral. You would only need to pay the premium on a $375,000 insurance policy to adequately protect this $600,000 mortgage loan.

4) Package Insurance for a Discount—
Some companies will lower your overall insurance bill by 5-15% if you "package" your insurance by buying two or more policies from them. For example, if you had your homeowner's and auto policy with the same company, this "packaged deal" could net you a reduction in your insurance premium.

The old man cautioned, "Do your homework," make sure this combined price is lower than buying the different coverage's from different companies.

5) Maintain Good Credit—some insurers will penalize you with higher insurance premiums if you have bad credit.

Translation: Good credit is the key to low insurance premiums.

To protect your credit rating you should a) pay your bills on time; b) don't obtain needless credit; c) keep your credit balances as low as possible; and d) check your credit report annually. If you find any misinformation, errors or discrepancies on your credit report, which can adversely affect your credit rating and erroneously raise your insurance premiums, you should promptly correct your credit to avoid overpaying. If derogatory information cannot be corrected because it really happened, you are entitled by law to add a statement of up to 100 words to your official credit report to explain the circumstances of your delinquent credit, like loss of job, death, divorce, sickness, etc.

*As a side note, the old man recommended obtaining a 1-2 million dollar umbrella policy for an even greater layer of protection from liability exposure.

The old man said the ultimate goal of increasing your positive cash flow is the creation of the **Pension Walker.** A Pension Walker is a tenant that pays for your retirement, in effect being your walking and talking pension by giving you maximum positive cash flow dollars by living in your paid off/free and clear "cash cow." The Pension Walker is not to be confused with a regular tenant. You might go through ten or fifteen tenants before you pay off the rental and arrive at your first **Pension Walker**. The amount of money that the Pension walker puts in your pocket each and every month commands your instant respect and admiration. A regular tenant helps you pay your bills by putting hundreds a month in your wallet; pension walkers can change your life by giving you the bankroll you need to enjoy a whole new style of living, namely the regal lifestyle of a King of the Middle Class The collective money generated by pension walkers every month is the hidden wealth created by the old man's investing system. The old man hid that wealth in plain sight; everyone knew he had rentals and made money with tenants; few people knew his rentals were paid off and he had pension walkers that were putting five figures a month in his coffers. The old man was silently rich.

The Pension Walker is the retirement vehicle of choice for the self-employed. The self-employed business owner, who does not have matching 401K contributions from a corporate giant like regular employees, can legally bury their money in real estate creating pension walkers that can outperform some of the better 401K 's. The self-employed who do not have the luxury of a fat pension from a fortune 1,000 company can no longer sit idle and wait for the government to subsidize their retirement through social security payments. The old man said, "Do the research," you could never retire and live comfortably on social security payments alone and furthermore, social security could be bankrupt by the time you reach entitlement age. I took the liberty of researching this fact in 2003, six years after his passing, and I was astounded to discover after 30 or so years of hard work the <u>average</u> dole out from Uncle Sam was only $895 per month. The old man had a valid point. You could not possibly survive on social security alone; you either needed to get a new job after you retired from your old job, or you needed supplemental income from another source like a corporate pension or dare I say the highly touted **Pension Walker**. The old man said, it's your call, **"You can retire like the average American on $895 per month social security or you can invest in real estate and retire like a self employed king with a stable of pension walkers putting $2-$10,000 per month in your pocket.**

Estimated Average Monthly Social Security Benefits Payable in January 2003:	Before 1.4% COLA	After 1.4% COLA
All Retired Workers	$882	$895
Aged Couple, Both Receiving Benefits	$1,463	$1,483
Widowed Mother and Two Children	$1,812	$1,838
Aged Widow(er) Alone	$850	$862
Disabled Worker, Spouse and One or More Children	$1,376	$1,395
All Disabled Workers	$822	$833

(<u>www.ssa.gov</u>)

The old man said if you are not looking to retire, the pension walker is the greatest part-time job in the world. Do the Math, Son! The numbers don't lie. Let's say you invested wisely and you have two paid-off rental properties generating a $1,000 per property positive cash flow. That's $2,000 per month.

Translation: You have two pension walker's putting a grand a month each in your pocket.

How many hours per week do you have to work to get that $2,000 per month? Lets see:

Average time the old man spent as landlord of two "Cash Cows:"

A. Hire Handyman —(avg. 1-2 hours for estimates)

B. Buy supplies for fix up—(avg. 2 hours @ Home Depot)

C. Monitor Handyman—(avg. 2-8 hrs.—periodic inspections)

D. Place classified ad for rental—(avg.—1 hour—½ hr to design ad, ½ hr phone call to place ad)

E. Show Unit to prospective tenants—(avg. 0 hrs—Save the time and let a professional realtor do it for you. It's FREE!)

F. Selecting tenants

1. Tenant application filled out—(avg. 0 hr-Save the time; Realtors do it for you for FREE!)

2. Run credit report—(avg. 0 hr-Save the time; Realtors do it for you for FREE!)

3. Run criminal check—(avg. 0 hr-Save the time; Realtors do it for you for FREE!)

4. Verify income—(avg. ½ hr—call employer)

5. Fill out lease / collect money—(avg. 1-2 hrs—in person)

G. Pay bills on property—(avg. 1hour—½ hr to pay bills, ½ hr for deposits)

H. Settle tenant disputes—(avg. 2 hrs—1 hr drive time, 1 hr resolve time)

I. Evict non-paying tenants—(avg. O hrs. —The old man never wasted his time going to court; he always hired an attorney to do it for him.)

The old man said on average he probably put in 10 hours per month per rental unit. That's 20 hours of work per month for $2,000.00. That's 240 hours of work per year. (20 hours X 12 months= 240 hours per year). That's about 5 hours per week (240 hours divided by 52 weeks = 4.62 average hours per week worked on rentals) Now lets do the math; $2,000 X 12 months = $24,000 for the year divided by 52 weeks = $461.54 per week. This $461.54 per week divided by the # of hours worked for the week (5) gives you a grand total of $92.31 per hour. The old man boastfully proclaimed, the pension walker is the greatest part-time job in the world it pays $92.31 per hour regardless of your education level, work experience or technical skills. The old man said the biggest perk of this extraordinary part-time job is that once your unit is fully rented you punch a time clock once a month, not twice daily like a regular job.

Now let's wrap up what we learned. What makes real estate a powerful investment?

1) **Forced Equity**—the natural by product of amortization
2) **Market Equity**—the increased value created by the laws of supply and demand
3) **Tax write offs**—pay less taxes with attractive real estate deductions and loopholes
4) **Positive Cash Flow**—the steady stream of passive income generated by Pension Walkers

The old man said, now let's prove it **Talk is Cheap, Results Speak**, lets crunch the numbers and prove the financial worthiness of the rental property investment. Let's say you had $75,000 to invest over a 10-year period, which investment vehicle would yield you the highest return on your money? The old man said, do the research, Son; show the average Joe or Jane what happens to $75,000 when you invest it in different financial products. The common choices for the average investor are:

a) Regular interest bearing savings account
b) Certificates of Deposit/ Bonds
c) Mutual fund
d) Stocks
e) Real estate

"Your mission, Son, is to research these investment vehicles and figure out which one on average will make you the most money over a 10 year consecutive period of time. I do not want you to blindly trust me on the merits of the rental property investment; I raised you better than that. I want you to prove it to yourself, so that you can confidently and safely park your hard earned dollars where the old man did: rental properties. I love you, Son, and I wouldn't steer you wrong, but you owe it yourself and your growing family's future to place your money in the investment that will yield you the most money. The only way you are going to figure that out is by doing your homework and compiling the data you need to make this all-important decision. Now, GO FIGURE!

I embarked on this fact-finding mission immediately after his death, but updated the results for this publication in late 2005. I started with the most obvious place that middle class people know of to place their money; the regular interest bearing savings account. According to bankrate.com the average yield in interest bearing accounts is a whopping .28% (that's less than 1/3 of 1%).

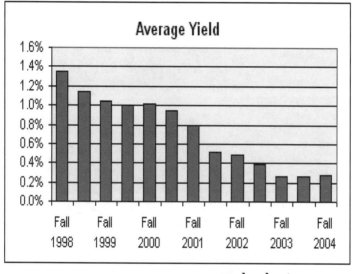

www.bankrate.com

For illustration purposes, I elected to give myself and other investors a much higher than average return on the money; a respectable 2% Personally, my own account at a major bank pays .40% if you have less than 10,000 in it, 2.0% if you maintain 10,000 or better.

Translation: unless you have an extra $10,000 you can park in a bank indefinitely you will be penalized with a paltry return on your money. A tall order for the average middle class investor struggling to make ends meet.

Regular Interest Bearing Savings Account
@ 2%

Year 1—$75,000—$1,500 = $76,500
Year 2—$76,500—$1,530= $78,030
Year 3—$78,030—$1,560.60= $79,590.60
Year 4—$79,590.60—$1,591.81= $81,182.41
Year 5—$81,182.41—$1,623.65= $82,806.06
Year 6—$82,806.06—$1,656.12= $84,462.18
Year 7—$84,462.18—$1,689.24=$86,151.42
Year 8—$86,151.42—$1,723.03=$87,874.45
Year 9—$87,874.45—$1,757.49= $89,631.94
Year 10—$89,631.94—$1,792.64= $91,424.58

> **Total Profit 10 Yrs. = $16,424.58 ($91,424.58—$75,000)**
> Monthly Profit =$136.87
> ($16,424.58 divided by 120)
> NET MONTHLY PRE TAX INCOME = $136.87 (Pre tax)

$136.87(Pre tax)

Rate of return for the interest bearing savings account

Calculated as (value now —value at time of purchase) / (value at time of purchase)

<u>Regular Savings account</u>

Value Now—$91,424.58

Value at time of purchase—$75,000

$91,424.58—$75,000= $16,424.58

$16,424.58 divided by $75,000= **10 Year Return 22%**

As the figures clearly show, if I took my $75,000 and conveniently parked it in a savings account for 10 years, I would have $91,424.58, a gain of $16,424.58 or an average monthly gain of $136.87 for 120 months. In 10 years I have increased the value of my money by a measly 22%. The numbers don't lie; there is only one group of investors that I know that fares worse than this—the "mattress money crowd." The people in society that don't trust banks and the protection of the FDIC, and choose not to invest their money, opting to hide their cash in a wall safe or some other proverbial "mattress" location. This is the same crowd that abhors credit and usually pays cash for everything, even depreciating assets like cars, boats, and computers. This group earns a dismal 0% return on their money after 10 years of non-investing. If you factor in inflation this group actually has a below zero return. The $75,000 they started with 10 years ago actually loses value over time due to the rising cost of living expenses. What cost $1.00 10 years ago might cost $1.25 or more today. This group brags about how much interest they are saving by not using credit cards, yet they are oblivious to how much money they are losing by not properly investing their hoarded money. They are one fire or robbery away from poverty.

The second investment vehicle I focused my energy on was certificates of deposit and bonds.

According to bankrate.com a certificate of deposit is:

"A time deposit, FDIC insured to $100,000 per person, with a fixed maturity date, usually from three months to five years. It usually pays higher interest than a savings account and a penalty is charged for withdrawing funds before the maturity date."

If I had $75,000 to invest over 10 years I would acquire a $75,000 5-year certificate of deposit and upon maturity roll it over into another 5-year certificate of deposit, completing my 10-year investment cycle. According to bankrate.com the average yield on a 5-year certificate of deposit is a little less than 7%.

According to Webster's dictionary a bond is:

"An interest-bearing certificate issued by a government or business promising to pay the holder a specified sum on a specified date."

Basically, you have two choices where to place your hard earned dollars in the bond market: the government or corporations.

According to bankrate.com, "Corporate bonds are the riskiest of the fixed income securities because only the individual corporation backs them and companies are much more likely to have serious financial problems." And conversely according to the same source, bankrate.com, "U.S. savings bonds are very safe: they are backed by the full faith and credit of the U.S. government." Naturally I would opt for the safety of patriotism over the higher risks associated with corporate greed and park my money with Uncle Sam. The government is less likely than a corporation to go bankrupt so I would proudly invest in government bonds. There are basically two types of government bonds you can invest in, Series-I and Series-EE.

You won't be able to buy these bonds all in the same year; there are annual limitations on how much bonds can be purchased. On the Series-I bonds, the annual purchase limit per social security number is $30,000 per year. The annual purchase limit per social security number on Series-EE bonds is $15,000. You can invest $45,000 one year and $30,000 the next year to complete your $75,000 investment. According to the bureau of public debt: Series-I bonds pay 6.73% per year and Series-EE pay 3.20% per year.

Current Rates:

(through Apr. 2006)

I Bonds = 6.73%

EE Bonds = 3.20% FIXED

New rates will be posted on May 1, 2006.

HH Bonds = 1.5%

Source—www.publicdebt.treas.gov

For comparison purposes, I chose to give myself a little better than average return on my government bonds investment, a 7% return to be exact, the same return I could receive on certificates of deposit.

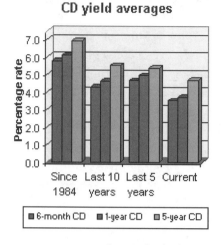

CD yield averages

Source: Bankrate.com

Certificates of Deposit / Government bonds
@7%

Year 1—$75,000—$5,250 = $80,250
Year 2—$80,250—$5,617.50=$85,867.50
Year 3—$85,867.50—$6,010.73=$91,878.23
Year 4—$91,878.23—$6,431.48= $98,309.71
Year 5—$98,309.71—$6,881.68=$105,191.39
Year 6—$105,191.39—$7,363.40 =$112,554.79
Year 7—$112,554.79—$7,878.84= $120,433.63
Year 8—$120,433.63—$8,430.35=$128,863.98
Year 9—$128,863.98—$9,020.48=$137,884.46
Year 10—$137,884.46—$9,651.91= $147,536.37

Total Profit 10 Yrs. = $72,536.37 (147,536.37—75,000)
Monthly Profit =$604.47
($72,536.37 divided by 120)
NET MONTHLY PRE TAX INCOME = $604.47 (Pre tax)

$<u>604.47</u>(Pre tax)

Rate of return for Certificates of deposit/Government bonds

Calculated as (value now —value at time of purchase) / (value at time of purchase)

Certificate of deposit/Government bonds

Value Now—$147,536.37
Value at time of purchase—$75,000
$147,536.37—$75,000= $72,536.37
$72,536.37 divided by $75,000= **10 Year Return 96.7%**

As the figures clearly show if I took my $75,000 and placed it in certificates of deposits or government bonds, for 10 years I would have $147,536.37, a gain of $72,536.37 or an average monthly gain of $604.47 for 120 months. In 10 years I have increased the value of my money by 96.7%.

Translation: in 10 years you almost doubled the value of your money.

The next investment vehicle I zeroed in on was mutual funds. Quite simply, a mutual fund is an investment company that pools money from many individual investors to purchase stocks, bonds, or other types of investments. Choosing which type of mutual fund to invest in is a daunting task for the average unsophisticated middle class investor. According to David Harrell of Morningstar. com, "It's gotten to the point where it's overwhelming even for an experienced investor." Harrell goes on to say, "A common mistake people make when choosing funds is to look at lists of funds with the biggest returns last year—and then buy them." Harrell states "…what's done well recently could easily have the lowest return in the near future; primarily because of the cyclical nature of the stock market." According to www.fool.com, "Almost all actively managed equity mutual funds over time lose to the market averages. And those funds that do beat the market's return typically do so for only a very short period of time, and then quickly reverse course." The lesson to be learned here is that past performance of a mutual fund is in no indication of its future success. The best advice I found on mutual funds was cut out the expense of the middleman (the proactive manager) and according to www.fool.com, "Buy an Index fund." According to www.Investopedia.com, "Index funds are simply mutual funds based on an index so as to mirror its performance." As per the Motley fool, "A index fund simply seeks to match "the market" by buying representative amounts of each stock in the index, rather than paying a manager to make bets on individual stocks, sectors, or investment strategies. Index funds do not even attempt to beat the equities market, they simply seek to come as close as possible to equaling it. The key to the unquestioned superiority of index funds is their extremely low expenses—they charge very low fees for providing the market's returns." Naturally I elected to place my hypothetical $75,000 investment in mutual funds in an index fund.

Now I had to figure out what was the average return I could realistically expect from investing in an index fund. According to www.fool.com, "On the whole, the average mutual fund returns approximately 2% less per year to its shareholders than does the stock market in general. The stock market's historical returns are roughly 11% per year…" (I confirmed the validity of the stock market's historical 11% average return on a website called www. finfacts.com, see chart), so a 9% return looked like a safe number to use for a regular mutual fund and 11% seemed like the right number to use for an index fund that mirrored the activity of the stock market. But before I used this number as my benchmark, I wanted to prove to myself that an index fund could actually outperform a regular mutual fund. I found that proof in a book written by Burton Malkiel, called *A Random Walk Down Wall Street*. His book begins by comparing a $10,000 investment in the S&P 500 Index to a $10,000 investment in an average actively managed mutual fund. The time period was the beginning of 1969 through June 30, 1998. The results were indisputable, the index investor was ahead nearly $140,000; the original $10,000 increased 31 times to $311,000 while the regular actively managed mutual fund investor ended up with only $171,950. Now I was sold; my hard earned dollars would migrate from my pocket to the S&P Index fund (**Translation:** Standard and Poor's 500—the stocks of 500 leading companies in leading industries). According to www.

Investopedia.com, "historically, the return of the S&P 500 has been around 10-11%…"

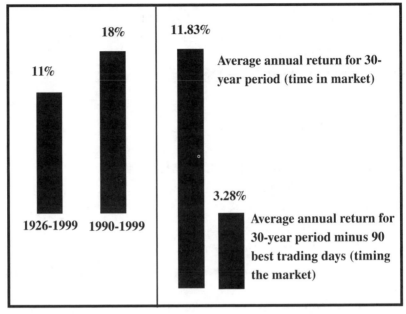

	18%	11.83%	
11%			**Average annual return for 30-year period (time in market)**
			3.28%
1926-1999	1990-1999		**Average annual return for 30-year period minus 90 best trading days (timing the market)**

**Source:
Ibbotson Associates**

Source: University of Michigan

www.finfacts.com

I opted for a little better than market average return and gave myself a pay raise and upped my 11% return to a more respectable 12%. Now I had to crunch my numbers and GO FIGURE.

Index Fund
@ 12%
**Year 1—$75,000-$9000= $84,000
Year 2—$84,000-$10,080= $94,080
Year 3—$94,080-$11,290= $105,370
Year 4—$105,370-$12,644= $118,014
Year 5—$118,014-$14,162= $132,176
Year 6—$132,176-$15,861= $148,037
Year 7—$148,037-$17,764= $165,801
Year 8—$165,801-$19,896= $185,697**

Year 9—$185,697-$22,283=$207,980
Year 10—$207,980-$24,958=$232,938

Total Profit 10 yrs. = $157,938 ($232,938-$75,000)
Monthly Profit = $1,316.15
($157,938 divided by 120)
Net Monthly Pre tax Income = $1,316.15

$1,316.15

Rate of return for Index Fund

Calculated as (value now—value at time of purchase) / (value at time of purchase)

Index fund

Value Now—$232,938

Value at time of purchase—$75,000

$232,938—$75,000= $157,938

$157,938 divided by $75,000= **10 Year Return 211%**

As the figures clearly show, if I took my $75,000 and parked it in a index fund for 10 years I would have $232,938, a gain of $157,938 or an average monthly gain of $1,316.15 for 120 months. In 10 years I have increased the value of my money by 211%.

I had a head start on the next stage of my exploratory mission— the stock market. I already confirmed from my research on mutual funds what return to typically expect from this investment vehicle; 11%. The real question was, do I choose individual stocks or do I stick with the same logic as mutual funds and invest in an index fund like the venerable SandP 500 Index fund. *Translation:* Do I want to have $311,000 in my pocket after 29 years of steady investing or did I want to take my chances at beating the market and wind up with $171,950 after 29 years of researching and investing in various companies (the commissions alone would run into the tens of thousands). Well, Momma didn't raise a dummy, this seemed like a no brainer decision. I would place my hard earned $75,000 in a historically proven winner the coveted index fund. But before I committed myself to this line of thinking I wanted to prove to myself how difficult picking winning stocks really was. The answer to this question was provided by Piper Jaffray, a brokerage and investment banking firm with five offices in northern California, they conducted a stock picking contest in 1997 in conjunction with the *San Francisco Business Times*. The contest was simple. Each contestant started the game with a hypothetical $100,000 bankroll to invest in the stocks of their choice, whichever investor had the greatest return on their money in 6 months won the game. To make the contest a little more interesting, celebrity contestants such as radio DJ Steven Seaweed, San Francisco Supervisor Barbara Kaufman, and Zura the gorilla (a real gorilla) from the San Francisco Zoo were entered into the competition. The results were astounding. The last place finisher was Karyn DiGiorgio of San Francisco, who lost almost 42% of the value of her hypothetical stock portfolio in six months. The big winner was a neophyte investor from Berkeley named Jocelyn Krygier, who posted an impressive 45% gain in value over the same six months. The big surprise came with the celebrity contestants, Zura, a primate with gorilla investing skills came in toward the middle of the pack and posted a 9% gain topping the other two celebrity investors, DJ Steven Seaweed (a 4% gain) and Barbara Kaufman (a 17% loss). I guess picking winning stocks isn't as easy as everyone thinks it is, and since I don't own a gorilla, I guess I'll stick with the original game plan and invest in an index fund.

So obviously, my research on investing in stocks is complete, all the previous calculations concerning mutual funds are fully applicable to the stock investment. The Index fund would be my choice for investing in either one of these financial vehicles. I now proved to myself with facts and figures how much to realistically expect from the most common investment choices presented to the average middle class investor. I now wanted to prove what my old man already knew; that real estate and the power of rentals could yield an even higher return than any other conventional financial products.

Unlike the other investment vehicles, where I gave myself a little better than average return, I opted to downplay the figures on real estate and be ultra conservative in my calculations. I figured if this investment vehicle (rental property) was as good as the old man said it was it wouldn't matter. I started my foray into real estate investing by taking my $75,000 and buying a rental property. Here's how it went down:

Purchase Price = $260,000
Down Payment = $52,000 (20% Down) No PMI
Closing costs = $13,000
Cash Reserve =$10,000 (repairs/eviction etc..)
Total $Invested =**$75,000** (Down payment and Closing costs and Cash reserve)

Mortgage (P&I)= $208k@ 7%= $1,384
Property Taxes (estimated $6,000)= $500
Homeowners Ins (estimated $600)=$50

Total monthly payment= $1,934

House—3-4 Br Ranch Full basement
Rental Value = estimated @ $2,500 month

I used $52,000 of my $75,000 investment as a down payment; I allocated $10,000 as a cash reserve to offset any unforeseen expense like an emergency repair or eviction. I used the remaining investment dollars ($13,000) to cover the closing costs associated with buying the rental. I now owned an investment vehicle called a rental property. Now I had to figure out what was the average return I could realistically expect from investing in my old man's favorite investing vehicle the revered rental property. I had to take those four reasons the old man cited previously 1) forced equity, 2) market equity, 3) tax write-offs, and 4) positive cash flow and plug them into the rental property investment to calculate an average return on my money. I had to crunch the numbers to prove to myself the financial worthiness of this investing product.

CRUNCH YOUR NUMBERS

- **Forced Equity**—Principal Balance Reduction
  Month-by-Month analysis (page 127-129)—10 year
  208,000 @7% 30 yr. $1,383.83 (round off $1,384)
  Year 1 = $208,000 to $205,887 = $2,113
  Year 2= $205,887 to $203,621 = $2,266
  Year 3 = $203,621 to $201,192 = $2,429
  Year 4 = $201,192 to $198,587 = $2,605
  Year 5 = $198,587 to $195,794= $2,793
  Year 6 = $195,794 to $192,798= $2,996
  Year 7= $192,798 to $189,587= $3,211
  Year 8 = $189,587 to $186,143= $3,444
  Year 9 = $186,143 to $182,450=$3,693
  Year 10= $182,450 to $178,490= $3,960
  Total 10 years =$29,510

$29,510 DIVIDED BY 120
MONTHS=$245.92 PER MONTH

- **"Market Equity"**—Appreciation
Historically New York has risen at 10.23% per year since 1990—Nationally, the entire USA has risen at 7.71% per year. Five percent per year is a very conservative estimate.

Assuming only a 5% Appreciation Rate Per Year

Year 1—$260,000—5%—$13,000—$273,000
Year 2—$273,000—5%—$13,650—$286,650
Year 3—$286,650—5%—$14,332—$300,982
Year 4—$300,982—5%—$15,049—$316,031
Year 5—$316,031—5%—$15,801—$331,832
Year 6—$331,832—5%—$16,592—$348,424
Year 7—$348,424—5%—$17,421—$365,845

Year 8—$365,845—5%—$18,292—$384,137
Year 9—$384,137—5%—$19,207—$403,344
Year 10—$403,344—5%—$20,167—$423,511

TOTAL APPRECIATION 10 YRS = $163,511

Bear in mind this gain will only be activated by selling the rental or cashing out tax-free by refinancing.

$163,511 DIVIDED BY 120 MONTHS= **$1,362.59 PER MONTH**

Historically New York real estate has risen 398.79% since 1980. If you bought a house in 1980 for $100,000, it would be worth almost $400,000 now.

Here's the proof for my conservative appreciation rate calculations ON THE NEXT PAGE:

Period Ended March 31, 2004 (Office of Federal Housing Enterprise Oversight)

State	*1-Yr.	1-Yr.	Qtr.	5-Yr.	Since 1980
Hawaii	1	15.16	3.89	43.98	236.60
Nevada	2	15.08	4.18	40.37	160.79
Rhode Island	3	14.80	1.26	80.24	361.36
District Of Columbia	4	14.33	3.20	92.96	302.84
California	5	13.94	2.11	76.97	314.95
Maryland	6	12.87	1.84	52.26	245.90
Florida	7	11.67	2.07	55.42	195.57
New Jersey	8	10.93	0.63	61.82	315.63
Delaware	9	10.38	1.60	44.61	265.53
New York	10	10.23	0.61	61.36	398.79
Virginia	11	10.12	1.66	48.66	223.63
Maine	12	9.86	1.01	56.68	302.32
Vermont	13	9.78	-0.68	43.84	238.71
Mass.	14	9.29	1.16	75.50	516.30
Montana	15	9.16	1.29	32.41	170.25
Conn.	16	9.10	0.90	50.49	273.03
New Hampshire	17	9.00	0.55	71.33	307.20
Minn.	18	8.04	0.40	56.18	216.43
United States **		7.71	0.96	41.73	209.60
Penn.	19	7.65	0.67	32.86	206.89
Alaska	20	7.40	-0.49	24.80	103.72
Arizona	21	7.19	1.12	34.78	152.85
Wyoming	22	6.58	0.90	31.40	93.22
Illinois	23	6.39	0.71	33.54	201.72
Wisconsin	24	6.01	0.27	29.86	172.41
Oregon	25	5.91	0.57	24.72	202.92
New Mexico	26	5.89	0.69	19.51	138.92
Washington	27	5.77	1.02	29.43	228.77
North Dakota	28	5.61	-0.39	21.84	96.35
Missouri	29	5.30	0.40	30.82	156.10
Arkansas	30	4.86	0.92	20.70	116.07
W. Virginia	31	4.82	0.57	20.68	100.06
S. Dakota	32	4.57	-0.54	24.46	135.12
Oklahoma	33	4.47	1.05	24.00	73.91
Iowa	34	4.45	-0.07	22.90	120.76
Louisiana	35	4.43	0.27	24.38	92.11
Kentucky	36	4.29	0.57	22.77	157.52
S. Carolina	37	4.01	0.84	24.81	161.67
Georgia	38	3.96	1.11	30.25	184.12
Idaho	39	3.94	0.61	18.61	136.88
Kansas	40	3.88	0.25	25.67	114.68
Michigan	41	3.75	0.27	29.28	202.55
Ohio	42	3.73	0.35	21.28	154.63
Nebraska	43	3.62	-0.01	19.43	129.16
N. Carolina	44	3.44	0.81	21.14	177.93
Mississippi	45	3.36	0.43	19.15	110.86
Tenn.	46	3.32	0.35	18.38	150.87
Alabama	47	3.18	0.80	19.67	134.49
Colorado	48	2.85	0.42	40.54	223.93
Indiana	49	2.80	0.10	18.01	137.09
Texas	50	2.34	0.20	26.03	88.60
Utah	51	1.95	0.77	9.98	162.56

* Note : Rankings based on annual percentage change.

** Note: United States figures based on weighted division average.

- ## TAX WRITE –OFFS
  Average tax savings per year could be $4,000-$5,000 a year (very conservative—a good CPA could probably double or triple this number).
  Interest on mortgage
  Property taxes
  Homeowners insurance
  Repairs
  Maintenance
  Depreciation
  Advertising/mileage/legal fees/ etc....

  $4,000 times 10 years= $40,000
  $40,000 divided by 120 months = **$333.33 per month**

- ## Positive Cash Flow-PITI= $1,934
  Rent Roll =$2,500

  $2,500 minus $1,934= $566 month

  PCF = $566 Per Month
  (Your P and I is a constant fixed number; the T for property taxes usually goes up year after year and the I for homeowners insurance can go up as well. For our illustration we will keep rent as a constant; bear in mind rent is normally adjusted upward to reflect any increase in prop tax or insurance).
  Year 1 = $566 times 10 months= $5,660 (**2 months per year vacancy factor**)($566 × 12=$6,792)
  Year 2= $5,660
  Year 3=$5,660
  Year 4=$5,660
  Year 5=$5,660
  Year 6=$5,660
  Year 7=$5,660
  Year 8=$5,660
  Year 9=$5,660
  Year 10=$5,660

<u>**Total 10 years = $56,600**</u>

$56,600 Divided by 120 months = $472 **NET PCF PER MONTH**

I was very conservative on the PCF calculations. I assumed 2 months per year vacancy and I did not adjust the rent for inflation.

<u>Rental Property investment</u>

<u>Real Estate Breakdown 10 year</u>

(Keys to chart—**FE**=forced equity/**ME**=market equity/
TW=tax write offs/**PCF**=positive cash flow)

YEAR 1	FE	2,113	YEAR 2	FE	2,266
	ME	13,000		ME	13,650
	TW	4,000		TW	4,000
	PCF	5,660		PCF	5,660
	TOTAL	24,773		TOTAL	25,576
YEAR 3	FE	2,429	YEAR 4	FE	2,605
	ME	14,332		ME	15,049
	TW	4,000		TW	4,000
	PCF	5,660		PCF	5,660
	TOTAL	26,421		TOTAL	27,314
YEAR 5	FE	2793	YEAR 6	FE	2996
	ME	15,801		Me	16,592
	TW	4,000		TW	4,000
	PCF	5660		PCF	5660
	TOTAL	28,254		TOTAL	29,248
YEAR 7	FE	3,211	YEAR 8	FE	3,444
	ME	17,421		ME	18,292
	TW	4,000		TW	4,000
	PCF	5,660		PCF	5,660
	TOTAL	30,292		TOTAL	31,396
YEAR 9	FE	3,693	YEAR 10	FE	3,960
	ME	19,207		ME	20,167
	TW	4,000		TW	4,000
	PCF	5,660		PCF	5,660
	TOTAL	32,560		TOTAL	33,787

Grand total = **$289,621**

Total Profit 10 yrs. = $214,621 ($289,621—$75,000 =$214,621)
Monthly Profit = $1,788.51
($214,621 divided by 120)
NET MONTHLY INCOME = $1,788.51

Rate of return for Rental Property Investment

Calculated as (value now —value at time of purchase) / (value at time of purchase)

Rental property

Value Now—$289,621

Value at time of purchase—$75,000

$289,621–$75,000= $214,621

$214,621 divided by $75,000=

10 Year Return 286%

As the figures clearly show, if I took my $75,000 and invested it in a rental property for 10 years I would have $289,621 a gain of $214,621 or an average monthly gain of $1,788.51. In 10 years, I have increased the value of my money by 286%. And 20 years from now (or sooner if I discipline myself and make regular unscheduled principal payments) when this asset is paid off, I will get a bonus for my patience. I will gain an additional $1,384 per month (when the mortgage is wiped out). This bonus will arrive just in time to make me retire like a well-compensated King.

The numbers don't lie, the jury's verdict is in—the rental property investment is the clear winner.

Rate of Return
- Regular savings account—10 year return
  22%
- Certificates of deposit/Government bonds—10 year return
  96.7%
- Index fund (Mutual fund/Stocks)—10 year return
  211%
- Rental property—10 year return
  286%

I now feel comfortable investing in a vehicle that made my old man obscenely wealthy because I took the time out of my valuable existence to confirm the validity of this highly touted wealth-building product. The hesitation of being an aggravated landlord has been eradicated by the indisputable proof of its superior investment potential. I have proved to myself that the aggravation of being a landlord pays big dividends. I have not disproved the merits of other investment vehicles. They are worthwhile financial products and should be used in conjunction with the rental property investment. A true King of the middle class is a well-diversified investor, whose financial basket includes many wealth-building products. My aim is NOT to have you invest solely in rental properties; but to add it as one of the many eggs in your investing basket. I purposely made sure I didn't exaggerate or fluff the numbers or bend my research to accommodate this endeavor. I wanted to paint an accurate picture of the rental property investment. I wanted to show how real estate performs in bad times not good times. I purposely omitted the high appreciation rates that ripped through this country the past 7-8 years.

In New York, we experienced almost quadruple the appreciation rate that I used to judge the rental property. I purposely did this to quiet any skeptics who might infer that real estate as an investment only generates a high return in a highly appreciating seller's market. I wanted to show the darker side of real estate, how it performs in a buyer's market, devoid of double digit appreciation jumps. I did this because the buyer's market is coming, and I want you to be prepared to prosper by providing you with the right information; so you can logically invest in this vehicle without relying on inflated or unrealistic expectations. My old man taught me well. He said, "The trick to investing in real estate is to invest in the bad times so you can reap your just rewards in the good times." You want to be buying when people are selling, and selling when people are buying.

You want further proof of the power of real estate as a viable investment, don't take my word for it or my old man's word for it, just ask another obscenely wealthy investor, Long Island's own

Charles Wang. Charles Wang had access to all the resources of the investing world, a direct plug into Wall Street. When his company, Computer Associates, went public and he made a gazillion dollars aside from his other investments, he bought half of Glen Cove, a prestigious town in Long Island. Obviously Charles Wang knew what the old man knew—real estate is a powerful, wealth-building vehicle that can drive you to a personal fortune.

Now that I was sold on the merits of real estate as a sound financial investment, I reflected back on the notes I took with the old man while he was alive in Southside and began to piece together his system of how to invest in real estate. I knew most of it from investing with him, but I transcribed his thoughts to paper as good measure lest I forget any crucial details. The old man said the best way to invest in anything is to do your research first and then develop a sound plan of action. The research part gives you the confidence you need to successfully carry out the plan without the hesitation of self-doubt. You will never invest your hard earned dollars in something unless you are 100% confident that it is the right thing to do, and that it will make you more money. The old man said he learned this valuable lesson his first year in real estate from his mentor, Raymond J. Connor of the Housing Exchange in Brentwood NY. The old man said Ray, his sponsoring real estate broker, approached him with an opportunity to invest in something quite foreign to him at the time—an FHA cashover. Ray wanted the old man to fork over $2,500 cash and partner up on a house with him. The old man said he balked because his ignorance of the profit potential of the FHA cashover stopped him from participating in the venture. This turned out to be a $7,500 education for the old man when weeks later Ray resold the same house for a tidy $15,000 profit. The old man apologized to his mentor for not believing in his judgment. His mentor turned to him and said, "Harry, real estate is a self taught business. You will only make the big bucks in real estate when you feed your mind with books, tapes, and seminars that give you the education and comfort level you need to successfully invest your money."

The old man said, "From that day forth, I had 7,500 reasons to fill my empty head with as much real estate knowledge as I could get my hands on. The system I am about to unfold to you, Son, is the culmination of those years of learning and earning I did with the greatest teacher of all, myself."

The old man said, "I pay respectful homage to my mentor, Raymond J. Connor, who was adroit enough to make me realize that."

My old man said that Ray told him, "One day in the future, Harry, you won't thank me for your riches. That distinct honor will be bestowed on you and the knowledge you filled your head with that got you there."

The old man said, "I give that same advice to you, Son. Don't feel compelled to thank me for your wealth. That honor falls on you for being stupid enough to listen to your old man and profit from his wisdom."

The Plan

- **Buy Appreciating Assets.** (Something that you buy today that in all likelihood over time will go up in value and cost you more to buy the same thing tomorrow) ie., Real Estate. A car is just the opposite—a depreciating asset. The time frame is the trick. In real estate, the time frame changes depending on when you initially invest. In a highly appreciating market (a seller's market), 1-5 year hold is all it takes. In a slowly appreciating market (buyer's market), it may take 10 years or more to see the same profit potential.

Real Estate
  - Hold it for a minimum of 10 years
  - Tenant pays all bills
  - You get all Tax Write-Offs
- You sell for Profit or Refinance (tax free) or you hold it for the rest of your life—and retire like a king by collecting

Positive Cash Flow Income from your **Pension Walker's** or exchange (1031 Tax Deferred Exchange) for even greater positive cash flow.

END GOAL—Have 2-4 properties paid in full and enjoy $4,000-$6,000 per month in **Passive Income.**

After doing what my old man instructed me to do (researching), I have added a thing or two to the Plan.
- **Invest in the stock market or mutual funds via Index Fund.** How could I ignore the logic of an investment that I proved to myself can increase the value of my money by 211% in 10 years. It came in a respectable 2nd place to my core investment vehicle, real estate rentals, and it definitely warrants the allocation of my investment dollars.

- **Invest in tax free municipal bonds** to offset the future expenditures of your children:
  1. Sweet 16 parties
  2. High School graduation parties
  3. New Cars/car insurance premiums for your kids
  4. College educations
  5. College graduation parties
  6. Weddings
  7. Grad school education
  8. Down payments for their first home

You should structure these investments based on the ages of your children, so when the money needed has to be allocated, it's there.

The old man said every Plan has to have its rules. These are the rules I established as a real estate investor from years of trial and error. I only added to his rules any applicable post-1997 (the year of his death) stratagems.

The Rules

- Rental Property(Bare minimum)
  3-4 Bedroom ranch with full basement
- Always try to maintain a 10,000—Cash Reserve Fund Per House—so you can sleep at night. Whenever you tap it, try to replenish it.
- Time Horizon—10-15 years. Allows a professional investor to realistically experience and profit from both a seller's market and a buyer's market. The professional knows: Instant riches ("get rich quick") are the result of years of focused dreams. The real millionaires reach their destination usually after 10-15 years of smart investing.

- Below average/ low property taxes on rental.
- Positive Cash Flow—(Bare minimum)—$200 per month— NO EXCEPTIONS—(protects you from down market, when rents could go down)
- Always try to increase your positive cash flow
  o Always be a disciplined saver and make unscheduled principal payments. The sooner you get your **Pension Walker**, the sooner you can realize your dream of retiring like a King at an early age.
  o Always pre-pay interest-only non-amortized loans.
  o Always refinance your way to increased positive cash flow
  o Always sell or trade your way to increased positive cash flow
  o Always protest your property taxes for increased positive cash flow
  o Always take full advantage of any and all property tax exemptions available in your locality. They will **respect** you for your knowledge and oft times **reward** you with lower property taxes.

- **Minimum Paid off Positive cash flow—**$1,000 per month per rental—when house is paid in full, you must make bare minimum $1,000 in pocket after paying property tax and insurance. Or don't buy. Otherwise, You won't respect your pension walker.

- Always use a **Line of Credit** on your primary residence as your personal piggy bank for short-term flips. Also, it is good cover for the King of the Middle Class lifestyle.
- Only use **interest-only** loans in isolated circumstances and stay away from the dangers of **ARM's.**
- Always pay your bills on time: a good credit rating is the fuel that powers your financial vehicle.
- **Incorporate** your holdings to add professional distance, a liability shield, and increased tax write-offs.
- Never invest in **rent control/rent stabilization** areas—it is an eviction nightmare
- **Evictions**—Always hire a lawyer to go to court for you and never fight for the money; always fight for possession.
- Always **invest in tomorrow not just today.**

The old man used to say, "People who buy homes to live in and raise families in are investing in **today**. These are not investors; these are homeowners. They need a place to live today.

People who invest in houses and rent them out to other families to live in are investing in tomorrow. These are investors that are holding assets that hopefully will appreciate in value and pay them **tomorrow.**

That's why you don't break up houses like the slumlord, who invests only in today's profits. You are a professional landlord; you play by the rules, and profit from tomorrow's higher returns. You don't get involved in illegal basement apartments; these are for the amateur landlords or strapped homeowners who blindly invest for today's profits. These amateurs are one complaint away from a possible $5,000-$10,000 legal problem that you, as a professional, will never have the honor of experiencing. Legal rents that guarantee a steady flow of passive income for a kingly retirement is the reward the professional landlord, like you, gets for investing in tomorrow.

- **Location/Location/Location**

  Always remember, whatever you buy you eventually must sell, so if you get a bargain price on a property in a poor location in a hot seller's market (busy street, great neighborhood), you may have a problem liquidating this undesirable property in the cold buyer's market that is coming. (Psst, if the bargain price is great enough to justify the risk, I am in).

- **Always consult your <u>Detractor Checklist</u> when investing in a rental (take value away)**

  Burn out
  Board up
  Wreck
  Busy Road
  Lot Size
  Excessive Repairs
  Neighborhood
  Near Commercial
  Small House (less than 3 BR)
  Small House (less than 900 sq ft)
  No Basement
  No Garage
  Corner Lot
  Back Yard Size
  No Rental unit
  Low wires
  Flood Zone
  Rodents (deer, rats, mice, etc…)

- **Repairs**—In a seller's market, buyers fight over **Handyman Specials**—the concept of fixing up property and activating the inherited equity. In a buyer's market, the real bargains exist in houses already fixed to the nines—saving you the time and expense of repairs. These same houses would command a premium in a seller's market (Exception to rule: Handyman house so severely discounted you can't say no).

  It is better not to buy rentals in a buyer's market that need heavy repairs; you never know how long it will take to recoup the money. You want to fix your properties in a seller's market, where the cost of renovations is justified by increasing values.

Translation: A professional real estate investor buys beat up rentals at a bargain price in a buyer's market and sticks around long enough to fix up and unload investment in new seller's market. The professional investor accomplishes this by investing with a realistic timeline of 10-15 years, so time can make the above event a realized dream.

- **Home Inspection (monster negotiating tool)**
  In a red hot seller's market, this negotiating tool was all but wiped out. If you found serious defects in a house you were buying, the agent would just sell house to less discriminating buyers waiting in the wings to outbid you on this gem. In a buyer's market, the seller will either adjust price against defects or risk losing the sale. The inspection will also be a guide to estimating fix up costs on rental.

  Roof
  Exterior (vinyl siding)
  Windows
  Doors
  Kitchen
  Bath
  Plumbing
  Electrical—outlets/switches/fixtures
  Service (100amp/200amp)
  Floors
  Boiler
  Cesspool
  Molding
  Landscaping
  Appliances
  Spackling
  Painting
  Extermination

- **Invest Local—30-40 minute drive max.** This was my old man's comfort zone. He said, "Once you stray out of this zone, you are more likely to bail on your investment before it bears its ripest fruit. I made that mistake in Florida—it'll never happen again."

- **PREPARE YOURSELF FOR THE APPRECIATION DOWNTIME And Don't Panic (The Greenspan Effect).**
  $438,950 value @ 6% (5%down) payment—$417,000 mortgage $2,502
  $300,000 value @ 10% (5% down) payment—$285,000 mortgage
  $2,502
  Affordability is the issue. Same house has two different values depending on interest rate (roughly same payment $2,502). If you bought the house at the top of the market ($438,950) and followed the rules of $200 minimum positive cash flow—you still win; the PCF and tax write offs and forced equity will eventually make you a winner. If rates go up, DON'T PANIC! You will lose equity; theoretically you could lose up to $140,000 based on affordability. But the smart investor knows that the same house could easily go back up to 440k when the rates go down again (and then some). What comes down must come up and vice versa.

- **Follow the FHA loan limits when investing**
  AFFORDABLE MARKET VALUES
  Your Maximum Buy Price Has been set for 1-4 family houses
  The Federal Government does not actually lend out the money, licensed mortgage bankers and banks lend out the money based on underwriting criteria set by the FHA. The FHA insures the repayment of the money by charging each borrower a MIP (mortgage insurance premium). The FHA decides how much money to allow lenders to lend in each area by putting caps on loan amounts in each area in each state.

The FHA mission is to make homeownership an affordable and possible dream for every qualified American. The FHA has low down payments (2.25%) and allows imperfect but explainable credit blemishes.

If you default on a FHA loan, the lenders, as directed by the FHA guidelines, have to bend over backwards to help you. The loan repayment is fully insured so the lenders are really not in jeopardy of losing any real money. The lenders will not receive a dollar of that money unless they abide by the rules of default set by the FHA. The rules change from time to time, but they usually involve mandatory counseling and restructuring of payments (adding arrear payments to principal balance and recalculating new P&I).

Translation: the government provides affordable housing by insuring lenders who lend money to otherwise risky borrowers. The FHA borrower puts little down (as little as 2.25%). (The government is even toying with the idea of 0% down). The buyer usually has bad but explainable credit; usually has a much lower FICO Score; and is afforded probably the highest form of protection in a foreclosure action.

*After the events of 9-11 the government imposed Mortgagee Letter 2001-21 giving "affected borrowers" a 90-day moratorium on any foreclosure action on their FHA Mortgage.

The government, with all its intelligence and resources, has decided to do all the homework for the average investor. The government has decided in numerical form what affordable is in each area of our wonderful country. An astute investor only wants to buy what is affordable. Now the investor has a benchmark, a reference point to determine affordability.(**see chart**). A good investor knows what is affordable today could be out-priced tomorrow. These government limits are not the *Fair market values* in the areas; they are the *affordable* market values in the area—the price of the property in a given area that the government feels confident enough to insure against loss from default. This free info from the government provides a **fixed price** that an investor can establish as the affordability ceiling in the area in which he/she plans on investing.

County	1 Unit Loan Limit
Albany	$ 228,000
Allegany	$ 200,160
Bronx	$ 362,790
Broome	$ 200,160
Cattaraugus	$ 200,160
Cayuga	$ 200,160
Chautauqua	$ 200,160
Chemung	$ 200,160
Clinton	$ 200,160
Columbia	$ 200,160
Cortland	$ 200,160
Delaware	$ 200,160
Dutchess	$ 308,750
Erie	$ 209,057
Essex	$ 200,160
Franklin	$ 200,160
Fulton	$ 200,160
Genesee	$ 200,160
Greene	$ 200,160
Hamilton	$ 200,160
Herkimer	$ 200,160
Jefferson	$ 200,160
Kings	$ 362,790
Lewis	$ 200,160
Livingston	$ 201,400
Madison	$ 203,300
Monroe	$ 201,400
Montgomery	$ 200,160
Nassau	$ 362,790
New York	$ 362,790
Niagara	$ 209,057
Oneida	$ 200,160
Onondaga	$ 203,300
Ontario	$ 201,400
Orange	$ 308,750
Orleans	$ 201,400
Oswego	$ 203,300
Otsego	$ 200,160
Putnam	$ 362,790
Queens	$ 362,790
Rensselaer	$ 228,000
Richmond	$ 362,790
Rockland	$ 362,790
Saratoga	$ 228,000
Schenectady	$ 228,000
Schoharie	$ 228,000
Schuyler	$ 200,160
Seneca	$ 200,160
St. Lawrence	$ 200,160
Steuben	$ 200,160
Suffolk	**$ 362,790**
Sullivan	$ 200,160
Tioga	$ 200,160
Tompkins	$ 200,160
Ulster	$ 246,300
Warren	$ 200,160
Washington	$ 200,160
Wayne	$ 201,400
Westchester	$ 362,790
Wyoming	$ 200,160
Yates	$ 200,160

(If investing outside of New York, check www.fhalibrary.com, for your county and loan limits)

For example—Suffolk County, NY—$362,790

If you find a house at or below this mark, it may, if it meets all the other **rules** we have established, be a good candidate for a rental property investment.

If the house is above this price, DON'T BUY IT—unless somehow it can meet our RULES OF INVESTING.

- Always remember the market you are investing in. If you are investing in a **Seller's market**, use **Yesterday's Game.** If you are investing in a **Buyer's market**, use **Today's Game.**

Yesterday's Game	Today's Game
Appreciation/Mtg. Leverage	Instant Equity/Free and Clear
NO $DOWN	20% DOWN/ Short Sale
LEVERAGE: *Investing with borrowed money as a way to amplify potential gains (at the risk of greater losses)./ARM / INT ONLY(No Equity)*	Instant equity: (DP is equity)
Rent	Rent
Hold (1-5years)	Hold (5-10 years)
Short-term Buy as many houses as Possible with as little as possible Down (LEVERAGE) and ride the Appreciation Wave Or Flip and cash out.	Short-term Buy 2 rental properties with healthy PCF, wait for market to appreciate, sell one pay off /pay down Mtg on other one OR FLIP properties using SHORT SALE. *
Long-term Own many rental properties with Little or no Positive cash Flow and Wait for Market to Appreciate and Cash Out.	Long-term Own 1-2 rentals, paid-in-full; and then Retire Early; and ride the PCF Wave.

NEGATIVE CASH FLOW Investors	Positive Cash Flow Investors Min 200 PCF—Flexible sellers—HOLD PAPER / PAY CLOSING COSTS
Lose 500-1000 month/ property appreciates At 30-40k year ——cash out #1 REASON, INVESTORS LOSE $$IN REAL ESTATE— APPRECIATION GREED	<u>Welcome to the Buyer's market</u> • Real Sellers Concession • Seller Held Financing • Negotiable sellers • Home Inspections that matter • Short Sale Bonanza

* A Short Sale is when a lender avoids the prohibitive costs of a foreclosure by cutting their loss and accepting less than what is owed to them in order to satisfy the lien on the property.

Most common conditions for a successful Short sale:
1. Borrower in foreclosure
2. Neglected property—in need of repairs
3. Slow moving Buyer's market

*<u>How to do a Short Sale</u>
- Contract of sale—non-involved party.
- Contact loss mitigation dept. of lender.
- Title report—Check for: Back taxes, judgments, other mortgages, ownership info on deed.
- Hardship letter—detailed account of reasons for default.
- Broker Price Opinion—establishes lender value.
- Estimation of repairs—provide photos to substantiate.

HUD 1—Fill out estimated HUD 1 detailing anticipated closing costs. Must show $0 going to borrower. The estimated HUD 1 justifies maximum payoff amount to lender. (The HUD 1 in a short sale always allows a little wiggle room for a real estate broker to charge a commission for providing this valuable service.

- **Minimal Education Requirements**

Rental Values—necessary to establish realistic Positive Cash Flow (PCF)

Resale Values—necessary to establish buying and selling Price

Fix-up costs—necessary to establish bottom line buying Price
You must know the market you are investing in. You must know what the houses are worth in your investment area, what the typical rents are and how much it realistically costs to rehab your investments.

How to Play Today's Game

- **Run Credit**—establish FICO score and borrowing power.
  30 year Mortgage—Fixed not adjustable. 1-year pre-pay penalty
- **20% Down Payment (Asset Check)**
  Primary Sources:
  1. Cash
  2. Line of Credit—Take equity out of primary residence use to invest. (Used primarily for flips, but can be used for rentals if PCF requirements are met) *Translation:* If you can still make a $200 PCF factoring in the added indebtedness of a line of credit payment; buy and prosper.
  3. Borrow from people who know you and trust you. (0% interest)
  4. Borrow IRA (talk to your CPA)

     5.   Sell underperforming stocks, bonds, mutual funds etc.

     6.   Relationship Selling—use $to buy rentals.

- **Follow the RULES (criteria for rental)**
- **Hunting for rental**—MLS, FSBO, estates, Handyman specials, Lis Pendens—Latin term for Litigation Pending / a foreclosure.
- **Acquisition of rental**—contracts, mortgage, insurance, estimated fix up, legal and accounting ramifications
- **Renting rental**—advertisements, qualifying the tenant, preparing lease
- **GET LICENSED—Become a Licensed RE Salesperson**
  1. Take 45-hour salesperson course—invest $160-$200 in your future.
  2. Take State test and get Licensed

WHY?

- **Knowledge**—The 45-hour course gives you the Real Estate Basics. It's like Boot camp for investors. The educated investor spends time in a classroom learning about Real Estate investing before she invests a dollar. Knowledge is power. The more knowledge, the less risk, the greater the reward.

Learn REAL ESTATE before you invest in it.(Mentally more comfortable)

- **Access** to MLS Stratus—As a member of MLS you can find bargain properties—Analyze multiple properties—Hunt for Rentals with inside scoop. Know the Marketplace Rental Values / Resale Values/ How to price properties—using a CMA (comparable market analysis).

- **SAVE $$$**—An investor invests $$in Real Estate to make Profits. The best way to increase profits is to lower your expenses. By getting licensed you will cut your commission costs (a large expense) in half on any house you buy or sell or rent. This savings could be used to offset any fix up costs.

Rental—$2,000—$1,000 in your pocket

Buy rental—SBC—2%—260= $5,200/2 = $2,600 in your pocket

Sell rental—6% —350= $21,000/2= $10,500 in your pocket

- **Earn Extra $$**—Relationship Selling. As a licensed RE salesperson you have an added bonus that could put lots of extra dollars in your pocket. It is not a Revolutionary Concept. It has been around for ages, it is called relationship selling. When you form a relationship or bond with someone, like a family member or close friend (it could take weeks, months or years to forge this relationship), you have earned the right to voice your opinion concerning their financial well being. By joining the real estate community and becoming a licensed real estate salesperson, you can now affix a price tag to the value of that solicited opinion. It is not selling real estate. It is Relationship selling real estate. It is friendly selling, no pressure. Non-threating/Non-confrontational. No real selling involved. Just be you. You are the best at being you. No set hours/ no complicated sales jargon to learn. Let your sponsoring real estate broker sell for you based on your relationships. Your sponsoring broker's job is to sell you on their integrity and years of experience in real estate. If you believe your sponsoring broker and trust that individual to guide you in your newly found real estate career, you will have no problem recommending him or her and the new company you are affiliated with to the people you love. The people you love will trust and value your opinion. You spent years building that trust. In the beginning of your fledgling career, you should be accompanied by your sponsoring broker or qualified staff member to your initial appointments. Your job is to be like an introductory referral service and hold your Uncle

Louie's or Aunt Sally's hand, and ease their concerns, while a highly trained professional from your new office helps you get them happily involved in real estate. The old man said, "Remember this…eventually all the people you love, people who trust and respect you, will touch real estate in one way or another, buy a home / sell a house / invest in rentals etc…Your goal is to tell these people you are now in real estate and do not lie—tell them the gospel truth—you are inexperienced and not looking to practice on them—instead you are bringing in a professional that you trust to take care of their needs—someone you can vouch for—someone you know won't violate them—your sponsoring real estate broker and his/her crew, of which you are a new member."

The people you love will respect you for your honesty and reward you with their business. Why should **You** allow another realtor to make a commission on the people that love and respect **You. You** know you would never do anything to harm your loved ones. I am sure the people in your trust circle would rather pay you than a total stranger; especially when you bring in trained competent professionals to handle their delicate transactions.

YOU SHOULD BE REWARDED FOR THE TRUST AND RESPECT THAT YOU EARNED WITH THESE PEOPLE.

The Rewards of Relationships

Explanation of commission splits: 50/50
- $500k @ 6% = $30,000

1) **They list, You sell** (The SBC (selling broker commission) on MLS decides how much you make).
   The SBC says 2% to the selling broker.
   We are the selling broker. (We would never know the true commission; we are only privy to our side of

transaction) (Also we would never know how the other broker splits his commission with agent)

2% of $500k= $10,000

50/50—SSP (selling sales person) = $5,000

SSB (selling sales broker)= $5,000 Your total= **$5,000**
You sold their listing.

2) **You list; they sell it** (We decide the SBC—how much they make)

The SBC says 2% to the selling broker. They are the selling broker (We know the true commission because we listed the deal—they will not know what we truly make until closing—if they attend).

6% of $500k = $30,000

2% of $500k = $10,000 (We give it to the selling broker who pays SSP)

4% of $500k = $20,000(Our booty)

50/50 = Listing Selling Person (LSP) = $10,000 Listing Selling Broker (LSB) = $10,000

Your total—**$10,000**—they sold our listing.
(You could be on vacation when this happens).

3) **You list, You sell own listing** (You are LSP (listing sales person) and SSP (selling sales person).

6% of $500k = $30,000

2% of $500k = $10,000 (You are SBC 10k ÷ 2 = 5000)

4% of $500k = $20,000 (You are LBC 20k÷ 2 = 10,000)

Your total —**$15,000**—You listed and sold own listing.

4) **You list, another salesperson from same office sells it** (You are LSP the SSP is fellow crew member).

6% of $500k = $30,000

2% of $500k = $10,000 (The SSP gets $5,000/ the broker SSB gets $5,000)

4% of $500k = $20,000 (the LSP gets $10,000/ the broker LSB gets $10,000)

Your total = **$10,000** as LSP/SSP (fellow crew member) $5,000

You listed and cooperated with fellow member and you both made money.

5) **You list, the Broker sells it** (You are LSP the Broker is SSP)
   6% of $500k = $30,000
   2% of $500k = $10,000 (The SSP is the SSB the broker gets full monty-$10k)
   4% of $500k = $20,000 (The LSP gets $10,000 / the broker LSB gets $10,000)
   Your total = **$10,000**, when you list and the broker sold it.

6) **The broker lists it, You sell it** (The broker is the LSP, You are SSP)
   6% of $500k = $30,000
   2% of $500k = $10,000 (The SSP gets $5,000/ the SSB gets $5,000)
   4% of $500k = $20,000 (The LSP is the LSB so the broker gets full monty-$20k)
   Your total = **$5,000** Broker listed you sold it.

The old man said, "Always remember commissions are always negotiable; there is no standard fixed price in the real estate industry; every real estate company can charge whatever they think they are worth and then some thanks to the virtues of the Sherman Anti-trust Act. The old man used to say, "What is the largest organized crime ring in America? The real estate industry, of which I am proud to be a card carrying (pulls out his real estate pocket card) member of. The old man said, when Al Capone gave his last interview from jail prior to his death, he said, ' When I sell liquor, it's called bootlegging; when my patrons serve it on Lake Shore Drive, it's called hospitality.'"

Translation: Get a license, in this country (USA), when you get a license, you can legally steal money from people without worrying about being locked up.

The old man said, "You won't go to jail if you join our crime ring; it's legal, highly respected, protected by powerful lobbyists and can give you the bankroll you need to become a bona fide member of the Kings or Queens of the Middle Class.

The Conclusion of the Book

P.S.—I know I promised to omit any reference to a conclusion at the end of the book, but if you honestly read the material, you earned my friendship and respect, and what kind of friend would I be if I didn't remind you? I figure I owe it to you; you invested your most valuable commodity (your time) to read it; the least I could do is to remind you to finish the job and **Don't Forget The Conclusion.** If you read the book, you should know where the conclusion is and proceed to it immediately. Your mission is almost over. This section does not apply to you, but I am sure by now you have a burning, yearning for learning, and you will read it anyway to validate your commitment to building **real** wealth for you and your loved ones.

As for the rest of you sneaky, non-reading book-scanners, your learning mission has just begun. This is your introduction. I will not divulge the exact location of the conclusion; you have to earn that right the old fashioned way, by reading the book. No short cuts /No Cliff Notes/ No cheating in my class. You just deprived your intellect of much needed mental nutrition. You are not hungry enough to be wealthy. You are not meant to be rich, your poor work ethic precludes you from accomplishing this dream. This dream is reserved for people who really want to experience this thrill, not occasional vacationers. The proverbial "ship" that you have been waiting for your entire life has finally come in and you missed it because you were too busy being preoccupied with your poor thoughts to **read** the boarding pass (knowledge) that gains you admission to the rich life you seek. You are the reason why it is so easy to be rich—most people want to just **pretend** to get involved in activities that can make them rich—not **actually** carry them out. The doors to the rich world are closed to the **wannabe,** who is in such a hurry to get rich, he/she doesn't realize that to unlock this information, they have to **slow down and learn** the combination first.

If you are not willing to sacrifice your time to completely read a book on how to be rich, you do not possess the determination and tools required to be rich. You are not worthy enough to command your riches. You are too quick to judge the merits of your choices concerning this quest. You will always settle for second best; you won't stick around long enough to be a grand prize winner. You are too comfortable being poor, and making up excuses why you aren't rich. (You are not alone. There must be a reason why some guru's are on TV for over twenty years hawking the same outdated dribble to millions of people). Maybe you are like the majority of people that attend the seminars or buy the tapes or books of these self-proclaimed financial prophets; you are only there to compile these various "get rich quick" books and tapes so you can line the shelves of your broken dreams and justify your poverty to your friends. Maybe you are a motivational book collector, accentuating your home or office décor with motivational "get rich" books so you can validate yourself as an ambitious "go getter" to prospective suitors. Maybe you want these books and tapes, prominently displayed in your bookcase for all to see, to serve as **proof** to whoever wanders in of your conviction to acquire the elusive American dream of being rich. Maybe you are now ready to improve your learning curve and live up to the conviction level of the books adorning your shelves by actually reading the material in its entirety.

The inaction of not reading this entire book in its correct order is your own Litmus test for your desire to be actually rich. You want to know what it is like to **try** to be rich, not actually be rich. This is your wake up call—you should really set your sights higher and stop misjudging information based on a cursory inspection. If, by reading the conclusion first, you determine that the material content must be recycled rubbish, you at least owe yourself the opportunity to prove it by completing the book in its entirety—

only then will you be able to **confirm** that misguided theory. How could you respect yourself otherwise? You don't want to guess at it. Your financial future is too important to leave to chance. I mean, you could be wrong and potentially lose millions of dollars by bowing out. Ignorance does have its educational rewards. You want to play the game until the end and see all the cards dealt, not just a few. A good gambler never bails out on a hand until he/she sees the entire flop. You never know when Lady luck is going to bless you with that winning Flush.

P.S.—If you read this entire book and still determine it is rubbish, I will graciously respect your opinion because at least you dedicated the right amount of time and mental energy to come to this erroneous conclusion. Besides, my perspective is a little skewed. I am already rich in thought and rich in monetary gain from the rubbish contained in this book that was passed down to me by my old man. I guess the old saying is apropos, "One man's garbage, is another man's riches."

There are no short cuts to being rich for the average middle class American. It is a slow, methodical, 10-15 year investing journey. If your car is too fast, you will miss the directional signs along the road to your wealth and remain forever stranded on the broken down poverty highway. The rich are rich because they learned to take the longer but surer scenic route to their wealth, slowing down long enough to get the right directions and information necessary to enjoy their wealth-building ride and successfully get to their destination of being rich. It is easy for the rich to remember this; most of us rich people had that concept drilled into our heads at an early impressionable age, by our loving mothers, who instead of spoiling us, taught us the virtues of the old adage, "Good things come to those who wait." You had to earn it with Mom. Extra chores or good grades, rewards were never free. You have to earn your riches the same way. It's **not free**. The mere cost of this book will not get you rich. Doing the work of learning and applying the information contained in this book will. You have to do the work. Pay your proverbial "Dues." I am here to show you what that right work is. I am here to make you a well-respected **earner**. I am here to help you earn your wings, so you can gain admittance to the secretive world of the rich that you covet so dearly. What you do with this ability is up to you. I can give you the tools; it's up to your ambition to actually use them. Being poor is a choice. You can chose to ignore this book and the years of wealth-building knowledge contained in it and blaze your own trail to your riches, or you can duplicate the success of a well-proven path to wealth, obtained from a deceased millionaire (my old man) and conveniently laid out for you in this book. It is your choice. Not everyone is cut out to be rich. I am doing you a favor by volunteering this information; most guru's would just take your money, smile, and give you some positive thinking mumbo jumbo bullcrap and invite you to their next seminar, not I. I am the real deal. I call it like it is. I don't pull any punches. Someone has to tell you the truth. Someone has to liberate you from your cloudy thinking. That honor will be mine. I will be the first to tell you the truth: not everyone that attends a "get rich quick" seminar **actually** gets rich. The paid participants usually become pretend-rich for an awe inspiring day.

I am here to make you really rich for the rest of your lifetime, not pretend rich for the day. I am here to help you change the "poor man mentality" inside you that blocks this event from actually happening. The truth is: Being rich is a full time job, a 24-hour state of mind. Only lottery winners are part-timers. For the rest of us, it's 10-15 years of constant work before we rightfully claim our earned prize of the rich life. You need faith to join this selective club. Not faith in me or any other guru, but faith in yourself and your ability to successfully carry out this life-altering mission. This book was written to give **you** the knowledge, so **you** can have the confidence and faith **you** need so **you** can become rich by **yourself**. Becoming rich is a solo operation. I can't do it for **you**. I can only guide you; ultimately only **you** can make the sound investments that catapult **you** into the stratosphere of the rich. The key to your future is not me, it's **You**.

Maybe you have watched so many guru's on TV, radio, and in person who promised to make you rich, get rich themselves, and because of that, you are preconditioned not to believe any of them (including me). "Once bitten, twice shy." Maybe you didn't receive the real message these highly compensated orators were delivering. These false financial prophets did teach you something: your money wasn't entirely wasted on them; you did get an education for the money you spent. These well-dressed, silver-tongued financial wizards proved one thing to you—financial dreams do come true, only it wasn't your dream that came true, it was theirs. But the question you have to ask yourself is, "What happens if out of the clear blue, the real McCoy does show up—the educator who can actually get you rich—appears on the scene? **Are you so shell shocked** from your prior bad experiences with other gurus that you refuse to open your heart and mind long enough to hear the legitimate guy's enriching message? It's like the lottery. **Hey, you never know what happens with a buck and a little luck**; maybe the cost of this book (a little more than a buck) and the teachings contained in it just might make you rich. GO FIGURE.

So if I ask somebody, "Did you read the book?" and they are oblivious to the conclusion section, I know the caliber of person, I am dealing with. Partial book readers do not get my undivided attention; they do not deserve that respect. You have to earn your respect with me. I do not give it away for the mere cost of a book; my old man's life and his teachings are worth way more than that. The expenditure of this item palls in comparison to the realistic content of this material. You robbed yourself of an education that might have propelled you into another league of thinking. You are so arrogantly smart that you think you can learn this information from social osmosis rather than the old fashioned way of reading and internalizing it. This thinking is flawed and should be corrected. I hope you read this and somehow you see the light; your future is only as bright as you want to create it. If you are not willing to put in the time needed to rise above the masses and challenge yourself, dare I say dream yourself, to be rich, you will always be a poor thinker and underachiever—A quality in life I refuse to accept from anyone, including myself.

If you are ready to acknowledge that "get rich quick" means 10-15 years of smart thinking and proper investing, you are ready to join me and my select group of young patriots in the "winners circle" as we forge ahead in our crusade to revolutionize the way all Americans conquer the American dream of being rich. The battle for your financial freedom has to start in your mind first, with ambitious dreamy thoughts of being rich. You have to believe your dream of being rich before you can live your dream of being rich. I am here to give you that belief by planting the revolutionary thoughts in your mind (via this book); that will enable you to realistically believe this dream can be your new reality. The old man said it best, **"Thunderous Dreams only happen when ambitious thoughts are raining in your mind."**

I am here to make sure you hungry young Americans don't get left out. You get your fair share, your piece of the American pie. And if you are real hungry, I am here to show you what's required to "Have your cake and eat it too." Being rich has its privileges. I am here to show you how you can **really,** "Be All You Can Be." Only **You** have the power inside **yourself** to make this really happen. Read the whole book and **"Go For It."** I know you are scared of your uncertain financial future, so was I when I attended college, and so was I when I wrote this book. I spent a year and a half of my rich life experience to work on a project with no guarantee of success except the faith and conviction of my focused dreams. I am in the same boat you are in. We are both taking a calculated risk on something that can make our dreams come true.

KING OF THE MIDDLE CLASS
ORDER FORM

TO ORDER ONLINE:

WWW.KINGOFTHEMIDDLECLASS.COM

DOWNLOAD VERSION $9.99

PAPERBACK $14.99 + SHIPPING

AND HANDLING Charge of: $5
Pay By PAY PAL Account or
Credit Cards Accepted:
VISA MASTERCARD AMEX DISCOVER

ORDER DIRECT FROM

QP DISTRIBUTION

ORDER BY PHONE TOLL FREE: 1-800-214-8110

TO ORDER BY FAX: 1-620-229-8978

DIRECT MAIL ORDERS MAIL CHECK TO:

QP DISTRIBUTION
22167 C STREET
WINFIELD, KS 67156